T0199231

Artificial Intelligence for Capital Markets

Artificial Intelligence for Capital Market throws light on the application of AI/ML techniques in the financial capital markets. This book discusses the challenges posed by the AI/ML techniques as these are prone to "black box" syndrome. The complexity of understanding the underlying dynamics for results generated by these methods is one of the major concerns which is highlighted in this book.

Features:

- Showcases artificial intelligence in the finance service industry
- Explains credit and risk analysis
- Elaborates on cryptocurrencies and blockchain technology
- Focuses on the optimal choice of asset pricing model
- Introduces testing of market efficiency and forecasting in the Indian Stock Market

This book serves as a reference book for academicians, industry professionals, traders, finance managers and stock brokers. It may also be used as a textbook for graduate-level courses in financial services and financial analytics.

Artificial Intelligence for Capital Markets

Edited by
Syed Hasan Jafar
Hemachandran K
Hani El-Chaarani
Sairam Moturi
Neha Gupta

CRC Press
Taylor & Francis Group
Boca Raton London New York

CRC Press is an imprint of the
Taylor & Francis Group, an **informa** business
A CHAPMAN & HALL BOOK

Front cover image: jamesteohart/Shutterstock

First edition published 2023
by CRC Press
6000 Broken Sound Parkway NW, Suite 300, Boca Raton, FL 33487-2742

and by CRC Press
4 Park Square, Milton Park, Abingdon, Oxon, OX14 4RN

CRC Press is an imprint of Taylor & Francis Group, LLC

Library of Congress Cataloging-in-Publication Data
Names: Jafar, Syed Hasan, editor.
Title: Artificial intelligence for capital markets / edited by Syed Hasan Jafar, Hemachandran K.,
Hani El-Chaarani, Sairam Moturi, Neha Gupta.
Description: Boca Raton : Chapman & Hall/CRC Press, 2023. | Includes bibliographical references and index.|
Identifiers: LCCN 2022051420 (print) | LCCN 2022051421 (ebook) | ISBN 9781032353937 (hardback) |
ISBN 9781032356303 (paperback) | ISBN 9781003327745 (ebook)
Subjects: LCSH: Capital market. | Artificial intelligence. | Machine learning
Classification: LCC HG4523 .A76 2023 (print) | LCC HG4523 (ebook) |
DDC 332/.0415--dc23/eng/20230111
LC record available at https://lccn.loc.gov/2022051420
LC ebook record available at https://lccn.loc.gov/2022051421

ISBN: 978-1-032-35393-7 (hbk)
ISBN: 978-1-032-35630-3 (pbk)
ISBN: 978-1-003-32774-5 (ebk)

DOI: 10.1201/9781003327745

Typeset in Minion
by MPS Limited, Dehradun

Contents

Preface

ARTIFICIAL INTELLIGENCE (AI) systems are machine-based systems with varying levels of autonomy, that are used to make predictions, decisions or recommendations for a given set of human-defined objectives. These systems have gained immense popularity in recent times and almost every sector and industry are exploring its application in some or another way. With the advent of big data and data analytics, there is an increase in the data sources and data volumes which have resulted in search of techniques which can help analyse such huge volumes quickly and efficiently. AI techniques such as machine learning (thereafter ML) present themselves as a feasible solution that uses massive amounts of data from alternative data sources to learn and improve predictability and performance through experience. Learning by experience is one characteristic of the AI models which caters to its immense popularity, without being programmed to do so by humans.

The global financial sector is also experiencing the deployment of AI models through algorithm trading, credit underwriting, blockchain-based financial services, asset management and many more. Many financial firms are adopting AI in order to drive their competitive advantage by improving the firms' efficiency via cost reduction and productivity improvement delivering higher profitability. And, by enhancing the quality of financial products and services, in terms of customization, presented to the customers. The AI/ML models help these firms in the optimization of processes, automation of functions, enhancing the decision-making processes, and improved risk management and regulatory compliance.

AI in Finance presents and explores the most recent advances in the application of innovative and emerging AI/ML models in the financial industry. The main contribution of this book is to provide new theoretical and applied AI perspectives to find solutions to unsolved finance questions. This volume presents the applicability of various machine learning models such as Support Vector Regression, Regression trees and Markov Switching Models in asset pricing and portfolio theory, Artificial Neural Networks (ANNs) in asset pricing, stock market forecasting utilizing a deep learning model, credit and risk analysis of borrowers using Random Forest Algorithms, examining market efficiency using news-driven sentiment, employing LSTM and RNNs for technical analysis, and price forecasting using deep learning and additive models in financial markets.

Apart from presenting the novel applications in the financial sector, this book also offers insights into the challenges presented by the adoption of AI/ ML models. It is necessary to talk about AI applications in finance that may create or intensify the financial as well as non-financial risks, leading to consumer and investor protection considerations. The complexity in understanding the functioning of these models and how they generate results could create possible incompatibilities with existing supervision and governance frameworks. The heightened risk of data breach and cyber security is accompanied with the lack of proper reasoning behind the results generated by these AI models which is one of the major disadvantages of their adoption.

About the Editors

Hemachandran K

Dr. Hemachandran Kannan has been a passionate teacher with 15 years of teaching experience and 5 years of research experience. A strong educational professional with a scientific bent of mind, highly skilled in AI & Business Analytics. After receiving a PhD in embedded systems, He started focusing on Interdisciplinary research. He served as an effective resource person at various national and international scientific conferences and also gave lectures on topics related to artificial intelligence. He was bestowed as Best faculty at Woxsen University in 2021–2022 and also at Ashoka Institute of Engineering & Technology in 2019–2020. He is having rich working experience in natural language processing, computer vision, building video recommendation systems, building chatbots for HR policies and education sector, automatic interview processes, and autonomous robots. He is working on various real-time use cases and projects in collaboration with Industries such as Advertflair, LLC, Course5i, and Apstek Corp. He has organized many International Conferences, Hackathons, and Ideathon. He owed four patents to his credentials. He has a life membership in estimable professional bodies. An open-ended positive person who has a stupendous peer-reviewed publication record with more than 35 journals and international conference publications. His editorial skills made him an editorial board member in numerous reputed Scopus /sci journals.

Syed Hasan Jafar

Professor Syed Hasan Jafar is a Program Chair of MBA Financial Services and Area Chair of Finance at Woxsen University. He is having around 13 Years of Experience in the field of Finance and worked as a Research Analyst, Deputy Research Head, and Corporate Trainer. He comes on several national media channels as a financial expert for sharing his view on the financial market. His areas of expertise are security analysis, corporate finance, equity and derivative research, and valuation. He has taken several sessions in top universities in India and abroad. He Awarded as Best faculty of the year 2020–2021 in Woxsen School of Business, Woxsen University. He conducted more than 50 Investor awareness programs across the country and was awarded the best Research Analyst several times during his corporate experience.

Hani El-Chaarani

Hani El-Chaarani is a full professor of finance. He is a financial consultant in many public and private institutions. He is a board member and financial advisor for many family firms in MENA region. He holds a PhD in Business Administration from the University of Bordeaux-IV (France), MSc in Business Administration from the IAE-Bordeaux (France), and MSc in Finance and Accounting from the Lebanese University. In addition, he holds a Rural and Economic Development diploma from Illinois University, USA, Excellence in Teaching diploma from Illinois University, USA, and Crisis Economic Leadership Diploma from London Business School, UK.

He is a charted accountant and a visiting professor at various universities, research centers and international organizations. He is the head of Business School at Beirut Arab University, Lebanon. He acted as the keynote speaker and delivered professional talks on various international forums. He is leading the IBERA (International Business and Economic Research Academy). He published close to 50 scientific works in high ranked journals and international conferences. He is a reviewer in several ranked journals. His research interests include financial behavior, corporate governance, SMEs performance, blockchain, big data management.

Sairam Moturi

Sairam Moturi is an Assistant Professor in Accounting and Finance area at Woxsen university. Mr. Moturi is having 10 years of work experience in Academia and Industry. He is currently pursuing his PhD in Accounting area from University of Hyderabad. His research focuses on Earnings manipulation, Rotation of Auditors and Audit Quality. Moturi is a dual post graduate with MBA (Finance & Human Resources) and Masters in Commerce focused in Accountancy and a Certified Accounting Technician by education. At Woxsen, he teaches Accounting and Management Accounting courses to undergraduate and postgraduate level programs.

Neha Gupta

Miss Neha Gupta is a Visiting Assistant Professor at Indian Institute of Management, Rohtak. Her previous association was with Woxsen School of Business, Hyderabad, where she headed Case Study Centre and was a part of Institutions of Innovation Council, Ministry of Education. She has pursued her PhD in the domain of Finance from Birla Institute of Technology and Science, Pilani campus. Her research interests constitute financial economics, behavioural finance and machine learning.

Contributors

Dheeraj Anchuri
School of Business
Woxsen University
Hyderabad, Telangana, India

Sunitha Purushottam Ashtikar
SR University
Warangal, Telangana, India

Hebatallah Badawy
Alexandria University
Egypt Japan University of Science
  and Technology
Egypt

Rohit Bakoliya
Sardar Vallabhbhai National Institute
  of Technology
Surat, Gujarat, India

Aleksander Bielinski
Edinburgh Napier University
United Kingdom

Daniel Broby
Ulster University
United Kingdom

Hani El-Chaarani
Business School
Beirut Arab University
Lebanon

Jay Chawla
Sardar Vallabhbhai National Institute
  of Technology
Surat, Gujarat, India

Hassan Dennaoui
University of Balamand
Lebanon

Deepika Dhingra
Bennett University
Greater Noida, Uttar Pradesh, India

Subhashini Durai
GRD Institute of Management
Coimbatore, Tamilnadu, India

Syed Hasan Jafar
School of Business
Woxsen University
Hyderabad, Telangana, India

Krupa N. Jariwala
Sardar Vallabhbhai National Institute
  of Technology
Surat, Gujarat, India

Jitendra Jat
Sardar Vallabhbhai National Institute of
  Technology
Surat, Gujarat, India

Jignesh Jinjala
Sardar Vallabhbhai National Institute
    of Technology
Surat, Gujarat, India

Pokala Pranay Kumar
MPS Data Science
University of Maryland
Baltimore County, USA

Madhavi Lokhande
ISME
Affiliated to the University of Mysore
Bangalore, Karnataka, India

Geetha Manoharan
SR University
Warangal, Telangana, India

Sam El Nemar
Azm University
Lebanon

Manali Patel
Sardar Vallabhbhai National Institute
    of Technology
Surat, Gujarat, India

Gunaseelan Alex Rajesh
Sri Venkateswara Institute of Information
    Technology and management
Coimbatore, Tamilnadu, India

S Rangapriya
ISME – Research Centre
University of Mysore
Bangalore, Karnataka, India

Mahmoud El Samad
Lebanese International University
Woxsen Lebanon

Muneer Shaik
School of Management
Mahindra University
Hyderabad, Telangana, India

Vaibhav Shastri
Birla Institute of Technology
    and Science (BITS)
Pilani, Pilani Campus
Rajasthan, India

Rola Shawat
Egypt Japan University of Science
    and Technology
Egypt

Yahya Skaf
Notre Dame University
Lebanon

Abanoub Wassef
Egypt Japan University of Science
    and Technology, Egypt

CHAPTER 1

Artificial Intelligence in the Financial Services Industry

Muneer Shaik

CONTENTS

DOI: 10.1201/9781003327745-1

1.1 INTRODUCTION

Four major revolutions have occurred in the history of the world. In 1784, the first revolution took place with the launch of the earth's foremost steam engine. The next occurred in 1870, with the invention of electricity. The third was in 1969, when the world was first introduced to information technology, and the fourth is the present artificial intelligence (AI) revolution. The contemporary revolutionary epoch is characterized by high levels of automation and global connectedness, both necessitate the use of AI.

AI has the potential to radically alter human history, and this is especially true in the case of massive data. Global funding to AI companies hit $15.1 billion in Q1 2022, according to CB Insights' State of AI Report 2022.[1] The overall number of AI unicorns has increased by 10% year over year to 141. The United States accounted for 79% of new unicorn births, whereas Europe accounted for 14%. In the first quarter of this year, only one new unicorn was born in Asia. In Q1'22, AI contributed for 12% of all fresh unicorns created throughout the venture capital landscape. In the first quarter of this year, 56 Fintech AI startups raised $900 million in 56 agreements. According to the research, Asia ($395 million) received the most Fintech AI funding in Q1'22, followed by the United States ($334 million), Europe ($112 million), Canada ($37 million), and all other areas ($3 million). In Q1'22, the United States and Asia each secured 36% of financial AI transactions. AI financing in India has increased by 519% year over year thanks to a $360 million mega-round.

The opportunities that AI technologies provide are reflected in their expanding acceptance and usage. Because of its potential to allow huge benefits for enterprises, individuals, and marketplaces, AI has risen to the top of corporate innovation agendas. Academicians and regulators are dedicating time and money to developing governance concepts, internal practices, and techniques for responsible and ethical AI, as it has the power to reshape financial services in new ways. It is our common responsibility to guarantee that this transition is carried out responsibly and also in a manner that benefits society.

The study probes the usage of AI in finance and discusses the questions like: What are the challenges of AI in the financial services industry? What function does AI serve in the financial sector? What does the future of AI in finance entail?

The rest of the chapter is organized as follows: section 1.2 discusses about AI and its types and subsets. Section 1.3 covers the applications of AI in finance. The issues of AI in finance are discussed in section 1.4, and then in section 1.5, we highlight the future trends of AI in finance and finally conclude in section 1.6.

1.2 ARTIFICIAL INTELLIGENCE

AI is a huge technological innovation that has us all buzzing about its amazing potential in the age of technology. "The application of cognitive tools to perform duties that traditionally involve human sophistication is widely referred to as AI" (Financial Stability Board, 2017).

1.2.1 Types of AI

AI is divided into two types: (1) symbolic AI and (2) statistical AI. Symbolic AI works by converting human understanding and rational arguments into rules that may be explicitly coded. "If a payment exceeds Rs. 10,000, then it should be flagged for review process," for example. Between the 1950s and the 1980s, symbolic AI was the most popular approach in AI research. Statistical AI, on the other hand, relates to the creation of data-driven, bottom-up systems. AlphaZero is an example of a computer software that can play extremely complex games.

Furthermore, advances in statistical AI enabled by rapid gains in computational capabilities, breakthroughs in algorithm methodologies, and considerable improvements in existing data can be separated into two subsets: general AI and narrow AI. General AI refers to systems that have universal abilities on par with those of the human mind. It is a goal rather than a reality. The AI systems that we see in business today are narrow AI systems. These systems' capabilities are constrained by the relatively restricted pre-defined tasks for which they were designed. The performance of narrow AI systems may possibly exceed that of humans for certain niche activities. Recent achievements in image recognition and sophisticated games such as chess demonstrate this. Unless otherwise stated, narrow AI is what we mean when we use the term "AI" (figure 1.1).

1.2.2 Subcategories of AI

Machine learning (ML) and deep learning (DL) are subcategories of AI applications. Although AI is described as a computer's ability to make intelligent human-like decisions

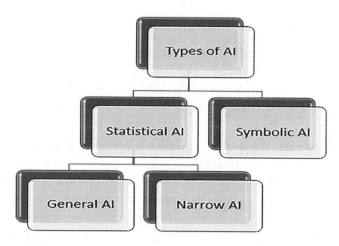

FIGURE 1.1   Types of AI.

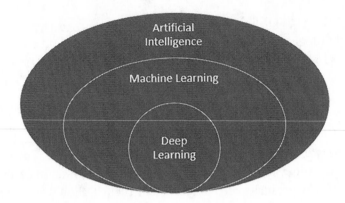

FIGURE 1.2 AI vs ML vs DL.

and improve over time, ML necessitates the development of models, primarily statistical methodologies that can be developed and provide accurate predictions. ML is a sub-category of AI, which is a wide field. ML is a tremendously active study topic that encompasses a wide range of methodologies that are constantly evolving. Supervised learning, unsupervised learning, and reinforcement learning are the three main methodologies that may be separated at a high level. These three approaches cover a wide range of individual ML methods, including linear regression, decision trees (DTs), support vector machines (SVMs), artificial neural networks (ANNs), and ensemble methods. Further, DL has recently produced impressive results in a variety of domains, including image identification and natural language processing (NLP; figure 1.2).

AI is a broad phrase that refers to all ways of making machines intelligent. ML is a subfield of AI that is normally utilized alongside AI. ML pertains to an information system that can self-learn using an algorithm. Machines which become better over time sans user intercession are referred to as ML. DL is an ML technique for analysing large volumes of data. ML is employed in the bulk of AI projects because intelligent behaviour needs a vast deal of knowledge.

1.3 APPLICATIONS OF AI IN FINANCIAL SERVICES

1.3.1 Robo-Advisory

Robo-advisors are completely automated digital advising systems that assist investors in wealth management by recommending portfolio allocations based on algorithms. Based on a study undertaken on a sampling of 2,000 US customers, according to the study by Piehlmaier (2022), while financial education appears to reduce robo-advice adoption, misplaced confidence in one's competence causes it to rise. The dramatically increasing acceptance of robo-advice among overconfident investors cannot be attributed to a willingness to take financial risk. Using risk of financial crime as an instrument variable, Chhatwani (2022) discovered that robo-advisory boosts retirement anxiety after adjusting for sociodemographic and financial literacy-related variables. According to Bhatia et al. (2021), several investors see robo-advisors as merely a substitute for wealth managers for research. Furthermore, they feel that human intervention is required to assess investor sentiments. The research by Atwal and Bryson (2021) finds that alleged risk, utility, ease of use, social factors, and intention to use are the characteristics that influence the desire to use AI to invest. According to a study by Rasiwala and Kohl (2021), the rise of robo-advisory services in many financial fields has posed a danger to the conventional investment and asset supervision industries.

1.3.2 Predictions

The use of AI and ML in predicting financial distress, stock market forecasting, portfolio administration, big data analytics, anti-money laundering, behavioural finance, and blockchain is on the rise (Ahmed et al., 2022). Adekoya et al. (2022) investigate the dynamic link between multiple indicators of investor attention and the stock returns of AI, Robotics, and Fintech stocks. To forecast the price movement of global financial indexes using technical analysis, Seong and Nam (2022) propose a unique DL method based on quantitative complex financial networks. Cura (2022) uses the artificial bee colony technique to give a heuristic approach to the portfolio optimization problem. The methodology developed by Petrelli et al. combines several AI methods to improve performance. Financial markets are increasingly employing AI techniques, such as fuzzy logic, which can capture nonlinear behaviour (Jankova et al., 2021).

1.3.3 Fintech

Traditional financial services are being transformed by financial technology advancements (Fintech). The paper by Vučinić et al. (2022) looks at the most recent advancements in the Fintech industry and explains the possible opportunities and concerns. The paper also examines cyber risk and "risk-based" thinking in the Fintech sector as the most recent and potentially most serious threat emerging during these chaotic and uncertain times. The traditional financial industry and banking sector have been impacted by the advancement of mobile technologies. Lee and Chen (2022) demonstrate mobile banking apps that provide practical advice for banks aiming to employ AI to retain customers. For the foreseeable future, risk mitigation necessitates a careful separation between AI and humans (Ashta and Herrmann, 2021). Mavlutova et al. (2021) investigate the role of Fintech and growth of alternative financial facilities and their parts in the financial segment's expansion. Boustani (2022) explores the use of AI in the banking sector, as well as its impact on bank personnel and consumer behaviour while purchasing financial services.

1.3.4 Risk Management

AI and ML's influence on banking risk management has received much interest in the aftermath of the global financial crisis. The study by Milojević and Redzepagic (2021) focuses on the potential of AI and ML and its application in risk management while taking into consideration potential hurdles and problems. It has the ability to help mitigate current global business issues, especially those brought on by the COVID-19 pandemic crisis. The impact of financial fraud on capital markets is significant. It deceives investors and the government, and it will stymie capital market growth. Qiu et al. (2021) propose an AI-based method to evaluate fraud risk to detect corporate fraud.

Governments all over the world have enlisted the help of financial services organizations to help detect and prevent money laundering. Canhoto (2021) investigates how ML algorithms' technical and contextual affordances may enable financial institutions to complete the mission. Zhao and Sun (2021) state that the advancement of modern information technology allows for the incorporation of AI technologies into credit risk evaluation, such as ANNs, genetic programming (GP), DTs, and SVCs.

1.3.5 Chatbot Technology

Customer service in financial organizations is predicted to be revolutionized by chatbot technology. However, in banking, the use of customer care chatbots is still limited. The purpose of Alt and Ibolya's (2021) article is to find specific categories of future financial services chatbot users related to technology user acceptance. The chatbots are significant in advertising and distribution automation, boosting conscience service for customers, and ensuring financial technology inclusion and economic stability, according to a study by Nair et al. (2021).

Li et al. (2021) offer a shared intelligence system that can abstract and integrate the sentiments articulated on the investing platform and build suitable portfolios by examining other depositors' expertise. In a variety of financial performance aspects, the suggested mechanism beats the market index and other standard methods. The article by Monkiewicz (2022) tries to identify and analyse important difficulties confronting financial sector oversight as a result of the digitization of securities industry and supervisory infrastructure.

1.3.6 Ethical AI

Bonson et al. (2021) discover that there is rising attention in the AI technology, despite the fact that 41.5% of European listed firms do not account for any AI activity. The adoption of ethical AI approaches is still in its infancy, with only 5% of businesses reporting on the subject. The paper offers a theoretical framework that integrates certain established theories, such as voluntary disclosure theory, signalling theory, and legitimacy theory, to analyse AI disclosure practices, which can aid in a more in-depth investigation of AI disclosure by merging multiple views.

1.3.7 Bank Lending Operations

Financial organizations can use document capture technology to automate their credit application evaluation processes. Rather than continuing the time-consuming procedure of manually studying invoices, payslips, and other permits, the job can be delegated to AI systems, which can impeccably handle these processes, robotically capture document information, and lever lending processes with negligible human intervention.

1.3.8 Credit Scoring

Financial institutions may employ AI to process credit applications quickly and accurately. AI technologies use predictive algorithms to examine applicants' credit ratings, resulting in lower regulatory costs and compliance, as well as better decision-making.

1.3.9 Debt Collection

Banks and other financial organizations employ AI to address the problem of delinquency and provide an effective debt collection system. TrueAccord is an example of AI in debt collection. The platform, which was founded in 2013 in San Francisco, promises to provide AI-based debt collection explanations to telecom, banks, and eCommerce firms. DL algorithms and document capture technology can be used by AI to avoid noncompliant expenditure and streamline approval operations.

1.3.10 Regulatory Compliance

Compliance with regulatory requirements is critical for all financial firms. AI may use NLP technology to scan regulatory and legal papers for any compliance concerns. This makes it a cost-effective and wise solution since it allows AI to quickly scan a large number of documents for noncompliant concerns without requiring any user intervention. Banks may detect any abnormal forms and identify danger parts in their Know Your Customer (KYC) procedures without involving humans. There are various advantages to using AI in KYC, including reduced mistakes, increased security and compliance, and faster processing.

1.3.11 Personalized Banking

With today's digitally aware consumers, traditional banking isn't cutting it. AI assistants, such as chatbots, use NLP to provide personalized investment assistance and identity-based client support.

1.3.12 Cybersecurity

Every day, users transfer money, pay bills, deposit checks, and buy stocks using online applications. Any bank or financial institution must now step up its cybersecurity efforts, and AI is playing a significant part in enhancing online finance security. Human error is thought to be accountable for up to 95% of cloud security breaks. AI may help businesses increase their security by studying and detecting regular data patterns and trends, as well as alerting them to any anomalies or odd behaviour (figure 1.3).

1.4 ISSUES WITH AI IN THE FINANCE INDUSTRY

1.4.1 Impact on Trading Based on Algorithms

Although AI is projected to deliver numerous profits when used in financial activities, new challenges have been found for market parties and governments. There are fears that high-frequency trading (HFT) and trading based on algorithms would increase market unpredictability, particularly if significant trading is based on the same algorithm, or that a probable exodus of market players who are unable to use HFT will reduce the variety of the market. As a result, applying AI to HFT and trading based on algorithms may exacerbate these undesirable consequences. In light of these differing viewpoints, policy-makers should keep a close eye on the potential effects of new technologies on market structure and price formation.

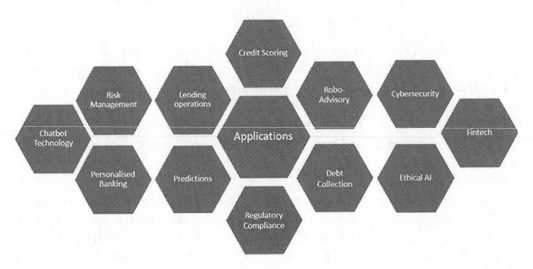

FIGURE 1.3   Some applications of AI in finance.

1.4.2 Assuring "Data Privacy" and "Information Security"

The potential advantages derived using information linked with financial operations are primary incentives for using AI in financial services organizations. As a result, data privacy and security of the information will become important in the provision of financial services. In this regard, stakeholders' earnest efforts will be critical in guaranteeing consumers' confidence as well as supporting their development.

1.4.3 Assuring "Governance" and "Trust"

Concerns have also been raised regarding whether the widespread use of AI will put financial system infrastructure beyond human control. Even though we now have very smart and experienced machines, limited people are willing to undergo entirely robotic procedures with no human participation, as we cannot eliminate jeopardies. To allow the application of AI to financial services, it will be necessary for key companies to build dependable frameworks for active governance and accountability in the event of negative outcomes, to maintain community confidence.

1.4.4 Risk of Relevant Laws and Regulations

Since the financial crisis of 2008, the global regulatory environment has risen in complexity and scale. The AI in the financial arena necessitates the establishment of a legal framework. The regulatory boundary is hazy due to the lack of rules and regulations. Following the occurrence of a disagreement, the assessment of legal culpability frequently lacks a legal basis. The financial regulatory system faces new issues as a result of AI's inventive use and development. The growing use of AI in the financial sector, which is leading to changes in financial operations and regulatory copies, as well as how to stay up with the times and incessantly enhance the legal system, is a significant problem that necessitates attention of key agencies.

1.4.5 Risk of Data Acquisition, and Leakage

To begin with, as an information-intensive sector, it frequently needs to evaluate, accumulate, and grip a huge quantity of consumer behaviour data in a financial company, as well as the extension of data collecting range, to assure the smooth flow of financial transactions. There is a legality issue with data collecting in explicit practices due to a lack of applicable collection standards and rules. When individuals lose data, whether purposefully or accidentally, there is a danger of data leakage.

1.4.6 Security Risks

To begin with, modern AI is still in its early stages of development, which means it will surely encounter several technical issues and pose significant hazards. For example, in the banking business, AI technology is widely employed, and many banks use facial recognition to withdraw money from ATMs. Face recognition technology has not yet matured to the point where it can be used effectively. There are various hazards with large-scale online face brushing transaction services, if solely facial recognition is used. Intelligent investment counselling, which relies on AI technology, also confronts many technical obstacles.

1.5 FUTURE TRENDS OF AI IN FINANCE

1.5.1 Use of Synthetic Data

From medical to financial services, businesses are resorting to synthetic datasets, which are artificial photos, recordings, or numerical information that imitate primary data obtained, in areas where enough actual data to train AI are inadequate or scarce, or where security and confidentiality are important problems. Despite the difficulties in effectively simulating real-world data, many businesses are depending on technology. In the financial sector, J.P. Morgan is training financial AI models with fake data.

1.5.2 Creating AI Legislation and Regulations

The smart revolution has ushered in a period of extraordinary crisis and challenge for contemporary ethical norms, legal laws, social order, and public management systems. It is the need of the hour to establish and enhance AI-related laws and regulations, fine-tune particular policies, identify the scope and direction of application, standardize, and offer support for AI's wider and faster adoption in the financial markets.

1.5.3 Increasing the Effectiveness of Financial Market Risk Mitigation

It is critical to recognize the relevance of AI, follow its growth trend, actively plan new intelligent business forms that match it, raise the degree of financial infrastructure building, and boost independent financial technology innovation. We should take steps to reduce the danger of financial fraud, develop a scientific and credible estimate of future trade trends, implement a security system, and keep technology up to date to prevent criminals from using it. According to CB Insights,[2] figure 1.4 depicts the future trends to watch out for AI in 2022.

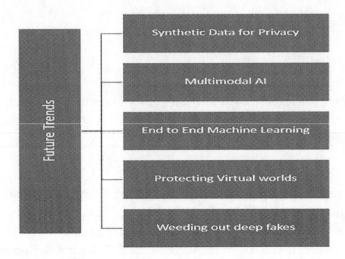

FIGURE 1.4 Future trends.

1.6 CONCLUSION

One of the most prominent progressive investigations in today's worldwide financial organizations is the adoption of AI into financial services. This chapter examines the use of AI in the financial services industry, its applications, challenges, and the present state of the technology, and future trends.

In our current day, technology is so widely used across the world that anybody with a basic understanding of finance may apply technology to their daily lives and make the most of it. Technology is no longer expensive or difficult to understand; everything is now encapsulated in a smartphone that anyone can operate without specialized training or experience. However, technical tools and skills are useless without financial understanding. AI has painted a clear picture of the role of Fintech businesses in improving financial literacy and inclusion. On the one hand, financial technology is advancing in banking and financial services, but the issues of AI and ML are also advancing at the same time. In this regard, the World Economic Forum has warned that AI would harm the financial system in the future by disrupting the employment market and posing financial risks.

Though there are huge opportunities for AI in financial services industry, it is important to investigate at the critical challenges as outlined by Ghandour (2021), which include job loss, user acceptance anxieties, confidentiality cracks, originality and compliance loss, digital divide, restrictive implementation and operational requirements, accessibility of massive quality information, and loss of emotional "human touch."

ACKNOWLEDGEMENT

I would like to mention and thank Mr. Akash Bahl, MBA, Krea University for providing assistance in collating relevant information required in writing this chapter.

NOTES

1 The report can be downloaded from https://www.cbinsights.com/research/report/ai-trends-q1-2022/
2 https://www.cbinsights.com/reports/CB-Insights_AI-Trends-2022

REFERENCES

Adekoya O.B., Oliyide J.A., Saleem O., Adeoye H.A. (2022), "Asymmetric connectedness between Google-based investor attention and the fourth industrial revolution assets: The case of FinTech and robotics & artificial intelligence stocks", *Technology in Society*, 68, 101925. doi: 10.1016/j.techsoc.2022.101925

Ahmed S., Alshater M.M., Ammari A.E., Hammami H. (2022), "Artificial intelligence and machine learning in finance: A bibliometric review", *Research in International Business and Finance*, 61, 101646. doi:10.1016/j.ribaf.2022.101646

Alt M.-A., Ibolya V. (2021), "Identifying relevant segments of potential banking chatbot users based on technology adoption behavior", *Market-Trziste*, 33(2), 165–183.

Ashta A., Herrmann H. (2021), "Artificial intelligence and fintech: An overview of opportunities and risks for banking, investments, and microfinance", *Strategic Change*, 30(3), 211–222. doi:10.1002/jsc.2404

Atwal G., Bryson D. (2021), "Antecedents of intention to adopt artificial intelligence services by consumers in personal financial investing", *Strategic Change*, 30(3), 293–298. doi:10.1002/jsc.2412

Bhatia A., Chandani A., Atiq R., Mehta M., Divekar R. (2021), "Artificial intelligence in financial services: A qualitative research to discover robo-advisory services", *Qualitative Research in Financial Markets*, 13(5), 632–654. doi:10.1108/QRFM-10-2020-0199

Bonsón E., Lavorato D., Lamboglia R., Mancini D. (2021), "Artificial intelligence activities and ethical approaches in leading listed companies in the European Union", *International Journal of Accounting Information Systems*, 43,100535. doi:10.1016/j.accinf.2021.100535

Boustani N.M. (2022), "Artificial intelligence impact on banks clients and employees in an Asian developing country", *Journal of Asia Business Studies*, 16(2), 267–278. doi:10.1108/JABS-09-2020-0376

Canhoto A.I. (2021), "Leveraging machine learning in the global fight against money laundering and terrorism financing: An affordances perspective", *Journal of Business Research*, 131, 441–452. doi:10.1016/j.jbusres.2020.10.012

Chhatwani M. (2022), "Does robo-advisory increase retirement worry? A causal explanation", *Managerial Finance*, 48(4), 611–628. doi:10.1108/MF-05-2021-0195

Cura T. (2022), "A rapidly converging artificial bee colony algorithm for portfolio optimization", *Knowledge-Based Systems*, 233, 107505. doi:10.1016/j.knosys.2021.107505

Ghandour A. (2021), "Opportunities and challenges of artificial intelligence in banking: Systematic literature review", *TEM Journal*, 10(4), 1581–1587.

Jankova Z., Jana D.K., Dostal P. (2021), "Investment decision support based on interval type-2 fuzzy expert system", *Engineering Economics*, 32(2), 118–129. doi:10.5755/j01.ee.32.2.24884

Lee J.-C., Chen X. (2022), "Exploring users' adoption intentions in the evolution of artificial intelligence mobile banking applications: The intelligent and anthropomorphic perspectives", *International Journal of Bank Marketing*, 40(4), 631–658. doi:10.1108/IJBM-08-2021-0394

Li Y.-M., Lin L.-F., Hsieh C.-Y., Huang B.-S. (2021), "A social investing approach for portfolio recommendation", *Information and Management*, 58(8), 103536. doi:10.1016/j.im.2021.103536

Mavlutova I., Volkova T., Spilbergs A., Natrins A., Arefjevs I., Verdenhofs A. (2021), "The role of fintech firms in contemporary financial sector development", *WSEAS Transactions on Business and Economics*, 18, 411–423. doi:10.37394/23207.2021.18.42

Milojević N., Redzepagic S. (2021), "Prospects of artificial intelligence and machine learning application in banking risk management", *Journal of Central Banking Theory and Practice*, 10(3), 41–57. doi:10.2478/jcbtp-2021-0023

Monkiewicz, J., Monkiewicz, M. (2022), "Financial sector supervision in digital age: transformation in progress", *Foundations of Management*, 14(1), 25–36. doi:10.2478/fman-2022-0002

Nair K., Anagreh S., Sunil A., Gupta R. (2021), "Ai-enabled chatbot to drive marketing automation for financial services", *Journal of Management Information and Decision Sciences*, 24, 1–17.

Petrelli D., Cesarini F. (2021), "Artificial intelligence methods applied to financial assets price forecasting in trading contexts with low (intraday) and very low (high-frequency) time frames", *Strategic Change*, 30(3), 247–256. doi:10.1002/jsc.2407

Piehlmaier D.M. (2022), "Overconfidence and the adoption of robo-advice: why overconfident investors drive the expansion of automated financial advice", *Financial Innovation*, 8, 14. doi:10.1186/s40854-021-00324-3

Qiu S., Luo Y., Guo H. (2021), "Multisource evidence theory-based fraud risk assessment of China's listed companies", *Journal of Forecasting*, 40(8), 1524–1539. doi:10.1002/for.2782

Rasiwala F.S., Kohl B. (2021), "Artificial intelligence in fintech: Understanding stakeholders perception on innovation, disruption, and transformation in finance", *International Journal of Business Intelligence Research*, 12(1), 48–65.

Seong N., Nam K. (2022), "Forecasting price movements of global financial indexes using complex quantitative financial networks", *Knowledge-Based Systems*, 235, 107608. doi:10.1016/j.knosys.2021.107608

Vučinić M., Luburić R. (2022), "Fintech, risk-based thinking and cyber risk", *Journal of Central Banking Theory and Practice, Central bank of Montenegro*, 11(2), 27–53.

Zhao Y., Sun Y. (2021), "Credit risk measurement study of commercial banks based on the innovation discrete Hopfield neural network model", *Journal of Global Business and Trade*, 17(2), 13–27. doi:10.20294/jgbt.2021.17.2.13

CHAPTER 2

Machine Learning and Big Data in Finance Services

Mahmoud El Samad, Hassan Dennaoui, and Sam El Nemar

CONTENTS

DOI: 10.1201/9781003327745-2

2.1 INTRODUCTION

Nowadays, the finance industry generates lots of data at a very high rate from different data sources (e.g., financial databases). The financial sector is working on improving the classical way of storing data in order to address new issues such as customer data management, risk management, workforce mobility and personalized marketing [1,2]. Financial organizations can benefit from big data as a long-term strategy, since it is now the fastest-growing technology adopted by many financial institutions [3].

Big data in finance can handle petabytes of data that can be analyzed to predict customer behaviors and propose intelligent strategies for financial institutions (e.g., banks, insurance companies, brokerage firms). Big data technology offers a set of services such as storing, processing and analyzing large amounts of data. These datasets can be structured (e.g., relational databases), semi-structured (e.g, XML, data collected from websites) or unstructured (e.g., emails, images, audios). These types of data cannot be treated by conventional database systems such as relational Database Management Systems (DBMS).

According to a recent survey published by Deloitte [4] in 2019, 64% of organizations rely on structured data collected from their internal data sources. Only 18% tackled the problem of handling unstructured data such as product images, customer audio files and social media comments. A solution to store this type of data, the Hadoop (an open-source project), enables handling of some types of unstructured data. The processing and analysis of big data plays a vital role in decision-making, forecasting, business analysis, product development, customer experience [5].

Moreover, big data technology can manage data with respect to the 3 Vs characteristics: volume, variety and velocity [6,7]. The volume means that the data generated are very big and cannot be processed by classical DBMS. The variety means that data can be of different types (e.g., structured, non-structured, semi-structured). The velocity means that data are generated at a very high speed such as in social medias, or data collected from sensors (e.g., Internet of Things). More Vs exist in the literature such as veracity, variability and value. Big data seem to be a very attractive solution for enterprises when dealing with this complex nature of data. More precisely, the finance industry is interested in the usage of big data technology in order to profit from its advantages. The finance sector covers a range of applications: banking, credit cards, stock exchanges, managing loans, stock brokerages and investment funds. Big data are well adapted as a solution for the finance field due to the enormous amounts of data generated in transactions in the financial market, whereas data might originate from different financial sources in different formats (e.g., stock trading).

Big data technology in combination with artificial intelligence (AI) (including machine learning (ML) algorithms and deep learning algorithms) is a very attractive solution in the financial sector since financial data can be collected, managed and analyzed. Recently, many studies [6,8–10] have shown the importance of combining big data and ML. ML is considered a branch or subset of AI. Intelligent algorithms are mainly applied during the data analysis stage in a big data framework. ML algorithms can also be used in other phases such as data collection [6] and data cleaning [11].

Consequently, the amalgamation of big data and ML is gaining more prominence in the academic and industry field. Many companies are focusing on how to benefit from big data and ML to enhance the level of productivity. ML can help to make predictions and to extract intelligent decisions. In the finance domain, ML can help to detect fraud, forecast trading [12,13], reach new customers, improve institutional risk and provide smart decisions [9]. ML relies on historical data collected from different data sources. In a nutshell, big data provide access to large volumes of heterogeneous data dispersed over the globe while ML enables to extract smart, quick and efficient decisions for financial institutions; however, there are still many challenges in this area (e.g., expanding the ML algorithms for big data environment).

The rest of the chapter is organized as follows. In section 2.2, we discuss big data technology including its characteristics and some applications in the financial domain. Section 2.3 presents ML while focusing on the financial service. Section 2.4 presents the current challenges of the integration between big data and ML with a focus on the financial sector. Finally, section 2.5 concludes this chapter.

2.2 BIG DATA CHARACTERISTICS AND CURRENT WORKS IN THE FINANCE SERVICES

2.2.1 Data Management

Data management can be achieved via centralized, parallel, distributed and big data systems. The centralized DBMS systems are classical systems that can handle data for a small company (most likely for hundreds to thousands of users). The parallel DBMS are used for highly intensive tasks requiring a lot of computations. It is a single machine with many processors that is stored in a single location, unlike distributed database system. The distributed database systems [14] enable the handling of a high number of users managing different data sources distributed geographically.

With the evolution of the abundance of continuous data, companies can no longer rely on traditional technology. These data amounts can be structured (such as relational database sources) or unstructured data. Unstructured data do not follow predefined models such as documents, texts, data collected from social media, emails, audios and videos.

Data are traditionally stored in classical relational models that rely on structured tables. Relational databases store data in tables with logical links between them. The querying of these structured tables is done using the well-known Structured Query Language (SQL). In order to query new types of data (i.e., semi-structured and nonstructured), new techniques exist such as NoSQL (not only SQL). NoSQL is a new technique that enables the processing of a wide variety of data including key-value, document, columnar and graph formats. Some examples of NoSQL DBMS are MongoDB, Casandra and CouchDB.

2.2.2 Big Data Characteristics

Data are the new oil that can lead the development in many fields such as finance, health, education, commerce and much more. Big data are characterized by the 4 Vs [7,15]: volume, variety, velocity and value. More Vs exist in the literature such as value, veracity, visibility, variability and venue.

- The term **Volume** refers to the management of huge amount of data that can reach Exabyte or even Zettabyte. When dealing with this size of data, we cannot use traditional approaches. Furthermore, data are now generated in massive amounts from countless data sources (e.g., data generated from online banking, insurance companies, stock exchange).

- The **Variety** refers to data from different types of formats (e.g., structured, XML, NoSQL, SQL files and text files). We can store structured data, semi-structured (machine-readable news) and unstructured data (documents on the web, posts on Twitter). These data sources can include valuable information to feed algorithm trading. More precisely, unstructured data are estimated to account for 70% to 85% of the total data [16]. Moreover, some financial data sources (e.g., Bloomberg) might be available to download as text files or excel files, while others might be stored in database systems.

- **Velocity** refers to the speed of data generation. The data generated by financial services such as banks, loans, insurance companies need to capture and analyze swiftly for better decision-making. For instance, the algorithm trading system [16] that can perform automated actions (e.g., buy/sell/hold), directly collects data from exchanges and web thus requiring quick decisions to avoid money loss.

- **Veracity** focuses on how accurate are the data collected. This term is very critical in the finance domain. Relying on inaccurate data can lead to inaccurate decision-making. In the finance domain, if we initiate our study based on inexact data, decision-makers will make poor decisions; for example, we advise investors to select weak stocks for investing. The storage of messy and noisy data can negatively affect our system.

- **Value** is related to extracting useful decisions for our business. More precisely, the idea is to deduct business rules.

Given this complex data nature, the business finance sector is relying on new big data technology as a solution that can enhance the quality of financial services (e.g., bank loans, insurance companies, forecasting). The challenge in big data is not only in storing and managing large amounts of heterogeneous data but to implement intelligent algorithms (e.g., ML) that can analyze big data to enhance the performance of the overall financial system.

2.2.3 Big Data Processing

In this section, the main phases needed for big data processing will be addressed. More precisely, the implementation of a big data framework should proceed in four main phases: (i) data collection, (ii) data processing, (iii) data analytics and (iv) data visualization.

The data collection consists of collecting data from different sources. For example, data sources can also be data generated from central banks, commercial banks and insurance companies. This phase requires the API (Application Programming Interface) that can retrieve data from different data sources. Data sources can be also social media comments, audio retrieved from a chatbot proposing, a loan for a customer. It should be kept in mind that data are generated in a very rapid manner when dealing with big data, which makes this phase more complex to handle [17].

Data processing consists of storing data that emerge from different sources (e.g., relational model, XML, text files) into one target database such as Hadoop [18]. Hadoop allows the distributed processing of high-volume sets of data (structured and non-structured) by using Hadoop Distributed File System (HDFS) for storing data efficiently [19].

The data analytics is a very important phase since data are analyzed in this phase for efficient decisions. This phase is realized, due to ML algorithms and data mining techniques, to produce meaningful value. The objective is to select the most suitable algorithm to analyze large amounts of data. In this phase, we can use MapReduce that allows parallel processing in a Hadoop framework.

The last phase is data visualization that enables visualization of the results; it is referred to data analytics at this stage, a trader can visualize, using sophisticated tools, which can advise customers to buy or sell share. The data visualization can help monitor the overall system.

2.2.4 Big Data and Financial Applications

Due to the success of the big data paradigm, many countries are investing in big data to help increase profits through financial services. In particular, big data can support the easing of access to financial products for economically active low-income families and micro-enterprises in China [20]. Moreover, characteristics of big data (e.g., volume, velocity, variety) complexity can help in the assessment of the creditworthiness of low-income families and micro-enterprises.

Another example in the banking sector that has relied on big data technology is the case in Spain of CaixaBank. CaixaBank is one of the banking leaders in the European region that contributes to research projects related to big data. This bank has 5000 branches using big data infrastructure with more than 40,000 employees managing 14 million clients. CaixaBank is connected to 300 heterogenous data sources reaching more than 4 PetaBytes of data. Due to this huge volume and variety of data, CaixaBank is relying on big data paradigm. More precisely, big data analytics is adopted to enhance the performance of the banking system and to increase the decision-making process. These include (1) analysis of relationships through IP addresses, (2) advanced analysis of bank transfer payment in financial terminals and (3) enhanced control of customers in online banking. Another example in the banking sector is the study conducted by Doerr et al. [21], who proposed the use of big data in combination with ML. In fact, the Banks' interest in the domain of big data and ML has increased by around 80% in the last few years. Many banks are leading new projects based on big data and ML to support their financial stability

When big data are combined with AI, it leads to a new paradigm known as "BDA (Big Data Analytic)". In the financial sector, BDA can forecast stock trading, detect a fraud and propose an adapted bank loan by using smart chatbot. BDA is gaining much importance [1] for finance services. The BDA utilizes millions of financial data records collected from different data sources (e.g., financial databases) distributed in a large-scale environment. The most interesting part when using big data technology is the capability of making analysis of data [22] coming from different data sources to take smart decisions. Moreover, the new trend is to focus on the customer behavior which is very important and critical for data analytics tools and how employees interact with the customers, utilizing big-data-as-a self-service [23].

2.3 MACHINE LEARNING

2.3.1 Definition and Characteristics

Machine learning, a subfield of AI [24], is an old concept that goes back six decades [25,26]. The ML concept is built around developing machines ready to execute many of the human activities through a self-learning and outside any human intervention.

Unlike traditional programming where the human role is essential, ML uses algorithms that initiate a self-learning process to repeatedly teach computers, from given data or its subsets and from the continuous outcomes of the performed operations, to execute several human tasks [24–29]. The ML methods can be categorized into four types each one of them used for solving specific problems: supervised, unsupervised, semi-supervised and reinforcement learning [25,28,30].

The importance of the ML development exists by adding to the machines/computers the capability of executing self-learning and self-programing without any human involvement [31]. When compared to the traditional computing or automation where the system/computer transforms the input (data and program) into multiple forms of outputs, ML is the technology that "*automates the process of automation*" [31]. With ML, problem solving will not rely upon a formula derived from human intervention, it relies on machine algorithms self-developed by the computer itself based on repeated patterns recognized over time when data change [32]. Accordingly, the algorithms are not static and do not require human intervention for updates, they are in a continuous self-update as long as there is a guaranteed big flow of data to the system to identify new patterns.

2.3.2 ML Types

As stated in the previous section, ML methods can be classified into four types, each one is applied for solving specific problems: supervised, unsupervised, semi-supervised and reinforcement learning [25,28,30].

2.3.2.1 Supervised Learning

Supervised learning algorithm deals with labeled data starting from the input data and reaching out the projected output. The input labeled data are split into various datasets including training, validation and test datasets. The supervised learning algorithm will identify patterns in the training and validation datasets. This training and validation process is repeated several times to improve the performance of the algorithm by comparing the training and validation dataset outcomes. Thus, a mapping function is created to identifying the relation between the expected output and the initial data. The evaluation of the algorithm or model, developed from the repeated training and validation process, is executed through the testing process that uses the invented algorithm/model on the test datasets determining the level of accuracy. The whole process is repeated until the desired level of accuracy is reached [25,27,29].

The well-known supervised learning algorithms are the regression (prediction of numeric data) and classification (prediction about the category an example belongs to). Other less-known supervised learning algorithms include Nearest neighbor, Naïve Bayes, Decision Trees, Linear Regression, Support Vector Machines and Neural Networks [25,27,29].

2.3.2.2 Unsupervised Learning

The unsupervised learning algorithm deals with unlabeled datasets to detect the existence of patterns, similarities or differences existing among the data, without setting initially any expected output or target or performing any training process, leaving to the algorithm the mission of determining those patterns, similarities or differences. In this ML category, the level of category is not evaluated as there is no predefined labeling or targeted outcome [25,27,29].

The well-known unsupervised learning algorithms are clustering, association and anomaly detection. Other less-known unsupervised learning algorithms include k-means algorithm for clustering and Apriori algorithm for association problems [27,29].

2.3.2.3 Semi-supervised Learning

Semi-supervised learning algorithm is considered as the model between supervised and unsupervised learning. It is mainly used for datasets combining both labeled and unlabeled data [29]. This model is used when we use some labeled datasets to train a model to be able after training, validation and evaluation to classify unlabeled datasets so that it can reach a trained model surpassing the performance and the accuracy of unsupervised models [29].

2.3.2.4 Reinforcement Learning

Reinforcement learning algorithm uses a training technique based on a trial and error concept to cumulate learning from self-actions and previous experiences. When machines use reinforcement learning algorithms, will get reward feedback when they reach the desired outcome based on a right decision [27–29]. The decision taken as well as the sequence of actions and attempts performed will be stored creating cumulative lessons learning to be used in the future for the purpose of improving the performance and the decision-making. The well-known reinforcement learning algorithms are Q-Learning and Markov Decision processes [27].

2.3.3 ML in Finance Services

During the last decade, the adoption of AI and ML in the financial sector has grown expeditiously, particularly because of the large financial data, where firms recognize the need and interest for continuous better and higher quality of services for their clients at affordable prices [33].

Financial firms, including trading and fintech firms as well as banks, are considering the use of AI/ML models and algorithms within their financial services as they expect, when integrated within their services, higher revenues by improving the company productivity and user experience, lower operational expenses by automating the processes and reinforcing the system security and its compliance with regulations and bylaws.

And since decision-making in the financial sector is very critical and requires high accuracy with reliable information, the ML algorithms improve financial services by applying the self-learning method starting from the initial and continuous flow of supplied data, processes and methods. With less human intervention, the ML/big data based financial services will benefit from the advanced data analytics performed by the powerful ML algorithms that, combined with big data collected from various sources, will capture and identify more relationships and patterns within the data and thus, when iteratively executed, will improve the accuracy of the results and accordingly reduce the error rate in the output data such as analytical data, and financial recommendations [33].

Hereunder, we will describe some of the growing AI/ML-based financial services before going in-depth with the well-known financial service providers 'Algo Trading' which is considered as one of the most mature ML-based financial services used widely by various financial firms worldwide.

2.3.3.1 Financial Monitoring Systems

Using ML algorithms, financial monitoring solution can improve a financial firm's network security, when combined with cybersecurity, it will be able to detect and identify various kinds of money laundry transactions even when using advanced techniques [34].

2.3.3.2 Investment Prediction Systems

ML algorithms play a significant role in enhancing the capabilities of financial prediction systems by allowing the identification of market changes through the continuous supply and analysis of the market insights. Those investment prediction systems will have the ability to predict potential trends in the financial market, as well as alerting earlier financial companies about potential risks, financial irregularities or any other threats that might arise from market changes [35,36] (figure 2.1).

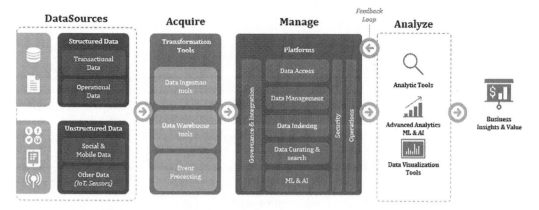

FIGURE 2.1   Investment prediction systems.

[Source: 35].

2.3.3.3 Process Automation Systems

ML algorithms improved the effectiveness of the process automation solutions in the finance sector by introducing new techniques and capabilities. The objective behind automating the repetitive tasks is to enhance companies' productivity, improve companies' services, increase customer's satisfaction and optimize cost. Accordingly, more powerful ML-based tools have been introduced such as document flow automation, chatbots, employee training gamification, customer request track and recognition, customer behavior interpretation [4].

2.3.3.4 Transaction Analysis and Fraud Detection Solutions

Nowadays, ML algorithms are supporting transaction analysis solutions by detecting internet and credit card frauds as well as reducing the false rejections of several clean transactions executed in the financial sector. Using huge amounts of data (real-time transactions and historical payments), the ML algorithms improve the solution capability by training itself for better understanding of the transactions' behaviors, detecting the existing trends within the data and being able to highlight potential frauds thus take preventive actions [33,37] (figure 2.2).

2.3.3.5 Financial Advisory Solutions

ML-based financial advisory solutions are becoming more powerful and necessity for many financial and non-financial firms by giving advisory for the management about the overall company budget management, daily spending, identification of spending patterns and highlight on some saving tricks. Moreover, the financial advisory solutions can support small- and medium-sized enterprises by managing their funds and loans by recommending some financial transactions such as trading, investments [34] (figure 2.3).

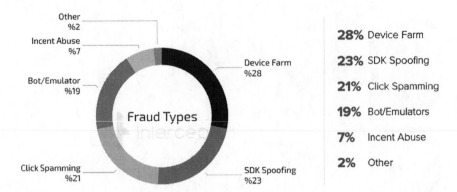

FIGURE 2.2   Security and fraud detection solutions.

[Source: 37].

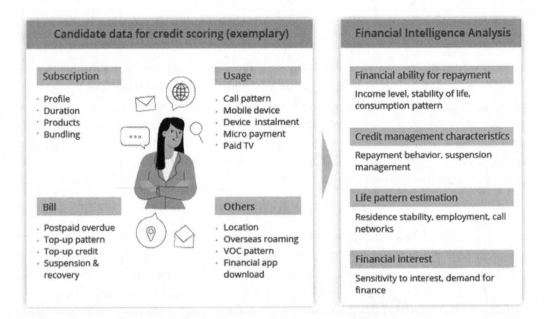

FIGURE 2.3   Credit scoring solutions.

(Source: [38]).

2.3.3.6 Credit Scoring Solutions

ML algorithms and big data empower credit scoring solutions when used in the banking or financing sectors. When traditional credit scoring is performed by humans, it is time-consuming especially when employees try to find the most accurate information to create an overall picture around clients with the powerful ML-based tool and big data. The loan manager will receive the needed and accurate information describing the candidate thus expecting the possibility of whether they are going to return or not the loan. Big data, such as social media and financial transactions of the candidate, will help the ML-based tool to analyze the candidate attitude and behavior by predicting and presenting its analysis to decision-makers [33,39].

2.3.3.7 Customer Service Solutions

ML algorithms enrich the customer service solutions used in financial and non-financial firms. For financial firms, the chatbots are used for many powerful transactions compared to the regular Q/A messaging tool chatbot used in the non-financial firms. The chatbots offer advanced services to the clients such as their monthly expenses, proposition of insurance plans, account analysis, money saving and growing plans, personalized investment plans, etc., all based on the customer available data to propose customized offers that fit within the client capability and profile [34].

2.3.3.8 Marketing Solutions

ML algorithms with the availability of big data help companies, using ML-based marketing solutions, to make accurate predictions when planning for upcoming years. Those ML-based marketing tools will be able to generate a strong marketing strategy using data from different sources such as company mobile application usage, company web activities, previous marketing campaigns and other marketing activities [34].

2.3.3.9 Customer Sentiment Analysis Solutions

ML algorithms do not work only on raw data related to the companies or to the market but also to individuals expanding its capabilities by analyzing their social media or financial data, to include also individual sentiments expressed either in texting or even through voice thus reaching a better understanding of the consumer behavior and reacting accordingly to respond to their needs [34].

2.3.3.10 Algorithmic Trading System

The ML algorithms enhance the trading services in multiple areas changing the way of trading globally. According to Johnson [39], Algorithmic Trading or Algo Trading (AT) is "*a computerized rule-based process for placing large orders in the market which almost eliminates manual human intervention of a trader*".

AT analyzes thousands of datasets at the same time collected from various sources, giving the traders a unique advantage in the market. The AT brings to the financial trading sector several benefits such as speed, competitive transaction cost, backtesting, precision and improvement of market liquidity. It allows financial trading firms to enhance their decisions by applying a deep observation of the trading results and real-time information, thus providing the AT with the capability of identifying the patterns affecting direct and indirect stock prices [33].

AT increases the trading accuracy which automatically reduces mistakes. AT is simply minimizing the human intervention and applying an automated self-learning process through a continuous update of the AT algorithms taking into consideration the real-time changes in the market conditions.

Accordingly, with the increase in system accuracy, decrease in system errors, decrease in trading execution time and decrease in human intervention and staff, AT will offer an execution of the financial trades at the best possible prices, increase in the trading [33].

2.4 CHALLENGES FOR THE INTEGRATION OF BIG DATA AND ML IN FINANCE SERVICES

Given the complex nature of big data, ML algorithms need to be expanded in order to deal with different types of data [8,10]. Moreover, many challenges exist in order to analyze unstructured and semi-structured data through ML techniques. Financial institutes such as banks, financial firms, governments and insurance companies should hire or take consultancy from data experts to handle the complexity of such environments.

On the other hand, the implementation of ML technologies in the financial services was not an easy decision by financial firms where several challenges have been identified by theory and practice [34] as described hereunder:

- Financial service providers do not have the full picture to understand the real capabilities of ML regarding a specific financial domain and thus could fail in setting realistic expectations.

- The fact of having multiple data sources stored in multiple locations and in different formats such as in big data frameworks will create greater challenges in data management and thus higher cost of research and development with lower return on investment when comparing the cost of the project to the value (financial and technical) of the proposed ML-based financial services.

- The need of huge amount of raw data is crucial to execute the process of training ML algorithms. Moreover, data supplied or collected cannot be treated equally where the need to identify sensitive data (such as financial data) using specific data security protocols to protect them from malicious accessibility.

- The need to have an infrastructure supporting ML algorithm implementation is essential considering that, reaching the desired outcomes, will require the availability of proper infrastructure and environment for testing and experimentation.

- The integration of ML algorithms in financial services requires the existence of potential business idea/case. Furthermore, the business idea should be translated into clear, agile and flexible business processes. This does not guarantee the success of the initial ML model implementation but will support the company in building a new strategy for future ML implementation based on lessons learned in the objective of developing a robust ML design.

- To develop robust ML algorithms in the finance sector, there is a need to have enough ML experts with financial services exposure. In general, there is a lack of qualified people in the AI industry, challenges will arise when recruiting AI/ML experts in the finance field.

- The implementation of ML in general will not solve the businesses' problem quickly, it is in fact a time-consuming process that requires continuous data gathering, algorithm training and algorithm re-engineering to reach the expected model that suits business.

- Finally, the initial question to be addressed by the financial or business firms: is it affordable to develop an in-house ML algorithm? And if not, which third-party consultancy firm will have the required capability to provide the needed ML algorithm within the allocated budget?

2.5 CONCLUSION

This chapter presented current works, applications and challenges related to the usage of big data and ML in the finance domain. The generation of the massive amount of financial data emerging from structured data sources (e.g., finance databases) and unstructured data (e.g., XML files, posts retrieved from blogs) is a real challenge since the need to expand current ML algorithms to treat this new dimension. Current financial institutions are now attempting to benefit from both big data technology and ML in order to increase profits and enhance the performance of the overall system. Yet there are many challenges in order to implement these technologies such as the Human Resource investment (hiring new data scientists in this area); the IT deployment where new hardware and software tools are now required to expand the IT infrastructure; the expansion of current ML algorithms in big data frameworks. Although we would like to cite some studies in this field, the study by Hasan [2] stated that the current works of big data in the finance area can be divided into three groups: the big data implications for financial markets, the big data implications for internet finance and the big data implications for risk management, financial analysis and applications. Another study by Cockcroft [40] in the area of big data and accounting and finance offers certain benefits; risk and security, data visualisation and predictive analytics, data management and data quality.

REFERENCES

[1] Alexopoulos, A., Becerra, Y., Boehm, O., Bravos, G., Chatzigiannakis, V., Cugnasco, C., & Vinov, M. (2022). Big data analytics in the banking sector: Guidelines and lessons learned from the CaixaBank case. In *Technologies and applications for big data value* (pp. 273–297). Springer, Cham.

[2] Hasan, M. M., Popp, J., & Oláh, J. (2020). Current landscape and influence of big data on finance. *Journal of Big Data*, 7(1), 1–17.

[3] Stockinger, K., Bundi, N., Heitz, J., & Breymann, W. (2019). Scalable architecture for Big Data financial analytics: User-defined functions vs. SQL. *Journal of Big Data*, 6(1), 1–24.

[4] Smith, T., Stiller, B., Guszcza, J., & Davenport, T. (25 July 2019). Analytics and AI-driven enterprises thrive in the Age of With The culture catalyst, Deloitte Article, Insight-driven organization | Deloitte Insights.

[5] Casado, R., & Younas, M. (2015). Emerging trends and technologies in big data processing. *Concurrency and Computation: Practice and Experience*, 27(8), 2078–2091.

[6] Roh, Y., Heo, G., & Whang, S. E. (2019). A survey on data collection for machine learning: A big data-ai integration perspective. *IEEE Transactions on Knowledge and Data Engineering*, 33(4), 1328–1347.

[7] Labrinidis, A., & Jagadish, H. V. (2012). Challenges and opportunities with big data. *Proceedings of the VLDB Endowment*, 5(12), 2032–2033.

[8] Zhang, F., Chen, Z., Zhang, C., Zhou, A. C., Zhai, J., & Du, X. (2021). An efficient parallel secure machine learning framework on GPUs. *IEEE Transactions on Parallel and Distributed Systems*, 32(9), 2262–2276.

[9] Vats, P., & Samdani, K. (2019, March). Study on machine learning techniques in financial markets. In 2019 IEEE International Conference on System, Computation, Automation and Networking (ICSCAN) (pp. 1–5). IEEE.

[10] Zhou, L., Pan, S., Wang, J., & Vasilakos, A. V. (2017). Machine learning on big data: Opportunities and challenges. *Neurocomputing*, 237, 350–361.

[11] El Samad, M., El Nemar, S., Sakka, G., & El-Chaarani, H. (2022). An innovative big data framework for exploring the impact on decision-making in the European Mediterranean healthcare sector, *EuroMed Journal of Business*, 10.1108/EMJB-11-2021-0168

[12] Abraham, R., Samad, M. E., Bakhach, A. M., El-Chaarani, H., Sardouk, A., El Nemar, S., & Jaber, D. (2022). Forecasting a stock trend using genetic algorithm and random forest. *Journal of Risk and Financial Management*, 15(5), 188.

[13] Henrique, B. M., Sobreiro, V. A., & Kimura, H. (2019). Literature review: Machine learning techniques applied to financial market prediction. *Expert Systems with Applications*, 124, 226–251.

[14] Özsu, M. T., & Valduriez, P. (1999). *Principles of distributed database systems* (Vol. 2). Englewood Cliffs: Prentice Hall.

[15] Sagiroglu, S., & Sinanc, D. (2013). Big data: A review. In 2013 international conference on collaboration technologies and systems (CTS) (pp. 42–47). IEEE.

[16] Qin, X. (2012, October). Making use of the big data: next generation of algorithm trading. In International Conference on Artificial Intelligence and Computational Intelligence (pp. 34–41). Springer, Berlin, Heidelberg.

[17] Al-Qirim, N., Tarhini, A., & Rouibah, K. (2017). Determinants of big data adoption and success. In Proceedings of the International Conference on Algorithms, Computing and Systems (pp. 88–92).

[18] Apache Hadoop. (n.d.). Https://Hadoop.Apache.Org/. https://hadoop.apache.org/

[19] Zomaya, A. Y., & Sakr, S. (Eds.). (2017). *Handbook of big data technologies*.

[20] Kshetri, N. (2016). Big data's role in expanding access to financial services in China. *International Journal of Information Management*, 36(3), 297–308.

[21] Doerr, B. S., Gambacorta, L., & Serena, J. M. (2021). How do central banks use big data and machine learning?. *In The European Money and Finance Forum*, 67, 1–6.

[22] Ravi, V., & Kamaruddin, S. (2017, December). Big data analytics enabled smart financial services: opportunities and challenges. In International Conference on Big Data Analytics (pp. 15–39). Springer, Cham.

[23] Passlick, J., Lebek, B., & Breitner, M. H. (2017). A self-service supporting business intelligence and big data analytics architecture. In 13th International Conference on Wirtschafts informatik, St. Gallen, February 12–15, 2017.

[24] Priyadharshini. (2017). Machine Learning: What it is and Why it Matters., from Simpli Learn: https://www.simplilearn.com/what-is-machine-learning-and-why-it-matters-article

[25] Choi, R. Y., Coyner, A. S., Kalpathy-Cramer, J., Chiang, M. F., & Campbell, J. P. (2020). Introduction to machine learning, neural networks, and deep learning. *Translational Vision Science & Technology*, 9(2), 14–24.

[26] Haenlein, M., & Kaplan, A. (2019). A brief history of artificial intelligence: On the past, present, and future of artificial intelligence. *California Management Review*, 61(4), 5–14.

[27] Sodhi, P., Awasthi, N., & Sharma, V. (2019). Introduction to machine learning and its basic application in python. In Proceedings of 10th International Conference on Digital Strategies for Organizational Success.

[28] Mahesh, B. (2020). Machine learning algorithms-a review. *International Journal of Science and Research (IJSR)*. [Internet], 9, 381–386.

[29] Hastie, T., Tibshirani, R., Friedman, J. H., & Friedman, J. H. (2009). *The elements of statistical learning: Data mining, inference, and prediction* (Vol. 2, pp. 1–758). New York: Springer.

[30] Salian, I. (2018). NVIDIA Blog: Supervised Vs. Unsupervised Learning. *The Official NVIDIA Blog*.

[31] Brownlee, J. (2016). Machine learning algorithms from scratch with Python. *Machine Learning Mastery*.

[32] Wagstaff, K. (2012). Machine learning that matters. arXiv preprint arXiv:1206.4656.

[33] OECD (2021), Artificial Intelligence, Machine Learning and Big Data in Finance: Opportunities, Challenges, and Implications for Policy Makers, https://www.oecd.org/finance/artificial-intelligence-machine-learningbig-data-in-finance.htm.

[34] Maruti Techlabs Inc., (2020) – source: https://marutitech.com/ai-and-ml-in-finance/

[35] OneGlobe, (2019) – source: https://www.oneglobesystems.com/blog/harnessing-the-power-of-ai-ml-for-analytics-in-banking-and-financial-services

[36] JPMorgan (2019), Machine Learning in FX, https://www.jpmorgan.com/solutions/cib/markets/machine-learning-fx (accessed on 14 December 2020).

[37] Interceptd, (2019) – source: The Interceptd Q2 2019 Mobile Ad Fraud Report. How severe is mobile ad fraud, and how hard could it hit your business? Get the facts and figures in our latest report.

[38] Intellias, (2018) – source: https://intellias.com/mobile-data-machine-learning-better-credit-scoring-for-the-underbanked/

[39] Johnson, B. (2010). *Algorithmic trading and DMA*. 4Myeloma Press.

[40] Cockcroft, S., & Russell, M. (2018). Big data opportunities for accounting and finance practice and research. *Australian Accounting Review*, 28(3), 323–333.

CHAPTER 3

Artificial Intelligence in Financial Services: Advantages and Disadvantages

Rola Shawat, Abanoub Wassef, and Hebatallah Badawy

CONTENTS

3.1 INTRODUCTION

The objective of the financial services sector is to offer different financial services to individuals and corporations. The financial services sector involves different participants. Technology companies that offer advanced and automated services to financial organizations and traditional financial companies that rely on technology in their operations are the main participants of such sectors (Hu, 2020). Banks are financial institutions that are eligible to receive deposits and offer loans to their customers.

In general, banks face different types of risks, such as credit risk, liquidity risk, technology risk, interest rate risk, market risk, operational risk, insolvency risk, and off-balance

DOI: 10.1201/9781003327745-3

sheet risk, and they are subject to very strict regulations. Market, credit, and operational risks are the primary risks that banks face. Credit risk refers to the borrower's failure to settle his/her obligations and is considered to be the greatest risk that banks face and the one that requires the most capital. Market risk refers to the risk that results from the trading operations of the bank and it encompasses risks related to changing interest rates, foreign currency exchange rates, and so on. Finally, operational risk represents the losses resulting from internal system breakdown or external events outside the bank or the financial institution. Banks are required to forecast and manage those risks (Leo et al., 2019).

AI and ML-related applications are broadly used in the financial services industry and specifically in the banking industry. The financial services industry is considered to be one of the early adopters and implementers of AI technology and its applications (Golić, 2019). This industry is one of the most comprehensive industries that rely on AI to a great extent (Hu, 2020). According to Hwang and Kim (2021), the investment in the area of AI in the financial sector is higher than that in other sectors such as the manufacturing, retailing, and non-private sectors. This industry relies on information technology to conduct its operations and integrate with AI because of the expected benefits resulting from its application.

There are four spectra for AI. The first one is automation, where programs do not think or make any decisions, beyond the pre-developed and programmed rules. The second one involves the classical and traditional statistical techniques and programs. Here the techniques draw inferences according to the quantifiable probability of a relationship. The third one involves ML and Robotic Process Automation (RPA), which are the systems that provide more benefits using more time and data. Here ML applications can detect anomalies to expect and prevent financial crises, like the 2008 financial crisis. The fourth and last one is Artificial General Intelligence (AGI), which makes computers able to behave and think like humans (Golić, 2019).

AI and ML applications are used in the financial services sector in different areas such as credit risk management, bank failure prediction, and customer services and support. Concerning the benefits expected from the integration and application of AI in the financial industry, Golić (2019) noted that it is expected that AI applications will enable its adopters to offer services of higher quality, at lower cost, and in the shortest time possible. The lower cost will result from replacing people in specific positions with chatbots, Robo-traders, and cobots that will reduce employment and also human errors. In addition, it is expected that the AI technology will change the relationship and the way of interaction between the financial services provider (for instance, banks) and the financial services user (client), and this will result in offering new products and services and new job opportunities. Finally, it is expected that AI technology will lead to better transaction security, data protection, and financial fraud prevention.

The objective of this chapter is to give a general overview of the AI and ML applications in the financial industry and specifically in the banking industry and discuss the advantages and disadvantages of these applications from different perspectives.

To fulfill the objective of this chapter, the rest of it will be organized as follows: Section 3.2 will provide a general overview of AI. Section 3.3 will discuss the AI applications in different areas in the financial sector. Section 3.4 will discuss the advantages and disadvantages of AI applications in the financial sector. Section 3.5 will summarize and present recommendations for future improvement.

3.2 OVERVIEW OF AI

To evaluate the AI applications in the financial services sector, it is essential to have a minimum understanding of the main terms in this regard. These terms are AI, ML, and deep learning (DL hereafter). These terms were used in different previous studies and the disagreements over their definitions are still unresolved (Wall, 2018).

"According to Oxford Dictionary, AI is the theory of the development of computer systems to be able to perform tasks normally requiring human intelligence, such as visual perception, speech recognition, decision making and translation between languages" (Wall, 2018). AI is a study area at the crossroads of computer, human, and social technologies. This technology development may help in simulating and expanding the applications of human intelligence technology (Khan et al., 2022). The technologies used in AI may include ML, expert systems, DL, audio processing, knowledge representation, natural language processing, and robotics (Ray et al., 2019).

ML is a part of AI and is a data analysis tool. It is a way to apply AI by having the machine learn directly from previous or training data (Wall, 2018; Wang et al., 2020), identify patterns, trends, or distributions of datasets, and make decisions (Wang et al., 2020). It involves different sciences, which are computer science, engineering, and statistics, and it becomes a common tool for nearly every task that requires extracting meaningful information from data sets (Leo et al., 2019). ML can be used in classifying objects, predicting values, and discovering structure and unusual data points (Wall, 2018). Generally speaking, ML is a system that automates analytical model building with the minimum level of human intervention (Wang et al., 2020).

To understand how machines can learn from data, it is important to discuss the three different classes of ML, which differ according to the degree of human involvement (Wall, 2018).

1. The first class is *supervised learning*. In this class, machines are trained to derive desired output from certain data. This class involves several algorithms such as Artificial Neural Network, Decision Tree, Random Forest, and K-nearest neighbor (Minastireanu and Mesnita, 2019).

2. The second class is *unsupervised learning*, where the data is not labeled, as in the clustering case. Here, the used algorithms classify the unlabeled data with similar attributes, and they are characterized by their lower accuracy level, in comparison with the supervised learning algorithms. Examples in this class involve Hidden Markov Model, Genetic algorithm, Expert system, Gradient Descendent, and Scatter search (Minastireanu and Mesnita, 2019).

3. The third and last class is *enforcement learning*, where the algorithm is rewarded for every decision taken at each stage.

Based on this section, it can be noted that AI is a disruptive technology that relies on computer, human, and social technologies. There are different AI and ML applications that differ according to the degree of human involvement.

3.3 AI APPLICATIONS IN THE FINANCIAL SECTOR

AI is now changing the financial services industry. There are different areas where AI technology is being used in the financial services industry and specifically in the banking industry. These areas might include fraud prediction, where the accuracy provided by AI techniques enables banks to predict fraud before it happens, chatbots, which offer 24/7 customer service and online conversations and help customers to open bank accounts and receive customer complaints and direct them to the appropriate unit, and customer relationship management, through offering facial recognition to use financial applications. AI is also used in predictive analytics (such as in revenue forecasting and risk monitoring) and credit risk management, as AI models and techniques are used to evaluate the creditworthiness of the borrower and predict the default risk (www.deloitte. com). In addition, AI applications can contribute toward financial inclusion by reducing information asymmetry problems, enhancing risk detection and management, enhancing the security of online finance, and improving the coverage, accessibility, and efficiency of financial services and credit risk assessment.

3.3.1 AI and Customer Services and Support

AI may be used in the customer services and support area. In this area, banks' use and application of AI technology will help them to adopt new customer support and help desks, which will result in higher efficiency and lower customer support cost (Mhlanga, 2020). This application might be in the form of using chatbots, which are increasingly adopted by Indian financial organizations to reap their benefits (Ray et al., 2019), and Robo-advisors (Belanche et al., 2019).

According to Hwang and Kim (2021), a chatbot combines the words "chatting" and "robot", and the chatbot is generally used in messaging. Chatbots offer customers previously prepared answers and other related information that resemble a great extent the case in the real world. They can make different functions such as providing contact data or information on the features of products and services, making financial recommendations to the customer, keeping track of personal finance, answering user questions, and making payments. To provide accurate and customized services, chatbots study customer-related information using ML and DL technologies.

Robo-advisors are online services that involve using computer algorithms to offer financial advice and help customers in managing their investment portfolios (Fisch et al., 2019). Robo-advice is being defined as "an automated investment platform that uses quantitative algorithms to manage investors' portfolios and accessible to clients online" (Waliszewski and Warchlewska, 2020, p. 400).

Robo-advisors are user-friendly. It follows certain steps. First, this automated service will assess the customer's profile based on an initial questionnaire that focuses on different aspects such as the customer's goal, risk, and expected return. Second, the offered service will make some recommendations or suggestions to the customer about investment, based on the customer's responses to the initial questionnaire, as would be the case of a human financial advisor (Belanche et al., 2019).

Robo-advisors are becoming an alternative to human financial advisors on banking issues and different cash transactions. They provide great advantages in the area of online trading, as they can open an account in real time and process a vast number of transactions immediately (Golubev et al., 2020). Accordingly, it can be expected that robo-advisors are in a better position compared to traditional human financial advisors. They enable its users to improve the access to financial services, reducing management fees and offering a wide range of investment opportunities without experiencing the influence of human motives (Faubion, 2016).

Hwang and Kim (2021) conducted a comparative study to investigate the effect of using automated customer service versus chatbots on the bank's financial performance. Based on 351,527 cases generated from banking data in Korea, the authors found that in the case of utility bills and loan interest payments, chatbots showed a positive impact on bank's profitability (in comparison to customer service).

3.3.2 AI and Bank Failure Prediction

Another area, where AI technology might be used and applied in the banking sector is bank failure or bankruptcy prediction.

Banks' functions are unique, and they are exposed to several types of risks such as market risk, interest rate risk, country risk, technology risk, foreign exchange risk, credit risk, liquidity risk, and other risks (Liu et al., 2021). Because of the negative effects of such risks on banks and the possible bank failure risk and their negative impact on society as a whole, banks are subject to very strict supervision and regulatory requirements in all countries. Meanwhile, banks are considered to be the major users of technology, and they can use ML techniques in bank failure and bankruptcy prediction. According to Liu et al. (2021), ML techniques can be used for bank failure prediction and are proven to be better and highly superior in their predictive ability than traditional statistical techniques. Examples of these techniques include decision trees, random forests, k-nearest neighbor methods, and artificial neural networks.

Prior studies analyzed the advantages and disadvantages of bank failure prediction techniques. It was found that, in general, AI and ML methods and techniques outperform the traditional statistical methods (Liu et al., 2021). Also, the ML techniques differ in their predictive accuracy. For instance, artificial neural networks and k-nearest neighbor methods are the most accurate models (Le and Viviani, 2017) and decision trees are superior in terms of their predictive ability to neural networks and support vector machine methods (Olson et al., 2012) and are efficient in their computing ability and data storage (Siswoyo et al., 2020).

Le and Viviani (2017) compared the accuracy of traditional statistical and ML techniques, which are used to predict bank failure. Based on a sample of 3000 banks in the US, the authors found evidence that ML techniques in general (artificial neural network and k-nearest neighbor) outperform the traditional methods (discriminant analysis and logistic regression) in their predictive accuracy.

In the same context, Siswoyo et al. (2020) developed a bankruptcy prediction model using five input variables that are related to total assets, which are working capital, sales, retained earnings, income before interest and tax, and market value of equity to book value of total liabilities. Using these five variables, the authors developed a hybrid model that involves a two-class boosted decision tree and a multi-class decision forest. After applying this model to the commercial banks in Indonesia, Siswoyo et al. (2020) found evidence that applying this model has proven to achieve higher bankruptcy prediction accuracy and can produce three major classifications of bankruptcy, which are bank-ruptcy, grey area, and non-bankruptcy.

To analyze the advantages and disadvantages of AI and ML techniques in the area of bank failure and bankruptcy prediction, these methods can be compared with the tra-ditional statistical techniques. Upon this comparison, it is found that AI and ML are found to outperform the conventional statistical techniques in terms of their predictive accuracy. Also, these methods are flexible and adaptable in comparison with the tradi-tional statistical methods which require strict assumptions concerning the normal dis-tribution of the data used and the absence of correlation between independent variables (Le and Viviani, 2017). On the other hand, it can be noted that the artificial neural network can't give a justification for the causal relationship between variables, and this reduces its applicability to different managerial problems (Lee and Choi, 2013).

3.3.3 AI and Financial Inclusion

Financial inclusion refers to the number of individuals who can reach banking or financial services (Ray et al., 2019). According to the World Bank, the importance of financial inclusion is increasing, as it contributes toward reducing the level of poverty and increasing prosperity (How et al., 2020). AI can offer considerable assistance in the area of financial inclusion (Mhlanga, 2020). Digital financial inclusion is of considerable importance to make sure that people who were at the lower level of the pyramid can now have access to different sources of finance (Mhlanga, 2020). AI applications will con-tribute toward financial inclusion in different aspects, by reducing information asym-metry problems, enhancing risk detection and management, enhancing the security of online finance, and improving the coverage, accessibility, and efficiency of financial services and credit risk assessment.

On one side, AI will help in enhancing the security of online finance and reducing the information asymmetry problem between the users and providers of funds, because the information offered through the social network, online services, and products will help in mitigating this problem between the people and financial institutions (Gomber et al., 2017).

In addition, the use of AI algorithms in risk detection and management in financial inclusion will enable more groups of women, adults, and small businesses such as small farmers, who were excluded previously from the traditional financial market because of the risk of providing funds to them, to access banking services (Mhlanga, 2020).

In the same context, Yang and Zhang (2020) found that digital financial inclusion will enhance the accessibility, efficiency, and coverage of financial services and will reduce information asymmetry. Accessibility of financial services will be improved as customers will be able to access financial services through their mobile phones and computers. The efficiency of financial services will be improved by reducing the entry barriers for customers and the related transaction costs, as a result of using big data and cloud computing to collect a large amount of customer data. Coverage of financial services will be better because financial services will be offered to small and micro enterprises at affordable costs and rural and underdeveloped areas will be included in the financial inclusion services. Information asymmetry will be mitigated as a result of broadening the sources of credit review data for financial institutions.

Finally, Mhlanga (2021) discovered that the application of AI and ML techniques and methods will lead to more accurate credit risk assessments, where alternative data sources such as public data may be used. This application will help in reducing adverse selection and moral hazard problems that are associated with the information asymmetry problem. AI and ML applications, through big data and DL, will enable grantors or funds to make accurate credit risk analyses, evaluate the behavior of the customer, and accordingly, evaluate the customer's ability to repay the loans and any related obligation, permitting less privileged people to access credit.

3.3.4 AI and Credit Risk Management

Banks are seeking more effective credit risk management using efficient credit scoring methods with high accuracy levels (Kumar et al., 2021). Traditionally, banks were testing the creditworthiness of the borrowers using subjective methods that focus on the 5Cs, which are the character of the borrower, his capacity, the collateral he/she is offering, his/her capital, and conditions. This traditional credit testing method is not efficient in case the borrower has no loan history or didn't conduct several banking transactions in the past, like those working in rural areas. As a result, banks started to apply digital methods to assess the creditworthiness of borrowers. AI and ML-based technologies can help in this regard and will enable bank managers to use large datasets and store and appropriately interpret them.

ML methods used in this regard may include generalized linear models, Bayesian models, ensemble models, support vector machines, and nearest neighbor models (Ifft et al., 2018). AI credit scoring techniques may include Genetic algorithm, decision tree, fuzzy logic, random forest, XGBoost, support vector machines, and artificial neural networks. Also, linear regression, logistic regression, and descriptive-analytical approaches are used to calculate the credit scores of the borrowers. Recently, financial institutions in general and banks, in particular, are using more innovative approaches, such as the hybrid model (whether it is AI-ML with AI-ML-based or AI with any other method of credit scoring), which could be the best fit for credit score assessment and credit risk management.

It is worth mentioning that using big data with the application of AI and ML techniques is very important, as they complement each other and will help banks to mitigate

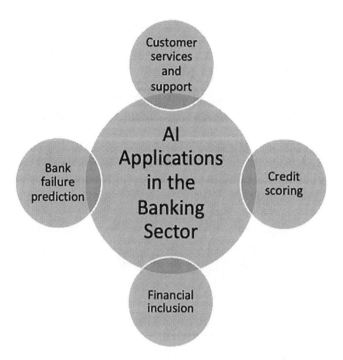

FIGURE 3.1   AI applications in banking sector.

the different risks that they face, such as operational risk, individual risk, market risk, and individual risk related to rural people and accordingly, they will predict loan default with high accuracy (Abuhusain, 2020) (figure 3.1).

3.4   ADVANTAGES AND DISADVANTAGES OF AI APPLICATIONS IN THE FINANCIAL SECTOR

When applying AI and ML technology in the banking sector, it is worth noting this application has its advantages and disadvantages. For instance, ML was adopted because it may help managers in cost reduction, productivity improvement, and risk management (Leo et al., 2019). In addition, ML is having the potential to deliver the analytical capability that financial organizations desire and is capable of affecting every aspect of the financial institutions' business model such as improving insight into client preferences, risk management, fraud detection, and client support automation (Leo et al., 2019). However, on the other side, it was argued that ML tools are sensitive to outliers, and they are a black box and so difficult to interpret their results in some time and they better fit for non-linear relationships (Bacham and Zhao, 2017). One of the potential problems of ML techniques is that they make assumptions about the structure of the data used in the analysis. Because of this problem, other techniques or methods were developed to allow the machines to learn from themselves. These methods are called DL (Wall, 2018).

Based on the discussion in the previous section, the advantages and disadvantages related to the AI and ML applications in the banking industry can be summarized as follows:

3.4.1 Advantages of AI Applications in the Banking Sector

- AI technology will increase the capability of small- and medium-sized banks to be competitive among the state and quasi-state banks (Golubev et al., 2020).

- Moving toward the digital financial sector will increase the quality and speed of interactions between financial services providers and consumers (Evdokimova et al., 2020).

- Financial innovation will help in reducing intermediaries and intermediating activities and will help in decentralizing decision-making, record-keeping, and risk-taking (Gąsiorkiewicz et al., 2020).

- RPA, which is one of the applications of AI and modern technology will allow companies to replace humans with software robots to a great extent, free them from repetitive, routine tasks, and make them available for more complex and value-added tasks. Also, RPA performs tasks faster than humans, without making mistakes, and software robots are available to perform tasks all the time, which results in the reduction of operating costs from 50 to 70% and this will be reflected in the firm's financial performance. Finally, RPA may be applied through the existing systems and applications, and accordingly, they do not require changes in the IT infrastructure of the company (Kanakov and Prokhorov, 2020).

- AI technology will enhance the online security of banks (Golić, 2019; Mhlanga, 2020).

- AI in banking and financial services will contribute towards offering better customer services, enhancing operational efficiency, and helping in cost saving (Srivastava and Dhamija, 2021).

- AI applications will enhance the bank customer relationship. Chatbots will bring a lot of information to the customer without going to a physical local bank branch or calling the bank.

- Banks are facing severe competition from Fintech companies and other non-bank institutions. Moving towards applying AI technology in the bank's operations and tasks will help the bank in competing with these institutions (Srivastava and Dhamija, 2021).

- AI has many applications in the banking sector, in addition to the areas being covered in these previous sections, which include underwriting, analysis of security markets, smart wallets, wealth management, blockchain-based payment, digitalization of documentation, and risk management (Srivastava and Dhamija, 2021).

- Artificial neural networks can model complex non-linear relations between variables without setting any previous assumptions regarding the linearity or normality of data used (Méndez-Suárez et al., 2019).

- The use of big data with AI applications will enable timely data processing and will make forecasting and prediction more accurate with data closer to reality (Da Costa, 2018).

- AI technology will help banks in making smarter and more accurate credit decisions using several factors and a vast amount of data (Golić, 2019).

- AI technology will help in quantitative trading because AI-powered computers will facilitate the analysis of complex and large amounts of data in a fast and efficient way that will save valuable time (Golić, 2019).

3.4.2 Disadvantages of AI Applications in the Banking Sector

Despite the advantages of applying AI and ML technology-based methods, it is worth noting that technology is a double-edged sword. Technology has its pros and cons and should be carefully used. The main disadvantages can be discussed as follows:

- Because financial institutions are relying on digital assets to a great extent, they are exposed to higher cyber risks and cyber attacks, especially that the financial services sector holds highly sensitive personal data, which makes it very attractive for data breaches. Also, it is worth noting that although FinTech is offering new opportunities to customers or financial services users, however, it is also bringing its risks, which are related to personal information disclosure, data security, privacy protection, and breaches (Evdokimova et al., 2020; Gąsiorkiewicz et al., 2020; Li, 2020).

- Although AI applications will help in forecasting and decision-making with a higher degree of accuracy, as in the case where humans are in place, however, AI can't explain the reasoning behind this (Srivastava and Dhamija, 2021).

- Losing control over big data might be one of the main disadvantages, as hackers may flood the data with fake information to affect the AI dynamics of decision-making (Srivastava and Dhamija, 2021).

- A higher level of the unemployment rate might be another side effect of applying AI technology in the banking sector, after replacing humans with robots.

3.5 SUMMARY AND RECOMMENDATIONS

This chapter aims at analyzing the AI applications in the financial sector and specifically in the banking sector. To fulfill this objective, the authors provided an overview of AI and ML and discussed the AI applications in the areas of customer services and support, bank failure prediction, financial inclusion, and credit risk management. Then, the authors summarized these applications' main advantages and disadvantages. It was found that the benefits resulting from the AI applications are quite considerable, as AI technology has proven to contribute to higher accuracy prediction, better customer services, bank-customer relationships, cost savings, higher operational efficiency, lower errors, and improving financial inclusion. On the other hand, AI applications have resulted in banks facing unique risks such as those related to information disclosure and data security.

As a result, the following recommendations might be considered:

- More emphasis should be placed on AI applications in the banking sector and more research is needed to analyze the positive and negative consequences of these applications.

- To reduce the AI-related risks, it is important to focus on the professional quality of financial practitioners (Li, 2020).

- Banks should invest more in AI technology to make sure that previously financially excluded people are now included and can access credit (Mhlanga, 2021).

- It is necessary to focus on interdisciplinary education, as practitioners should have a comprehensive background in computer and information technology. Accordingly, universities should pay more attention to the intersection of finance and other disciplines in their curriculum design. Meanwhile, it is necessary to include new related courses such as big data analysis and financial integration to improve the comprehensive ability of graduates and make them ready for practice (Hu, 2020).

REFERENCES

Abuhusain, M. 2020. The Role of Artificial Intelligence and Big Data on Loan Decisions. *Accounting*, 6: 1291–1296.

Bacham, D. and Zhao, J. 2017. Machine Learning: Challenges and Opportunities in Credit Risk Modeling. Available online: https://www.moodysanalytics.com/risk-perspectives-magazine/managing-disruption/spotlight/machine-learning-challenges-lessons-and-opportunities-in-credit-risk-modeling (accessed on 30 April 2022).

Belanche, D., Casaló, L. and Flavián, C. 2019. Artificial Intelligence in Fintech: Understanding Robo-Advisors Adoption among Customers. *Industrial Management and Data Systems*, 119 (7): 1411–1430.

Da Costa, 2018. How Artificial Intelligence Is Changing the Banking Sector? Thesis, La Rochelle Business School, France.

Evdokimova, Y., Egorova, E. and Shinkareva, O. 2020. *E3S Web Conf.*, 2008: 03017. 10.1051/e3sconf/202020803017.

Faubion, B. 2016, Effect of Automated Advising Platforms on The Financial Advising Market. *Bachelor's Thesis*, Sam M. Walton College of Business, University of Arkansas, Fayetteville, AR, available at: https://core.ac.uk/download/pdf/72841372.pdf (accessed May 3, 2022).

Fisch, J. E., Labouré, M. and Turner, J. A. (2019). The Emergence of the Robo-advisor. In J. Agnew and O. S. Mitchell (Eds.), *The Disruptive Impact of FinTech on Retirement Systems*: 13–37. Oxford, UK: Oxford University Press. 10.1093/oso/9780198845553.003.0002.

Gąsiorkiewicz, L., Monkiewicz, J. and Monkiewicz, M. Technology-Driven Innovations in Financial Services: The Rise of Alternative Finance. *Foundations of Management*, 12. 10.2478/fman-2020-0011.

Golić, Z. 2019. Finance and Artificial Intelligence: The Fifth Industrial Revolution and Its Impact on the Financial Sector. *Proceedings of the Faculty of Economics in East Sarajevo*, 19: 67–81.

Golubev, A., Ryabov, O. and Zolotarev, A. 2019. Digital Transformation of the Banking System of Russia with the Introduction of Blockchain and Artificial Intelligence Technologies. *Materials Science and Engineering*, 940: 012041. 10.1088/1757-899X/940/1/012041.

Gomber, P., Koch, J. and Siering, M. 2017. Digital Finance and FinTech: Current Research and Future Research Directions. *Journal of Business Economics*, 87: 537–580.

How, M., Cheah, S., Khor, A. and Chan, Y. 2020. Artificial Intelligence-Enhanced Predictive Insights for Advancing Financial Inclusion: A Human-Centric AI-Thinking Approach. *Big Data and Cognitive Computing*, 4: 8; 10.3390/bdcc4020008.

Hu, Z. 2020. Research on Fintech Methods Based on Artificial Intelligence. *Journal of Physics*. 10. 1088/1742-6596/1684/1/012034.

Hwang, S. and Kim, J. 2021. Toward a Chatbot for Financial Sustainability. Chatbot for Financial Sustainability. *Sustainability*, 13: 3173. 10.3390/su13063173.

Ifft, J., Kuhns, R. and Patrick, K. 2018. Can Machine Learning Improve Prediction—An Application with Farm Survey Data. *International Food and Agribusiness Management Review*, 21: 1083–1098.

Kanakov, F. and Prokhorov, I. 2020. Research And Development of Software Robots for Automating Business Processes of A Commercial Bank. *Procedia Computer Science*, 169: 337–341.

Khan, H., Malik, M., Alomari, M., Khan, S., Al-Maadid, A., Hassan, M. and Khan, K. 2022. Transforming the Capabilities of Artificial Intelligence in GCC Financial Sector: A Systematic Literature Review. *Wireless Communications and Mobile Computing*, 10.1155/2022/8725767.

Kumar, A., Sharma, S. and Mahdavi, M. 2021. Machine Learning (ML) Technologies for Digital Credit Scoring in Rural Finance: A Literature Review. *Risks*, 9; 192. 10.3390/risks9110192.

Le, H. and Viviani, J. 2017. Predicting Bank Failure: An Improvement by Implementing Machine Learning Approach on Classical Financial Ratios. *Research on International Business and Finance*. 10.1016/j.ribaf.2017.07.104.

Lee, S. and Choi, W., 2013. A Multi-Industry Bankruptcy Prediction Model Using Back-Propagation Neural Network and Multivariate Discriminant Analysis. *Expert Systems with Applications*, 40: 2941–2946.

Leo, M., Sharma, S. and Maddulety, K. 2019. Machine Learning in Banking Risk Management: A Literature Review. *Risks*, 7: 29. 10.3390/risks7010029.

Li, P. 2020. Research on the Application and Security of Artificial Intelligence in the Financial Industry. *Materials Science and Engineering*, 750. 10.1088/1757-899X/750/1/012102.

Liu, L., Liu, S. and Sathya, M. 2021. Predicting Bank Failures: A Synthesis of Literature and Directions for Future Research. *Journal of Risk and Financial Management*, 14: 474. 10.3390/ jrfm14100474.

Méndez-Suárez, M., García-Fernández, F. and Gallardo, F. 2019. Artificial Intelligence Modelling Framework for Financial Automated Advising in the Copper Market. *Journal of Open Innovation: Technology, Market, and Complexity*, 5: 81. 10.3390/joitmc5040081.

Mhlanga, D. 2020. Industry 4.0 in Finance: The Impact of Artificial Intelligence (AI) on Digital Financial Inclusion. *International Journal of Financial Studies*, 8: 45. 10.3390/ijfs8030045.

Mhlanga, D. 2021. Financial Inclusion in Emerging Economies: The Application of Machine Learning and Artificial Intelligence in Credit Risk Assessment. *International Journal of Financial Studies*, 9: 39. 10.3390/ijfs9030039.

Minastireanu, E. and Mesnita, G. 2019. An Analysis of the Most Used Machine Learning Algorithms for Online Fraud Detection. *Informatica Economică*, 23 (1): 5–16.

Olson, D., Delen, D. and Meng, Y. 2012. Comparative Analysis of Data Mining Methods for Bankruptcy Prediction. *Decision Support Systems*, 52: 464–473.

Ray, S., Paul, S. and Miglani, S. 2019. Use of Blockchain and Artificial Intelligence to Promote Financial Inclusion in India Smita Miglani Indian Council for Research on International Economic Relations. *Asia-Pacific Tech Monitor*, 36 (1), Jan – Mar.

Siswoyo, B., Herman, N. and Dewi, D. 2020. Machine Learning Approach as An Alternative Tool to Build a Bankruptcy Prediction Model in Banking Industry. *Materials Science and Engineering.* 10.1088/1757-899X/830/2/022083.

Srivastava, K. and Dhamija, S. 2021. Paradigm Shift in Indian Banking Industry with Special Reference to Artificial Intelligence. *Turkish Journal of Computer and Mathematics Education*, 12(5): 1623–1629.

Waliszewski, K. and Warchlewska, A. 2020. Attitudes Towards Artificial Intelligence in the Area of Personal Financial Planning: A Case Study of Selected Countries. *Entrepreneurship and Sustainability Issues*, 8 (2) (December) 10.9770/jesi.2020.8.2(24)

Wall, L. 2018. Some Financial Regulatory Implications of Artificial Intelligence, *Journal of Economics and Business.* 10.1016/j.jeconbus.2018.05.003.

Yang, L. and Zhang, Y. 2020. Digital Financial Inclusion and Sustainable Growth of Small and Micro Enterprises—Evidence Based on China's New Third Board Market Listed Companies. *Sustainability*, 12: 3733.

CHAPTER 4

Upscaling Profits in Financial Market

Jay Chawla, Rohit Bakoliya, Jitendra Jat, Jignesh Jinjala,
Manali Patel, and Krupa N. Jariwala

CONTENTS

4.1 INTRODUCTION

In recent times stock market investment is considered to be a smart and profitable choice among other investment options such as fixed deposits, mutual funds, real estate, gold, etc., as it offers better long-term and short-term returns, dividend income and hedge against inflation. Even though stock trading has seen massive growth compared to the past, only 55% of people in the USA, 33% in the UK, 13% in China and 3% in India are engaged in the stock market. According to risk attitudes [1], financial knowledge and financial self-efficacy can affect stock market prediction.

Predicting stock prices is a challenging task due to the highly non-linear and volatile nature of stock data because it can be affected by many factors such as global crisis, political factors, news articles, investor's psychology [2], etc. The Global Financial Crisis of 2008 and COVID-19 outbreak revealed the volatile nature of the Indian stock market as well as other developed countries.

DOI: 10.1201/9781003327745-4

Stock market forecasting has two well-known analytical approaches: fundamental and technical analyses. Fundamental analysis considers a company's intrinsic value i.e., revenues and expenses, position in the market, growth rate, balance sheets. Technical analysis is a study of historical data to predict movement of stock prices by constructing various technical indicators [3].

Technical analysis is widely used by traders as it helps traders make conclusive decisions based on historical data and identify entry and exit points that can minimize the risk. Choosing a particular indicator is a subjective choice which reflects the psychology of an investor. By combining various technical indicators we can make more accurate predictions and minimize this subjectivity. Based on this observation we have proposed a trading strategy using multiple technical indicators which utilizes prediction values of deep learning (DL) model.

Our main contribution is the following:

- We have applied various DL models to predict the future stock price of companies listed on the National Stock Exchange (NSE) of the Indian stock market.

- A comprehensive analysis is done to choose appropriate DL models and hyperparameters such as lookback window and forecasting horizon.

- A trading strategy is built using multiple technical indicators that can generate accurate Buy/Sell signals.

- The results show that our strategy can upscale the profit with a high return ratio.

The rest of the chapter is organized as follows: section 4.2 reviews recent methods and various technical indicators, our methodology is represented in section 4.3, dataset and evaluation metrics are discussed in section 4.4, result and analysis are discussed in section 4.5 followed by conclusion and future work.

To avoid any ambiguity, we will use the words forecasting and prediction interchangeably.

4.2 LITERATURE REVIEW

Stock market data are treated as time series data that are collected at regular intervals of time i.e., hourly, daily, monthly, weekly or annually. Stock market forecasting techniques are broadly classified into two types: statistical and machine learning approaches. Statistical approaches include various autoregressive methods like Autoregressive Integrated Moving Average (ARIMA) [4,5], Seasonal Autoregressive Integrated Moving Average (SARIMA) [6], Vector Autoregressive (VAR) [7] and volatility-based Generalized AutoRegressive Conditional Heteroskedasticity (GARCH) [8] models. These parametric methods require stationary data. In practice, stock market data are non-stationary data that limit the use of these methods.

Various machine learning approaches include Support Vector Machine (SVM) [9,10], K-nearest Neighbors (KNNs) [11], Random Forest (RF) [12] and Fuzzy methods [13].

But these approaches require handcrafted features and fail to capture long-range dependence of time series data. Apart from this they fail to capture the latent dynamics existing in stock data.

With recent advancement of DL methods in various domains, it has also been applied to time series forecasting. These methods are self-adaptive and non-linear function approximators which make them suitable choices for this task. These methods include Artificial Neural Network (ANN), Convolution Neural Network (CNN) and Sequence-to-Sequence models based on various architectures. Sun et al. proposed ARMA-GARCH-NN model [14] that combined traditional and data-driven approaches to predict intraday market shock. Kale et al. [15] trained ANN with Backpropagation Technique to predict the next day's opening price of NIFTY 100 index. Since neural networks are efficient for modeling complex interactions, they are not interpretable.

Recently, there have been attempts to apply CNN and its variants to time series data. Chen et al. [16] applied a 1D CNN to predict stock price movement on the China Market. Selvin et al. [17] proposed CNN Sliding Window to predict stock prices of NSE-listed companies for a short time interval of 10 minutes. Hoseinzade et al. [18] proposed 2D- and 3D-based CNNPred models using 82 different technical indicators for five markets. The 2D model utilizes markets separately but the 3D model makes predictions based on combined information of all different markets. Dai et al. proposed and applied Attention-based Temporal Convolution Model [19] on Chinese Shenzhen Stock Exchange 100 Index to predict probability of price change category. Although it has shown significant improvement, choice of filter size, data arrangement affects its performance. Sidra et al. [20] proposed CNN Regression model for multivariate time series forecasting on NIFTY 50 dataset.

Recurrent neural networks are sequence-to-sequence models that can capture temporal dimension of data effectively. It suffers from vanishing and exploding gradients. To alleviate this, Long Short-Term Memory (LSTM) and Gated Recurrent Unit (GRU) networks are proposed that have the ability to process sequential data and long-range dependencies. Qiu et al. [21] proposed Attention-based LSTM model to predict opening price of Standard and Poor's 500 (S&P500), Dow Jones Industrial Average (DJIA) and Hang Seng Index (HSI). Fischer et al. [22] applied the LSTM model to predict next day movement of the S&P500 index. Ji et al. [23] applied sentiment analysis to forecast stock prices of medical companies in China and proposed the Doc-W-LSTM model that uses the Doc2Vec algorithm to extract text features. Zhu et al. [24] applied recurrent neural network (RNN) network to predict closing price of Apple company using previous ten years' historical data.

GRU [25] works slightly better than Vanilla RNN and LSTM for commercial banks listed on Nepal Stock Exchange. Zulqarnain et al. [26] proposed a hybrid CNN-GRU model to predict trading signals. Lu et al. [27] proposed a hybrid CNN-LSTM model to forecast future prices of the Shanghai Composite Index.

In this work, we have implemented GRU model [28] to forecast future prices as it requires fewer parameters than LSTM, thus leading to less computational complexity. The proposed methodology is discussed in the following section.

4.3 PROPOSED METHODOLOGY

The proposed methodology is divided into two modules: prediction module and trading strategy module.

4.3.1 Prediction Module

The main objective of this module is to predict daily future closing prices. In this work, we have considered only the closing price as an input feature. With GRU model this can be extended to include multiple features. The GRU model has two gates: Reset and Update gates. The hidden state is updated using following equations:

$$z_t = \sigma\left(x_t U^z + h_{t-1} W^z\right) \tag{4.1}$$

$$r_t = \sigma\left(x_t U^r + h_{t-1} W^r\right) \tag{4.2}$$

$$\underline{h}_t = tanh\left(x_t U^h + (r_t * h_{t-1}) W^h\right) \tag{4.3}$$

$$h_t = (1 - z_t) * h_{t-1} + z_t * \underline{h}_t \tag{4.4}$$

Here, x_t represents input features at timestamp t, Update and Reset gates are represented by z and r respectively, whereas U and W are learnable parameters. In our work, two GRU layers are used with 50 and 100 units respectively. The model is trained using a learning rate of 0.001, ReLU activation function and a look-back period of 120 days, batch size of 4. To overcome the overfitting problem, a dropout layer is introduced. The complete flowchart of the proposed work is shown in figure 4.1.

4.3.2 Trading Strategy Module

The results obtained from the prediction module are used to build a trading strategy that can generate Buy/Sell signals. Technical indicators are powerful tools to determine entry and exit points for short-term trading. Investors rely on multiple indicators before making a trading decision. Based on this observation we have created two strategies consisting of three different indicators. By following this strategy, traders can gain maximum return compared to Buy and Hold Strategy. These are explained below.

Strategy 1:

- Exponential Moving Average(EMA): When short-term EMA moves across long-term EMA, Buy signal is generated and Sell signal for vice-versa.

- Moving Average Convergence Divergence (MACD): When MACD value crosses over the MACD signal line, a Buy signal is generated and Sell signal for vice-versa.

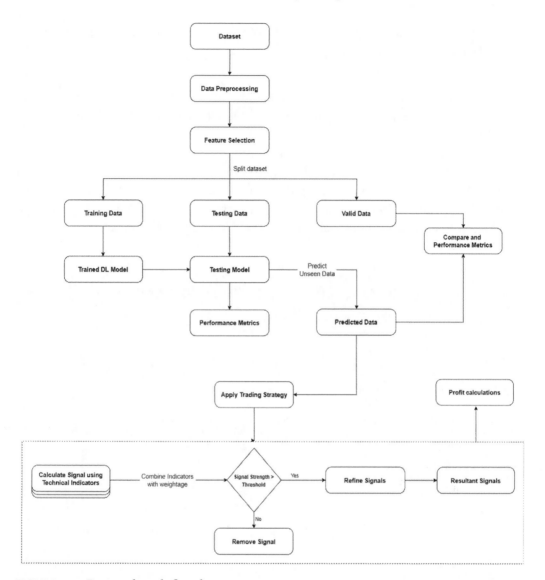

FIGURE 4.1   Proposed work flowchart.

- Relative Strength Index (RSI): When a price of commodity crosses RSI value of 70 indicates overbought condition, a Sell signal is generated. Likewise, when the price falls below RSI value of 30 indicates oversold condition, a Buy signal is generated.

Strategy 2:

- Stochastic Relative Strength Index (STOCHRSI): When a price of commodity crosses over the value of 80 indicates overbought condition, a Sell signal is generated. Likewise, when the price falls below the value of 20 indicates oversold condition, a Buy signal is generated.

- On Balance Volume (OBV): When OBV value rises above the average line then a Sell signal is generated and a Buy signal is given when OBV value falls below the average line.

- Bollinger Band (BB): If the price of commodity crosses over the upper Bollinger Band then a Sell signal is generated and if it falls below the lower Bollinger Band then a Buy signal is generated.

Each technical indicator is given weight manually depending on its significance for both strategies. Only a Buy/Sell signal with more than 30% signal strength is considered. The procedure to generate Buy/Sell signals from the above two strategies is explained in Algorithm 4.1. Each strategy is evaluated on the basis of profit earned, which is represented in section 4.5.

ALGORITHM 4.1 GENERATE BUY/SELL POINTS USING STRATEGY:

Input: Data D, Weight W, Signal Strength delta

Output: Buy/Sell Signals S

1. Sort data D based upon date

2. *BuySellArray ← empty list*

3. *ProbabilityArray ← empty list*

4. *Weighted sum ← SUm of Weight W*

5. for all datapoints D

6.   *Score ⇐ 0*

7.   for all weights W_j do

8.   *Score ⇐ Score + D_i * W_j*

9.   end for

10.   *Score ⇐ Score/Weighted sum*

11. if *Score ≤ delta*

12.   *BuySellArray$_i$ ⇐ Buy*

13.   *ProbabilityArray$_i$ ≤ Score*

14. else

15.   *BuySellArray$_i$ ⇐ Sell*

16.   *ProbabilityArray$_i$ ≤ Score * (−1)*

17.   end if

18. end for

19. return BuySellArray

4.4 IMPLEMENTATION DETAILS

4.4.1 Dataset

The dataset used here is of "RELIANCE" company, from 1 January 1996 to 15 March 2022 as it is the top-ranked Indian firm in the Forbes Global list 2022. The dataset is divided into training and testing sets which consist of 80% and 20% of the data, respectively. The aim is to predict the next day's closing price and generate a trading strategy. To prove the effectiveness of the proposed model, it has also been applied to different NSE-listed companies.

4.4.2 Tools

To implement the DL models, Google Colaboratory is used. It provides access to various DL libraries such as Tensorflow, Keras. To plot the figures, Matplotlib library is used. Finance library from Yahoo Finance is used to extract historical data of RELIANCE company.

4.4.3 Evaluation Metrics

We have evaluated our model on most commonly used evaluation parameters i.e., mean absolute error (MAE), root mean square error (RMSE) and Accuracy. These are calculated using below formulas:

$$\text{MAE} = \frac{1}{n}\Sigma|y - \hat{y}| \tag{4.5}$$

$$\text{RMSE} = \sqrt{\frac{\Sigma|y - \hat{y}|^2}{n}} \tag{4.6}$$

To calculate Accuracy, a confusion matrix is created which is represented by table 4.1 and is calculated using equation 4.7.

$$\text{Accuracy} = \frac{TP + TN}{TP + TN + FP + FN} \tag{4.7}$$

TABLE 4.1   Confusion Matrix

Predicted Values	True Values	
	Positive	Negative
Positive	True Positive	False Negative
Negative	False Positive	True Negative

TABLE 4.2   Analysis on Models for RELIANCE Company Data

Model	RMSE	MAE	Accuracy
CNN	113.77	40.74	48.17%
CNN-LSTM	104.22	84.85	64.29%
RNN	77.43	65.32	60.67%
LSTM	37.28	31.54	82.02%
GRU	**17.07**	**13.79**	**91.01%**

4.5 RESULT AND ANALYSIS

We have considered RNN, CNN, LSTM and CNN-LSTM models as baseline models to verify our work. The number of prediction days considered is 120 days and the results obtained are represented in table 4.2. Statistically, it can be verified from table 4.2 that GRU model outperforms all other baseline models on RELIANCE company data. All the models are evaluated on the basis of evaluation parameters discussed in the above section. For an accurate model, lower values of MAE, RMSE and higher value of Accuracy are preferred. From the results obtained, GRU model is outperforming other models. Another conclusion is that the sequence-to-sequence models such as RNN, LSTM and GRU are outperforming CNNs and hybrid models on RELIANCE company data. This is due to the fact that the sequence-to-sequence models are better at capturing the long-range dependencies.

Figures 4.2–4.6 depict the actual and closing price predicted by CNN, RNN, LSTM, GRU and CNN-LSTM models, respectively. From this we can verify that LSTM and GRU models are giving less deviation from actual prices compared to other models.

The trading strategies discussed in section 4.3 are applied on prediction results obtained from different models and profit is calculated. Figures 4.7 and 4.8 illustrate the

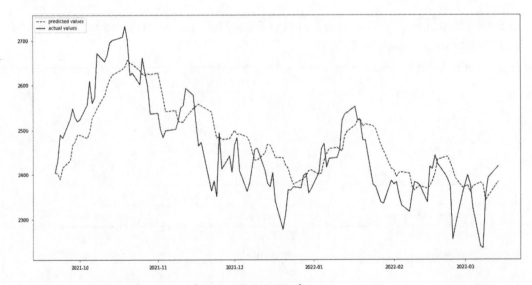

FIGURE 4.2   CNN prediction results on RELIANCE data.

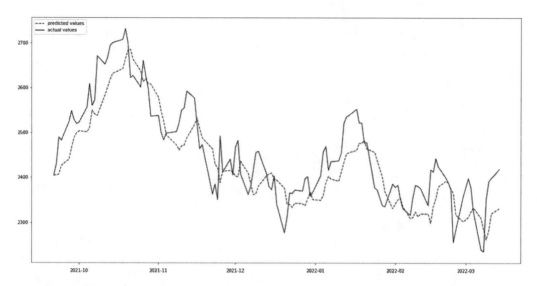

FIGURE 4.3   RNN prediction results on RELIANCE data.

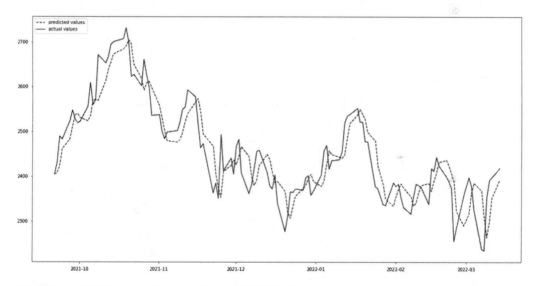

FIGURE 4.4   LSTM prediction results on RELIANCE data.

generated Buy/Sell signals from strategy 1 and strategy 2 on GRU-predicted values, respectively. It is clear from the figures that the proposed trading strategy is following basic "Buy low and Sell high" stock market ideology. It is generating Buy signals on lower-side peaks and Sell signals on higher-level peaks with the depicted probabilities. To compare both strategies, actual and predicted profits are calculated.

Table 4.3 represents the profit values calculated for 300 days (30 December 2020 to 15 March 2022) using Buy/Sell signals generated from the above-mentioned two strategies. As CNN-LSTM is not giving satisfactory results on prediction, we have applied strategies on CNN, RNN, LSTM and GRU models. It is clear that strategy 2 (STOCHRSI-OBV-BB)

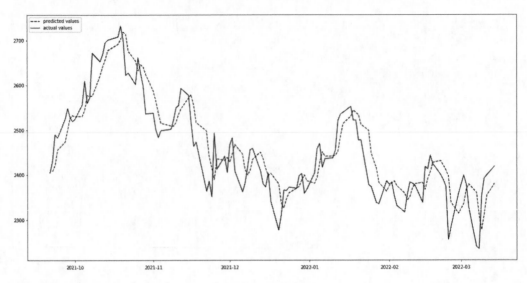

FIGURE 4.5   GRU prediction results on RELIANCE data.

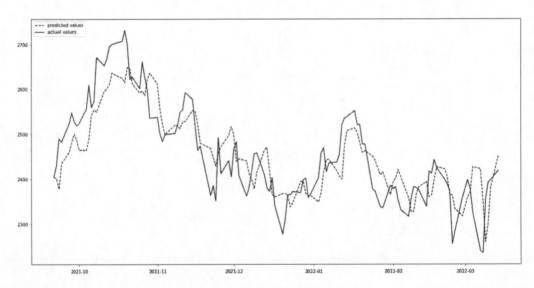

FIGURE 4.6   CNN-LSTM prediction results on RELIANCE data.

is better than strategy 1 (EMA-MACD-RSI) and is giving less deviation between actual and predicted profits on the GRU model. This is due to the fact that the strategy 2 consists of a volume indicator as well as a volatility indicator that can capture the dynamics existing in the data. Applying strategy 2 on prediction values obtained from GRU model shows less deviation from the actual profit which proves efficiency of the prediction module proposed.

To further verify the correctness of the proposed model, various companies from the different sectors are selected for the duration from 3 January 2000 to 22 June 2022. Table 4.4 represents the analysis on DL models for TATA STEEL company. It can be verified that the GRU is again outperforming other models on RMSE, Accuracy values.

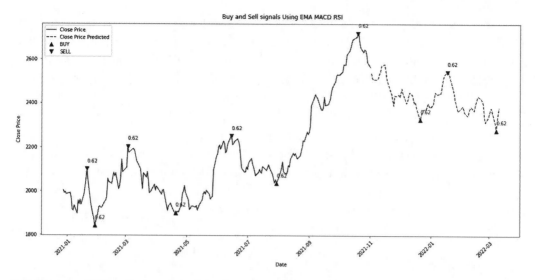

FIGURE 4.7   GRU and strategy 1 (MACD-EMA-RSI).

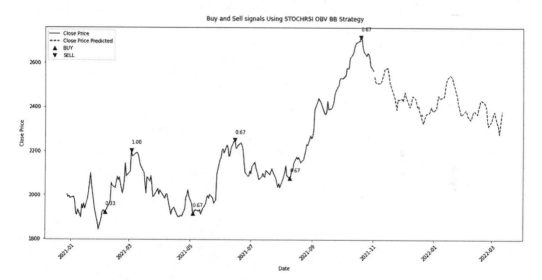

FIGURE 4.8   GRU and strategy 2 (StochRSI-OBV-BB).

TABLE 4.3   Analysis on Strategies for RELIANCE Company Data

Model/Strategy	Strategy 1 (MACD-EMA-RSI)		Strategy 2 (STOCHRSI-OBV-BB)	
	Predicted	Actual	Predicted	Actual
CNN	1620.48	1600.45	1664.09	1379.60
RNN	1440.36	1600.45	1301.26	1379.60
LSTM	1345.55	1600.45	2027.21	1379.60
GRU	1499.32	1600.45	1370.78	1379.60

Moreover for MAE, CNNs are giving more promising results but performance of the GRU is comparable to the CNN with only 2% error gap. Figure 4.9 represents the actual and prediction results obtained for TATA STEEL using the GRU model. Further, it can be verified from table 4.5 that strategy 2 is again giving more actual profit compared to strategy 1 for TATA STEEL company. From the table, we can observe that the GRU-predicted profit is less than the LSTM predicted profit, but it is misleading due to the fact that the prediction accuracy of GRU is more promising, proven in table 4.4.

For further verification from the IT sector, WIPRO is selected and DL model prediction results are represented in table 4.6. Again the GRU model is outperforming other

TABLE 4.4   Analysis on Models for TATA STEEL Company Data

Model	RMSE	MAE	Accuracy
CNN	20.26	**15.53**	71.19%
CNN-LSTM	57.5	47.88	63.56%
RNN	42.01	35.86	74.58%
LSTM	25.0	20.96	88.98%
GRU	**19.36**	17.34	**90.68%**

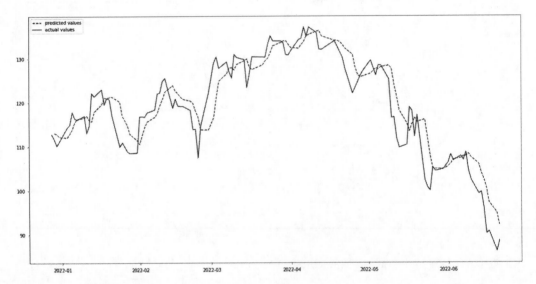

FIGURE 4.9   GRU prediction results on TATA STEEL data.

TABLE 4.5   Analysis on Strategies for TATA STEEL Company Data

| Model/Strategy | Strategy 1 (MACD-EMA-RSI) | | Strategy 2 (STOCHRSI-OBV-BB) | |
	Predicted	Actual	Predicted	Actual
CNN	657.76	703.05	639.41	984.5
RNN	526.1	703.05	880.67	984.5
LSTM	704.52	703.05	923.17	984.5
GRU	687.41	703.05	823.02	984.5

TABLE 4.6   Analysis on Models for WIPRO Company Data

Model	RMSE	MAE	Accuracy
CNN	70.07	63.95	66.65%
CNN-LSTM	83.28	75.4	67.8%
RNN	43.18	39.23	69.49%
LSTM	18.3	16.8	78.81%
GRU	**11.81**	**10.46**	**83.39%**

models. Figure 4.10 represents the actual and prediction results obtained using the GRU model. From table 4.7, it can be seen that strategy 2 is giving more profit compared to strategy 1 on prediction results obtained from the GRU model. TECH MAHINDRA company from automobile sector is selected for an analysis that is represented in table 4.8. For this company also strategy 2 is giving more returns compared to strategy 1 as represented in table 4.9. Figure 4.11 depicts the pictorial representation of actual and predicted values.

From the analysis done on various companies from different sectors, we can confirm that our proposed method is outperforming other DL models in most of the cases and

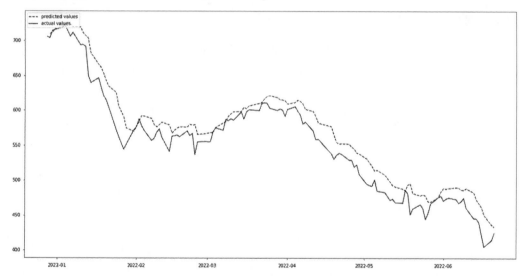

FIGURE 4.10   GRU prediction results on WIPRO data.

TABLE 4.7   Analysis on Strategies for WIPRO Company Data

Model/Strategy	Strategy 1 (MACD-EMA-RSI)		Strategy 2 (STOCHRSI-OBV-BB)	
	Predicted	Actual	Predicted	Actual
CNN	246.10	300.79	275.40	312.05
RNN	272.261	300.79	297.76	312.05
LSTM	297.16	300.79	326.46	312.05
GRU	292.51	300.79	321.81	312.05

TABLE 4.8   Analysis on Models for TECH MAHINDRA Company Data

Model	RMSE	MAE	Accuracy
CNN	264.88	249.05	58.47%
CNN-LSTM	98.53	94.79	47.5%
RNN	133.04	125.93	69.49%
LSTM	96.35	92.54	66.10%
GRU	**85.76**	**52.29**	**83.39%**

TABLE 4.9   Analysis on Strategies for TECH MAHINDRA Company Data

Model/Strategy	Strategy 1 (MACD-EMA-RSI)		Strategy 2 (STOCHRSI-OBV-BB)	
	Predicted	Actual	Predicted	Actual
CNN	940.62	1051.45	1041.92	1061.65
RNN	1057.61	1051.45	1158.91	1061.65
LSTM	1058.71	1051.45	1160.61	1061.65
GRU	1035.35	1051.45	1136.65	1061.65

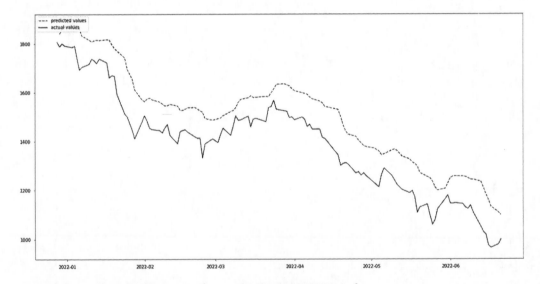

FIGURE 4.11   GRU prediction results on TECH MAHINDRA data.

giving comparable results. By incorporating strategy 2 (STOCHRSI-OBV-BB), we can upscale the profits.

4.6 CONCLUSION AND FUTURE WORK

Technical analysis plays an important role to decide entry and exit points in the market. Each investor has its own trading strategy which reflects the psychology of an individual. Therefore, choosing an appropriate strategy is a crucial task. Based on this observation we have built a model that forecasts future closing prices using DL model and two trading strategies (strategy 1: MACD-EMA-RSI; strategy 2: STOCHRSI-OBV-BB) consisting of multiple indicators that generate Buy/Sell signals. Both strategies are compared in terms of profit earned. The results show that strategy 2 outperforms strategy 1 on predicted values obtained using the GRU model on RELIANCE company data. From the analysis done on different companies from different sectors, we conclude that sequence-to-sequence model GRU is more promising. Trading strategy consisting of accurate technical indicators can upscale the profits.

This work further can be extended by considering multiple features. In addition to this, sentiment analysis can be included to predict future prices.

REFERENCES

[1] Nadeem Khemta, M., Qamar, J., Nazir, M. S., Ahmad, I., Timoshin, A. & Shehzad, K., "How investors attitudes shape stock market participation in the presence of financial self-efficacy," *Frontiers in Psychology*, vol. 11, pp. 1–17, 2020.

[2] Naseem, S., Mohsin, M., Hui, W., Liyan, G. & Penglai, K., "The investor psychology and stock market behavior during the initial era of COVID-19: A study of China, Japan, and the United States," *Frontiers in Psychology*, vol. 12, pp. 1–10, 2021.

[3] Mailagaha Kumbure, M., Lohrmann, C., Luukka, P. & Porras, J., "Machine learning techniques and data for stock market forecasting: A literature review," *Expert Systems with Applications*, vol. 197, pp. 116659, 2022.

[4] Adebiyi, A., Adewumi, A. & Ayo, C., "Stock price prediction using the ARIMA model," Proceedings - UKSim-AMSS 16th International Conference on Computer Modeling and Simulation, UKSim 2014, 10.1109/UKSim.2014.67.

[5] Banerjee, D., "Forecasting of Indian stock market using time-series ARIMA model," 2014 2nd International Conference on Business and Information Management, pp. 131–135, ICBIM 2014.

[6] Tewari, A., "Forecasting NIFTY 50 benchmark Index using Seasonal ARIMA time series models," 2020. [online]. Available: 10.13140/RG.2.2.10332.95364.

[7] Gupta, R. & Wohar, M., "Forecasting oil and stock returns with a Qual VAR using over 150 years of data," *Energy Economics*, vol. 62, pp. 181–186, 2017.

[8] Vasudevan, R. D. & Vetrivel, S., "Forecasting stock market volatility using GARCH models: Evidence from the Indian Stock Market," *Asian Journal of Research in Social Sciences and Humanities*, vol. 6, p. 1565, 2016.

[9] Li, X., Wu, P. & Wang, W., "Incorporating stock prices and news sentiments for stock market prediction: A case of Hong Kong," *Information Processing & Management*, vol. 57, pp. 1–19, 2020.

[10] Yang, R., Yu, L., Zhao, Y., Yu, H., Xu, G., Wu, Y. & Liu, Z., "Big data analytics for financial market volatility forecast based on support vector machine," *International Journal of Information Management*, vol. 50, pp. 452–462, 2019.

[11] Zhang, N., Lin, A. & Shang, P., "Multidimensional k-nearest neighbor model based on EEMD for financial time series forecasting," *Physica A: Statistical Mechanics and Its Applications*, vol. 477, pp. 161–173, 2017.

[12] Manojlovic, T. & Štajduhar, I., "Predicting stock market trends using random forests: A sample of the Zagreb stock exchange," pp. 1189–1193, 2015.

[13] Zhang, W., Zhang, S., Zhang, S., Yu, D. & Huang, N., "A novel method based on FTS with

both GA-FCM and multi-factor BPNN for stock forecasting," *Soft Computing*, vol. 23, pp. 6979–6994, 2019.

[14] Sun, J., Xiao, K., Liu, C., Zhou, W. & Xiong, H., "Exploiting intra-day patterns for market shock prediction: A machine learning approach," *Expert Systems with Applications*, vol. 127, pp. 272–281, 2019.

[15] Kale, A., Khanvilkar, O., Jivani, H., Kumkar, P., Madan, I. & Sarode, T., "Forecasting Indian Stock Market Using Artificial Neural Networks," 2018 Fourth International Conference on Computing Communication Control and Automation (ICCUBEA), pp. 1–5. 10.1109/ICCUBEA.2018.8697724.

[16] Chen, S. & He, H., "Stock Prediction Using Convolutional Neural Network," IOP Conference Series: Materials Science and Engineering, vol. 435, pp. 012026, 2018.

[17] Selvin, S., Ravi, V., Gopalakrishnan, E., Menon, V. & Kp, S., "Stock price prediction using ISTM, RNN and CNN-sliding window model," 09 2017, pp. 1643–1647.

[18] Hoseinzade, E. & Haratizadeh, S., "CNNPred: CNN-based stock market prediction using several data sources," 2018.

[19] Dai, W., An, Y. & Long, W., "Price change prediction of ultra high frequency financial data based on temporal convolutional network," 2021. [online]. Available: https://arxiv.org/abs/2107.00261.

[20] Mehta, S. & Sen, J., "Stock price prediction using convolutional neural networks on a multivariate time series," *TechRxiv*, 2021.

[21] Qiu, J., Wang, B. & Zhou, C., "Forecasting stock prices with long-short term memory neural network based on attention mechanism," *Plos One*, vol. 15, no. 1, pp. 1–15, 01 2020. [Online]. Available: 10.1371/journal.pone.0227222.

[22] Fischer, T. & Krauss, C., "Deep learning with long short-term memory networks for financial market predictions," *European Journal of Operational Research*, vol. 270, no. 2, pp. 654–669, 2018.

[23] Ji, X., Wang, J. & Yan, Z., "A stock price prediction method based on deep learning technology," *International Journal of Crowd Science*, 2021.

[24] Zhu, Y., "Stock price prediction using the RNN model," *Journal of Physics: Conference Series*, vol. 1650, p. 032103, 2020.

[25] Saud, A. & Shakya, S., "Analysis of look back period for stock price prediction with RNN variants: A case study on banking sector of NEPSE," *Procedia Computer Science*, vol. 167, pp. 788–798, 2020.

[26] Zulqarnain, M., Ghazali, R., Ghouse, M., Mazwin, Y., Mohmad Hassim, Y. M. & Javid, I., "Predicting financial prices of stock market using recurrent convolutional neural networks," *International Journal of Intelligent Systems and Applications*, vol. 12, pp. 21–32, 2020.

[27] Lu, W., Li, J., Li, Y., Sun, A. & Wang, J., "A CNN-LSTM-based model to forecast stock prices," *Complexity*, vol. 2020, pp. 1–10, 2020.

[28] Cho, K., Merrienboer, B., Gulcehre, C., Bougares, F., Schwenk, H. & Bengio, Y., "Learning Phrase Representations using RNN Encoder-Decoder for Statistical Machine Translation," 2014. [online]. Available: 10.3115/v1/D14-1179.

CHAPTER 5

Credit and Risk Analysis in the Financial and Banking Sectors: An Investigation

Geetha Manoharan, Subhashini Durai,
Gunaseelan Alex Rajesh, and Sunitha Purushottam Ashtikar

CONTENTS

5.1 INTRODUCTION

Understanding consumer behaviour is critical for a business organisation's success. A customer's or a group of customers' selection, purchase, use, and discarding of ideas about products or services is the focus of consumer behaviour. Personalised marketing involves analysing a customer's purchasing habits. Predicting future trends is easy after analysing individual behaviour. Problem recognition, information search, alternative evaluation, purchase decision, and post-purchase behaviour are the five stages of the consumer buying decision process. Consumer behaviour is a broad term. Consumer

DOI: 10.1201/9781003327745-5

behaviour is always a hot topic among academics and researchers. However, further research into consumer behaviour, such as the factors that influence consumer purchasing behaviour, could be conducted in the future. This study only focuses on the consumer buying process. Putting this theoretical process into practice will allow for more investigation. Research can be carried out on an entire sector as well as on a particular product or brand. The empirical study takes into account other studies that will be conducted in the future on this subject. Only the consumer's purchasing decision is being studied in this process; further research into the consumer's purchasing behaviour can be conducted digitally (Hemachandran et al. 2022a).

One can study many different aspects of consumer behaviour. How, why, and when people buy a product or brand are all questions of consumer behaviour. The way people buy things is still a mystery because it has so much to do with the mind. But with a wide range of analytical software, it is possible to find out more about how people buy things on digital platforms like Facebook or Twitter. However, a complete understanding of consumer purchasing habits is still a mystery. The act of making purchases is known as "consumer behaviour." Being happy is a universal desire. A person's basic human needs cannot be denied. A person will go to the market in order to satisfy a desire by exchanging their money for various goods. Marketers must be able to understand the habits and preferences of their customers. In consumer behaviour, the focus is on how people make purchases. Pre-purchase and post-purchase behaviour can be observed. Businesses can also use it to look for new opportunities because of its versatility.

It is important to know how people buy things. The consumer buying decision process is made up of the different steps a consumer goes through before, during, and after buying a product or service. It helps the seller or marketer sell their products or services to the market. To be successful in selling products or services, a marketer must first understand consumer behaviour in relation to the purchasing decision process. Customers go through five stages before making a purchase decision: initiation of a problem-solving process, collection of relevant data, evaluation of potential solutions, selection of a product, and subsequent behaviour. Consumers begin to think about purchasing a product when they see it on television. When purchasing a product, a customer may proceed through any or all of the five stages of the decision-making process. One or more stages may also be skipped by the buyer; it all depends on the consumer's mindset. It is impossible to compare the minds of different people. Every time a person needs milk, he or she will go to the store and buy the same brand. As a result, when compared to products that are more involved, there is a higher likelihood of skipping information and evaluation. We are all flawed in some way. It is different when we are buying a car and have a lot invested in it. Each of the five steps in the car-buying process must be completed. This method is particularly useful for first-time or complicated consumer purchases. The education of the customer, their choice of product, their utilisation of that product, and their eventual disposal of it are all aspects of the experience that some companies prioritise.

5.1.1 Objective of the Study

To carry out credit and risk analysis in the financial and banking sectors.

5.2 LITERATURE REVIEW

Brody et al. (2007) reveal in their research that the novel strategy for modelling credit risk sidesteps the need to make use of inaccessible stopping times. The failure of obligors to make payments that were contractually agreed upon is directly linked to the occurrence of default events. There is a great deal of chatter going on about the up-coming cash flows that are available to market participants. Within the confines of this framework, one or more independent market information processes are assumed to produce market filtration. Only a small proportion of the market factors that influence future cash flows are communicated by each of these information processes. A model parameter is the rate at which market participants are given accurate information about a market factor's expected value. This rate is different for each market factor. Analysis that can be easily simulated is presented for defaultable bond price processes with stochastic recovery. Other forms of debt instruments, such as multi-name products, can be characterised using the terms analogous to those presented here. An explicit formula is developed here for calculating the value of a risky discount bond option. When more accurate information about the bond's final payoff is made available, it has been demonstrated that the value of such an option will rise. Consistency is a key feature of the framework, which makes it suitable for use in practical modelling situations where frequent recalibration is necessary.

According to Kumari et al.'s (2022) research, an Online Customer Experience-Attitude Behaviour Context model is recommended as a comprehensive model for online grocery retailing in a digital world. The study also looks at value co-creation from the perspective of a moderated mechanism. A total of 526 people who had purchased groceries online were surveyed for the purpose of the study. In order to perform additional analysis, test hypotheses, and formulate models, the Analytical Hierarchy Process, SPSS 23, AMOS 22, and PROCESS Macro were used. The results showed that the antecedent's convenience, recovery, and delivery experience influenced the attitude significantly. On the other hand, at a lower level of value co-creation, the newly emerging concept of value co-creation had an impact on the overall relationship between the antecedent of online customer experience and attitude. It may be beneficial for retailers to periodically involve their customers in creating a delightful online customer experience in order to increase the attitude and likelihood of repeat purchases among online grocery customers.

Haralayya (2022) enhances with this summary that we can get an overview of a Ford car study among Indian residents of the Bidar district, which looked at the "impact of branding on consumer purchasing behaviour." This summary also includes a quick rundown of marketing strategies that can be used to entice customers to look for a more youthful Indian vehicle logo. These strategies can be used to draw customers' attention to the fact that the Indian vehicle logo features young people. A brand can guarantee brilliant principles established at the right time and place, but it cannot guarantee inferior principles. However, while competing in the product sector, it has an impact on the logo's specific seal but not on the customer's mind. A brand created from the personalities of clients will become inseparable from clients who become acquainted with the image. This report seeks to investigate the impact of manufacturers' products on customer purchasing trends. Customers are typically influenced to pay for a logo design based on price, brand, or other factors throughout the purchasing process. The record is a comprehensive writing outline of suppliers; consideration for logo decency, price, and logo photograph dependability.

Laloan et al. (2022) intend that the phenomenon of the pandemic shows a before and after effect, which needed to be taken into consideration regarding the research. During the pandemic era, the current situation is highly associated with consumer decision-making; there are determinants that needed to be taken into account in order to find the current situation of people who want to use car wash service. The goal of this study is to discover how the company set up the car wash service with the intent of influencing consumer purchasing decisions. This study employs a qualitative approach, with informants interviewed to learn more about the phenomenon. The service quality of a car wash will eventually play a role in a customer's purchasing decision. It can be seen that service quality is closely related because it talks about the quality of service or products that will be received by the customers. The service is expected to maintain the current quality of service and keep on maintaining the implementation of health protocol. It can boost the trust of the customers toward the service given by the car wash and also retain a good number of customers as well.

Millatina et al. (2022) say that many groups are now paying attention to the current growth of this industry, which has seen a significant increase in order to attract their attention. Islamic finance, halal food and beverages, halal tourism, fashion and entertainment media, and halal pharmaceuticals and cosmetics are just a few of the seven industries where halal business trends can be found. Halal food and beverage labels in Indonesia need to be better known, and that is why this research is being conducted. The quantitative research method that was utilised in this investigation was known as PLS-SEM, and it was carried out with the assistance of the Smart-PLS software. In this particular research project, a total of one hundred individuals took part in the surveying process. Non-probability sampling was combined with the method of purposive sampling to select these individuals. It is clear from this study's findings that halal food products in Indonesia are more likely to be purchased if they have the halal label. Alternatively, halal awareness has begun to rise in Indonesian society, and halal is now a way of life.

Jadwal et al. (2022) investigate that their study focuses on segmenting Taiwanese credit card customers into optimal groups. When it comes to categorising customers, unsupervised learning can be very useful. Machine learning models trained on data from customers in optimally clustered groups have higher precision. To compare the predicted accuracy of the K-means, hierarchical, and HK Means clustering algorithms to the accuracy obtained by applying these machine learning models to all of our data, we used linear discriminant analysis, logistic regression, and random forest. This was done so that the accuracy of the predicted accuracy could be compared to the accuracy of the actual accuracy. In this particular piece of research, both hierarchical clustering and the K Means method are utilised. Customers are divided into optimal groups using the HK clustering algorithms, which are applied to the factorial coordinates obtained through multiple correspondence analyses. The accuracy of clustering methods is significantly influenced by how thoroughly inertia is broken down. According to the findings, the most efficient method for clustering customers is to use K-Means in conjunction with hierarchical clustering as a clustering technique. This will allow for a better understanding of the credit risk associated with each customer.

Da and Peng (2022) attempt that their research is on the technological innovation, job creation, and economic growth, which are important roles played by TMSEs. Due to the fact that they are fraught with danger and require a significant number of resources, the government of China has set aside funds and encouraged financial institutions to lend money to TMSEs. Methods used to evaluate TMSE credit cannot be used because they differ from those used for traditional enterprises. Credit risk assessment for TMSEs, a new and challenging topic, is difficult to understand. TMSE credit characteristics are being studied in order to discover new indicators. According to their findings, TMSE credit risk can be identified using innovation capability and business models. Using both traditional and novel financial indicators, they established that the latter were indeed more accurate. In the case of TMSEs, the findings showed that incorporating innovation and business model indicators improved classifier performance significantly.

Wu (2022) states that there is not a theory that has been sufficiently developed to measure credit risk or conduct decision analysis for large amounts of financial data, and there is also no evaluation system that is both effective and scientific that has been developed. Reading a brief summary of each of the aforementioned subjects and how they are connected can be helpful if you are interested in gaining additional knowledge about the topics and how they are connected. In addition, this paper suggests four directions for research in the areas of measuring credit risk and making financial decisions based on big data. Because of this, anyone who works in the field of making decisions based on big data can learn something from reading this paper. This includes practitioners, researchers, financial institutions, and government agencies.

According to Bu et al. (2022), the goal of their research is to look into the different ways that individual ratings and credit performance can be used to analyse and monitor portfolio credit risk. Rating specific exposure to observable macro variables, industries, and a latent mean-reverting macro fragility factor are all taken into account within the context of the proportional model that we implement. In order to make an accurate estimation of the model's parameters, an algorithm based on the Markov chain Monte Carlo method is implemented. We are able to precisely measure parameter uncertainty using this method, which is necessary for forecasting, and it also provides a practical way to update the model. Both of these benefits are essential for accurate prediction. We use a large default data set spanning 45 years, including the financial crisis of 2008, to show the link between individual frailty and exposure to systematic risk factors on credit ratings. This data set contains information from both before and after the 2008 financial crisis. According to testing done outside of the sample set, our model has been shown to be capable of forecasting the number of defaults across business cycles, particularly during the financial crisis. Even though the companies in the CLO were not included in the initial calibration of the model, we were still able to demonstrate that our model is capable of performing reasonably well in surveillance as long as timely updates are applied to it.

Augustin et al. (2022), inferring as a result of the COVID-19 pandemic, stated that they have the extraordinary chance to investigate the connection between unexpected increases in economic growth and the risk of default by sovereign governments. They discovered a positive and statistically significant relationship between the probability of a sovereign default and the extent to which the virus is spreading in a sample of 30 developed countries with budgetary restraints. In support of the fiscal channel, the results of fiscal policy are confirmed for the countries of the Eurozone and the states of the United States where monetary policy can be maintained at its current level. As a result of their susceptibility to shocks from the outside world, governments with limited fiscal space are punished in the global financial markets, as all have learned.

Roeder et al. (2022) narrate that the non-financial institutions, such as banks, keep a close eye on credit risk and perform in-depth analysis of it in order to forestall the possibility of counterparty default. There is a diverse collection of financial instruments that, when combined, can reveal information about the creditworthiness of a counterparty. Despite the fact that this metric has the potential to provide essential information, the fundamental price dynamics are frequently unknown and require further explanation. Making decisions based on the analysis of data is an important concept that can help identify these reasons and support and justify these decisions. The justifications in this research paper by using sentiment and topic analysis on financial analyst reports are used. Because analysts use their reports to communicate the findings of extensive research to the general public, these reports are an excellent source of information for experienced investors. From 2009 to 2020, this study examined 3,386 reports on the Dow Jones Industrial Average Index's components. Changes in sentiment, as well as certain topics, are correlated with changes in the CDS spread, even when traditional credit risk indicators are factored in. This implies that quantitative risk metrics and analyst reports are intrinsically linked. It is possible to find CDS spreads in analyst reports, which enables us to have a better understanding of our current risk assessments. According to the findings, financial institutions and corporate risk managers can improve their existing financial metrics and financial news data by making use of new insights gleaned from analyst reports.

Yfanti et al. (2022) investigate on policymakers and market practitioners who are concerned about systemic risk are particularly interested in the connections between sectoral corporate credit risk and each other. In this paper, they investigated the macroeconomic factors that have an effect on the dynamic correlations between the sectoral credit default swaps (CDS) markets in Europe and the United States. The CDS conditional equicorrelations can be explained using macro-financial and news proxies, respectively. Their research indicates that the behaviour of sectoral CDS interdependence is counter-cyclical. Higher sectoral correlations are linked to increased economic policy and financial uncertainty, a stronger impact of infectious disease news on stock markets, tighter credit conditions, a slowdown in economic activity, and negative sentiment. One of the primary factors that contribute to the integration of the CDS market is economic policy uncertainty (EPU), which, according to our findings, amplifies macro effects across credit risk correlations. Other significant factors, such as crisis events, exacerbate the time-varying effects of correlation macro drivers. It is possible for macro factors to have a significant influence on the development of credit risk relationships, which can lead to credit risk contagion and pose a potential threat to financial stability. For operational research applications involving risk and portfolio management, a solid understanding of the mechanisms underlying credit contagion is essential.

Wang et al.'s (2022) work on machine learning and data mining algorithms to improve credit risk assessment accuracy is well known. However, only a few methods can meet both its universal and efficient demands. A new multi-classification assessment model of personal credit risk based on the theory of fusion of information (MIFCA) employs six machine learning algorithms. This paper suggests the MIFCA model can reduce the interference of uncertain information by combining the benefits of multiple classifiers. MIFCA was tested with data from a Chinese commercial bank and found to be accurate. Research shows that MIFCA has a number of outstanding points across various evaluation criteria. Both its multi-classification accuracy and its universal applicability make it ideal for a wide range of risk assessments. The first is that it is more precise. Banks and other financial institutions can use the findings of this study to improve risk prevention and control, as well as their ability to identify credit risk and avoid financial losses.

Yu et al. (2022) enhance in their research that in credit risk assessment, a small sample size makes it difficult to build a reliable machine learning model; so many methods of virtual sample generation (VSG) for sample augmentation based on sample distribution have been proposed. For financial institutions, predicting a customer's creditworthiness becomes more difficult when the data sets they use contain a small sample with low dimensionality. An ELM-based VSG method with feature engineering for credit risk assessment with data scarcity is proposed to address these issues. First, the ELM-based VSG methodology is used to generate virtual samples and solve the data scarcity (i.e., small sample) problem. There are two ways to deal with the problem of data attribute scarcity (i.e., low dimensionality). The predicted performance of generated virtual samples is then predicted using various classifiers. When data are scarce, two public credit data sets are used for credit verification in credit classification. The experimental results show that the proposed methodology significantly improves classification performance for credit risk assessment using limited data.

Abdesslem et al. (2022) underwent research using data from 2006 to 2017. The impact of credit and liquidity risks, as well as the role of managerial ability, on the likelihood of European commercial banks defaulting is investigated in this study. According to data envelopment analysis and to bit modelling, bank efficiency and default risk are measured with a z-score while the endogeneity and model specification robustness tests are used to evaluate the performance of the banks. Their findings demonstrate that both of these risks have a significant impact on the likelihood of bank failure, and that managerial skill has no effect on this effect. Management ability, on the other hand, mitigates credit risk. Arrogance and a lack of empathy could be to blame for what happened. This could be explained by the fact that senior managers who are likely to be compensated on the basis of performance are more likely to keep bad news under wraps. The likelihood of a bank failure would rise in such a scenario.

In Zhang et al.'s (2022) research, supply chain finance (SCF) SMEs' credit risk is defined as the probability that the SME will default on loans derived from financing for the SCF platform. There are currently no models that can accurately predict the creditworthiness of small- and medium-sized enterprises (SMEs) in SCF using only static data from the businesses themselves. However, these models do not take into account the dynamic financing behaviour of SMEs in SCF, limiting their ability to predict credit risk. SCF SMEs' credit risk can be predicted using Deep Risk, a new approach that integrates enterprise demographic data with financing behaviour data. Using a multi-modal learning strategy, we are able to combine the two different sets of data. A feed-forward neural network is fed the concatenated vectors produced by data fusion in order to predict the credit risk of SMEs. On a real-world SCF data set, experiments show that the proposed Deep Risk approach outperforms the baseline methods in credit risk prediction for precision, recall, F1, AUC, and economic loss. SCF SME's credit risk can now be predicted with greater accuracy thanks to the combination of two previously unrelated data sources. It is essential to have both static and dynamic data on SMEs in order to better predict their credit risk. It is still better to look at financial behaviour than company demographics when it comes to making predictions. Decision makers involved in SCF should be aware of the managerial implications for maximising the benefits of SCF while minimising credit risk.

From 2003 to 2018, Bannier et al. (2022) conducted research on the relationship between corporate social responsibility and credit risk for US and European businesses. Only environmental aspects of corporate social responsibility, according to a study, have a negative impact on various measures of credit risk for US companies. Credit risk is affected by a number of external and internal factors for European businesses. Credit ratings, to their dismay, do not reflect the same contemporaneous relationship between corporate social responsibility and financial performance. Different estimation techniques have no influence on reliability.

According to Chen et al. (2022), the attention of ordinary people has shifted from the professional term of credit risk in the financial world to the social focus. Credit risk is a significant factor in determining a country's social and economic stability. The fact that society as a living environment and credit between individuals in each network will invariably lead to relevance, infection, and relevance risk issues, regardless of the shape or structure of the economic system, is one of these. To conduct a visual comparison of relevant research on credit risk contagion in the United States and elsewhere from the year 2000 to 2020, the WOS and CNKI databases are used as data sources, CiteSpaceV is used as a tool, and scientific measurement and knowledge map analysis methods are used. Despite the fact that China began late and progressed slowly in comparison to related research both at home and abroad, key words in the related literature show that China has begun to discuss both the universality and the particularity of each credit risk network individual; domestic research is rather fundamental. However, China has been attempting to catch up with and surpass the United States. Current efforts are focused on determining how the network's credit risk data are organised, what types of connections are made between the nodes, and who exactly belongs where. Related networks and individual responses to those networks are currently under consideration. According to these findings, research into credit risk contagion and related topics is increasing. It also looks at the research framework from the standpoints of fundamental knowledge, core expertise, and applied expertise, both domestically and internationally.

Hemachandran et al. (2021) made a performance analysis of K-nearest neighbour machine learning algorithm for bank loan sector. It is mainly used to identify the good customers for sanctioning loans. The accuracy of this model is 70%. Whereas the performance metric Jaccard is 0.70 and F1 Score is 0.68.

In Hemachandran et al.'s (2022a) research, an attempt was made to analyse the performance of the different machine learning models such as K-nearest neighbour, decision tree, support vector machine, and logistic regression for identifying the good customer for sanctioning bank loans. Comparing the accuracy of all these models, support vector machine model performs well with an accuracy of 79.6%.

5.3 METHODOLOGY OF RESEARCH

This study uses the data set available online in kaggle.com. The data set name is "bank loan." The data set has been downloaded for the website which can be used for any type of data analysis. The data set consists of nearly 1,500 data of customers who had availed bank loan. From these only 700 customer data were considered for data analysis as there were no data for "default" available for other customers except the first 700 customers. These data consist of the customers demographic details such as age, education, income, and details of credit or debt availed by the customers having variable name "debtinc," "creddebt," and "otherdebt." To calculate the total debt of the customers, all the debt value are added together and named as "totaldebt." Also, there is another detail named "default" where it is stated "0" for no default to pay loan amount availed and "1" for those who default to pay back the loan availed from the bank.

Credit and risk analysis has been performed using this data set. For performing this analysis, basic MS excel and SPSS have been used to analyse whether there is any

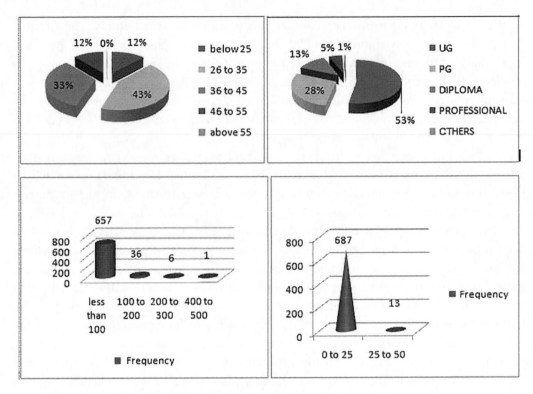

FIGURE 5.1   Demographic profile of the respondents.

significant difference among the group of the demographic variables and default made by the customers (figure 5.1).

5.4 DATA ANALYSIS

5.4.1 Interpretation 1

It is observed that 43% of the respondents belong to the age group of 25–35 years. Most of the respondents have completed their undergraduate education. Nearly 93% of the respondents were having the income less than $100 and 74% of the respondents were having total debt of less than $25 (figure 5.2).

5.4.2 Interpretation 2

It is observed that 73.9% (517) of the respondents have no default to pay the debt, whereas 26.1% (183) of the respondents have default to pay the debt (figure 5.3).

5.4.3 Interpretation 3

It is noted that 6.6% (46) of the respondents of age group less than 25 years have no default of loan and 5.7% (40) are default to pay the bank loan. When it comes to the age group of 26–35 years, it is noted that 31.6% (221) have not default and 11.6% (81) are default to pay loan. With regards to the age group of 36–45 years, it is seen that 27.0% (189) are not default and 5.9% (41) are default. And among the age group of

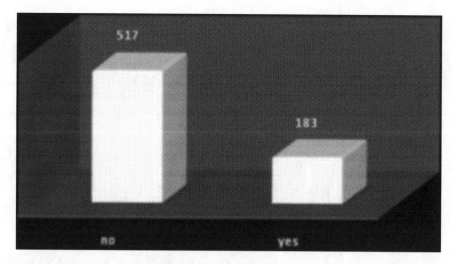

FIGURE 5.2   Default to pay the debt by the respondents.

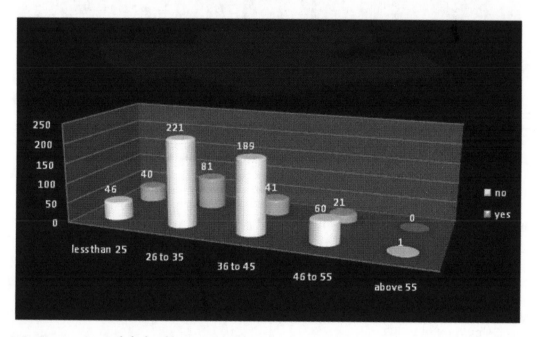

FIGURE 5.3   Age * default of loan payment.

46–55 years, 8.6% are not default and 3.0% are default. Overall, it is seen that 73.9% (517) of all the age groups are not default and 26.1% (183) are default to pay the loan amount (figure 5.4).

5.4.4 Interpretation 4

It is noted that 41.9% (293) of the respondents of UG education have no default of loan and 11.3% (79) are default to pay the bank loan. When it comes to the education of PG, it is noted that 19.9% (139) have not default and 8.4% (59) are default to pay loan. With

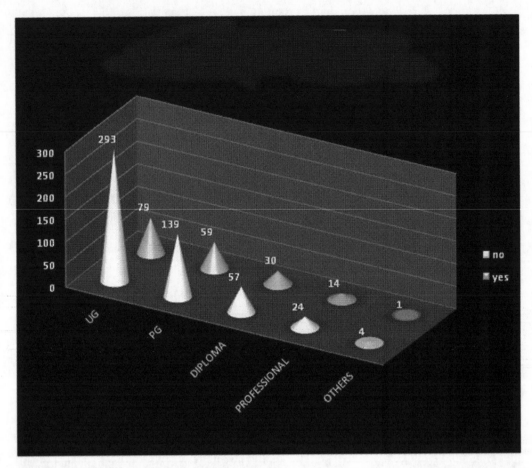

FIGURE 5.4   Education * default of loan payment.

regards to the education group of diplomas, it is seen that 8.1% (57) are not default and 4.3% (30) are default. Among the education group of professionals, 3.4% (24) are not default and 2.0% (14) are default. And among the education group of others, 0.6% (4) are not default and 1% (1) are default. Overall, it is seen that 73.9% (517) of all the education groups are not default and 26.1% (183) are default to pay the loan amount (figure 5.5).

5.4.5 Interpretation 5

It is noted that 68.9% (482) of the respondents of income less than $100 have no default of loan and 25.0% (175) are default to pay the bank loan. When it comes to the income of $100–$200, it is noted that 4.4% (31) have not default and 0.7% (5) are default to pay loan. With regards to the income of $300–$400, it is seen that 6% (4) are not default and 3% (2) are default. And for the income group more than $400, only one person has default to pay the loan back. Overall, it is seen that 73.9% (517) of all the education groups are not default and 26.1% (183) are default to pay the loan amount (figure 5.6).

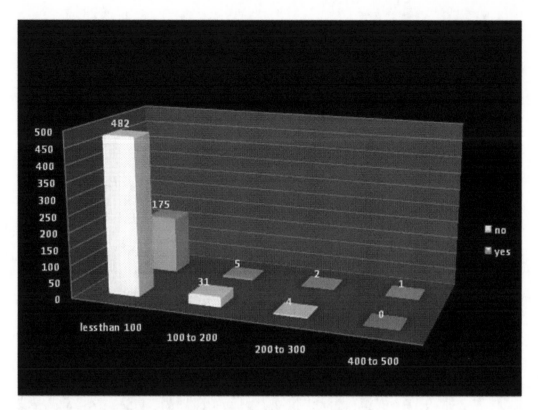

FIGURE 5.5   Income * default of loan payment.

5.4.6 Interpretation 6

It is noted that 72.6% (508) of the respondents of debt amount to less than $25 have no default of loan and 25.6% (179) are default to pay the bank loan. When it comes to the debt amount to more than $25, it is noted that 1.3% (9) are not default and 6% (4) are default to pay loan. Overall, it is seen that 73.9% (517) of all the education groups are not default and 26.1% (183) are default to pay the loan amount (table 5.1).

5.4.7 Interpretation 7

It can be inferred that the default status of the respondents significantly influences various age groups of the respondents (F value = 14.684, p value = 0.000), respondents' educational attainment (F value = 9.301, p value = 0.002), which is represented by the significance level for each of these variables less than 5%, which means that the p values are less than 0.05.

Default status of the respondents do not significantly influence various groups of income (F value = 0.025, p value = 0.874), and total debts of the respondents (F value = 0.146, p value = 0.702), which is represented by the p values of less than 0.05 at a level of significance of 5% considered significant for each of these variables.

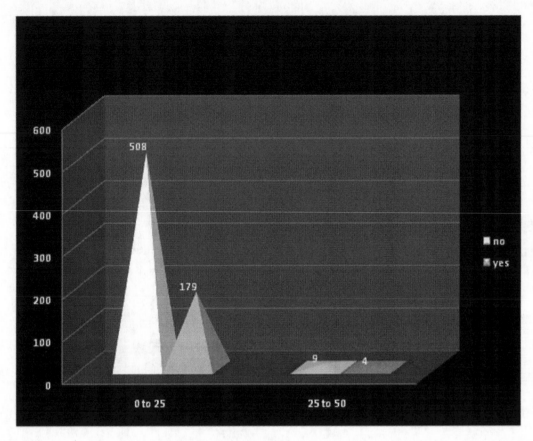

FIGURE 5.6   Total debt * default of loan payment.

TABLE 5.1   Difference Between Groups of Demographic Variable and Default to Pay the Debt by the Respondents

		ANOVA				
		Sum of Squares	df	Mean Square	F	Sig.
Age	Between groups	10.561	1	10.561	14.684	0.000
	Within groups	502.037	698	0.719		
	Total	512.599	699			
Education	Between groups	7.92	1	7.92	9.301	0.002
	Within groups	594.315	698	0.851		
	Total	602.234	699			
Income	Between groups	0.003	1	0.003	0.025	0.874
	Within groups	72.135	698	0.103		
	Total	72.137	699			
Total debt	Between groups	0.003	1	0.003	0.146	0.702
	Within groups	12.756	698	0.018		
	Total	12.759	699			

5.5 CONCLUSION

With regards to the age of the respondents, the bank has to concentrate more on the age group of 26–35 years as the default is more with this age group. Also, the bank has to concentrate on the age group less than 25 years and 36–45 years. When it comes to the education group, both who have completed their undergraduation and post-graduation are default to pay the debts. So the bank has to concentrate more on these groups. Respondents with income less than $100 have more default to pay the debts and people having their debts less than $25 have more defaults in paying the debts. Thus, it is concluded that the bankers need to do more analysis on the credit and risk analysis before providing the loan to their existing and new customers. Based on this study, it can be concluded that the bankers should be more careful when they provide further loan to the aforementioned age, education, income, and total debt groups. And it is important to consider these results before providing new loans and additional loans to their customers. Thus, the analysis helps the decision makers to take appropriate decisions in case of providing loans and also take some necessary steps to avoid delays in repayment of loans and defaults.

REFERENCES

Abdesslem, Rim Ben, Imed Chkir, Halim Dabbou. (2022). Is managerial ability a moderator? The effect of credit risk and liquidity risk on the likelihood of bank default. *International Review of Financial Analysis*, 80, 102044. doi:10.1016/j.irfa.2022.102044

Augustin, Patrick, Valeri Sokolovski, Marti G. Subrahmanyam, Davide Tomio. (2022). In sickness and in debt: The COVID-19 impact on sovereign credit risk. *Journal of Financial Economics*, 143(3), 1251–1274. doi:10.1016/j.jfineco.2021.05.009

Bannier, Christina E., Yannik Bofinger, Björn Rock. (2022). Corporate social responsibility and credit risk. *Finance Research Letters*, 44, 102052. doi:10.1016/j.frl.2021.102052

Brody, Dorje C., Lane P. Hughston, Andrea Macrina (2007). Beyond hazard rates: A new framework for credit-risk modelling. In Fu, M.C., Jarrow, R.A., Yen, J.Y.J., Elliott, R.J. (eds.) *Advances in Mathematical Finance. Applied and Numerical Harmonic Analysis*. Birkhäuser Boston. doi:10.1007/978-0-8176-4545-8_13

Bu, Shang, Nan Guo, Lingfei Li. (2022). Rating frailty, Bayesian updates, and portfolio credit risk analysis*. *Quantitative Finance*, 22(4), 777–797. doi:10.1080/14697688.2021.2013519

Chen, Shuai, Yating Zhang, Li Li. (2022). A comparative study of credit risk infection at domestic and abroad based on knowledge map. *Procedia Computer Science*, 199, 215–222. doi:10.1016/j.procs.2022.01.027

Da, Fang, Yi Peng. (2022). Non-financial indicators for credit risk analysis of Chinese technology-oriented micro and small enterprises. *Journal of the Operational Research Society*. doi:10.1080/01605682.2022.2072781

Haralayya, Bhadrappa. (2022). Effect of branding on consumer buying behaviour in Bharat Ford Bidar. *Iconic Research and Engineering Journals*, 5(9), 150–159.

Hemachandran, K., P. M. George, R. V. Rodriguez, R. M. Kulkarni, S. Roy. (2021). Performance analysis of K-nearest neighbor classification algorithms for bank loan sectors. *Advances in Parallel Computing*, 38, 9–13.

Hemachandran, K., R. V. Rodriguez, R. Toshniwal, M. Junaid, L. Shaw. (2022a). Performance analysis of different classification algorithms for bank loan sectors. In *Intelligent Sustainable Systems*, Springer, 191–202.

Hemachandran, K., S. Khanra, R. V. Rodriguez, J. Jaramillo (Eds.). (2022b). *Machine Learning for Business Analytics: Real-Time Data Analysis for Decision-Making*. CRC Press. doi:10.4324/9781003206316

Jadwal, Pankaj, Sunil Pathak, Sonal Jain. (2022). Analysis of clustering algorithms for credit risk evaluation using multiple correspondence analysis. *Microsystem Technologies*, 1–7. doi:10.1007/s00542-022-05310-y.

Kumari, Anshu, Loveleen Gaur, Gurmeet Singh. (2022). Impact of customer experience on attitude and repurchase intention in online grocery retailing: A moderation mechanism of value co-creation. *Journal of Retailing and Consumer Services*, 64, 102798. doi:10.1016/j.jretconser.2021.102798

Laloan, Dwi Putra Kristian, James D. D. Massie, Fitty Valdy Arie. (2022). Consumer buying decision of car wash service during COVID-19 pandemic case study: Car wash Tugu Kacang Kawangkoan. *Jurnal EMBA*, 10(1), 1449-1457. doi:10.35794/emba.v10i1.39420

Millatina, Afifah, Fifi Hakimi, Risanda Budiantoro, Muhammad Arifandi. (2022). The impact of halal label in halal food buying decisions. *Journal of Islamic Economic Laws*, 5, 159–176. doi:10.23917/jisel.v5i1.17139

Roeder, Jan, Matthias Palmer, Jan Muntermann. (2022). Data-driven decision-making in credit risk management: The information value of analyst reports. *Decision Support Systems*, 158, 113770. doi:10.1016/j.dss.2022.113770.

Wang, Tianhui, Renjing Liu, Guohua Qi. (2022). Multi-classification assessment of bank personal credit risk based on multi-source information fusion. *Expert Systems with Applications*, 191, 116236. doi:10.1016/j.eswa.2021.116236

Wu, Wenshuai. (2022). Credit risk measurement, decision analysis, transformation and upgrading for financial big data. *Complexity*. doi:10.1155/2022/8942773

Yfanti, Stavroula, Menelaos Karanasos, Constantin Zopounidis, Apostolos Christopoulos. (2022). Corporate credit risk counter-cyclical interdependence: A systematic analysis of cross-border and cross-sector correlation dynamics. *European Journal of Operational Research*. doi:10.1016/j.ejor.2022.04.017

Yu, Lean, Xiaoming Zhang, Hang Yin. (2022). An extreme learning machine based virtual sample generation method with feature engineering for credit risk assessment with data scarcity. *Expert Systems with Applications*, 202, 117363. doi:10.1016/j.eswa.2022.117363

Zhang, Wen, Shaoshan Yan, Jian Li, Xin Tian, Taketoshi Yoshida. (2022). Credit risk prediction of SMEs in supply chain finance by fusing demographic and behavioral data. *Transportation Research Part E: Logistics and Transportation Review*, 158, 102611. doi:10.1016/j.tre.2022.102611

CHAPTER 6

Cryptocurrencies and Blockchain Technology Applications

Yahya Skaf

CONTENTS

6.1 INTRODUCTION

The recent technology advancements and the related customers' dependence have incited financial institutions to offer e-finance services such as e-banking and trading platforms [1]. The latest technological advancements have changed financial services drastically in the past decade [2]. Financial institutions have now recognized the importance of adopting information technology in terms of increasing efficiency, security, and cost reduction [3]. Furthermore, customers' increased reliance on the internet and smartphones has prompted financial organizations to offer e-finance services [1]. E-finance is the delivery of financial services to clients through the Internet, thus representing a shift

DOI: 10.1201/9781003327745-6

from the physical delivery of financial services to the virtual world [4]. E-services incorporate all types of financial services including e-banking, market trading, brokerage, and so on. Despite the different benefits of E-finance services, security remains the major concern and barrier to its adoption. Trust and security of transactions in trading are key elements for business success [5]. Furthermore, when dealing with the digital world, critical data representing rights and ownership of assets faces serious cyber threats [6]. Thus, data must be protected against any fraudulent activities, and Blockchain technology is a relatively great tool to address the issue [7]. The Blockchain is a new architecture of data governance that is essentially based on the creation of linked blocks identified with cryptographic hashes [8]. Data is stored in blocks after the confirmation of all participants in the network through the consensus mechanism with no need for a central authority. Data stored using Blockchain technology is immutable and unalterable due to the distributed ledger technology and any fraudulent activity to alter the data can be detected by the consensus mechanism [9]. Bitcoin can be referred to as the first enactment of Blockchain technology to the world, and it was first restrained for the development of Bitcoin and its related transactions [10]. Blockchain technology is expected to change the way people do business and to rapidly develop financial technologies [11].

However, recent years witnessed increased propagation of Blockchain technology [12]. The application of Blockchain has extended from Cryptocurrencies with Blockchain 1.0 into other financial areas with the second generation (Blockchain 2.0) and extended to other industries with Blockchain 3.0 [13]. The market of the Blockchain is growing quickly as a result of its many key features such as transparency, trust, efficiency, and so on [14]. Revolutions in industrial and commercial sectors are expected to ignite with this technology (Underwood, 2016). Based on recent studies, the market of Blockchain would be worth more than eight billion dollars by 2025 with increased popularity in many sectors such as governmental services, healthcare, media, industrial sector, and so on [15]. The exponential growth of this technology urged many scholars to conduct various studies on the potential usage of the Blockchain [16]. For instance, reference [17] studied smart contracts as an underlying technology for Blockchain.

Therefore, this chapter demonstrates an overview of Blockchain technology and focuses on the application of Blockchain technology in the financial markets. We aim to present comprehensive literature on Blockchain technology, how it works, and its current and potential applications in the financial markets. Additionally, we hope to provide some recommendations for businesses willing to implement the technology and offer some directions for future research. The rest of the chapter is structured as follows: Section 6.2 introduces the working mechanism of Blockchain, and its evolution and provides a comparison between permissionless and permissioned Blockchain. Section 6.3 explains how this technology is applied in the financial industry and focuses on three main areas: Cryptocurrencies, financial markets, and the banking sector. Section 6.4 discusses the main benefits of adopting the Blockchain as well as the challenges of its implementation. Finally, section 6.5 provides a conclusion, recommendations, and future scope of research.

6.2 BLOCKCHAIN TECHNOLOGY, EXPLAINED

In recent years, finance and technology were strongly associated, and this marriage between both fields is now known under the name of FinTech [18]. FinTech requires the use and integration of technology for financial firms [19]. Fintech is also the upgrade of the services of the traditional financial enterprises by using technology, it also refers to the use of technology to develop new financial services [5]. Fintech includes the integration of many technologies in finance such as artificial intelligence, Data Science, mobile payment, and smart contracts but the most popular is the Blockchain [20].

Blockchain technology is a new and improved approach to database architecture compared to the traditional design of databases [21]. Traditional databases are organized in several ways but most traditional databases organize and store data in tables for fast search, update, and retrieval [22]. The traditional databases are relational and centralized where a master copy of data is stored and controlled by a central authority. Thus, the users of traditional databases must have confidence in the central authority that should safeguard the data by maintaining the necessary infrastructure to prevent data loss from equipment failure or cyber attacks. Therefore, the major threat to a traditional database is the loss of data due to the failure of the central authority.

Hence, Blockchain technology is a new architecture for data management that offers a decentralized design of data due to the distributed nature of the leger with no control of central authority, the immutable character of transactions, and the use of a consensus mechanism to store the data [23]. While the development of Blockchain technology is still in its infancy stage, the application of this technology is highly promising in the financial markets [24].

6.2.1 How Does It Work?

Blockchain technology is based on three main elements: a Network of Node Operators, a Consensus Mechanism, and a Digital Ledger with immutable character.

The Network of Node operators is a group of connected users. Each user stores an identical copy of the data, thus giving birth to another term for the Blockchain technology "Distributed Ledger Technology (DLT)" [25]. This technology referred to as a peer-to-peer (P2P) distributed database is based on the creation of unalterable records of transactions that each user in the network can read and write into the database [26]. If the transaction appears the same in all users' ledgers, these transactions are confirmed by the agreed-upon consensus mechanism and each user's copy of data is then updated to reflect the change, thus all users will update their version of the ledger, and the records are validated and final [27]. After a transaction is added to the Blockchain, it cannot be modified or deleted. Thus the only option is to add data to a Blockchain but not to delete or modify any record [28]. On the other hand, when a user submits a transaction to the network and this new transaction is in conflict with the state of other users' ledgers, the network discovers this transaction and the consensus mechanism breaks. As a result, the consensus mechanism forces the other users to reject the new update of the ledger.

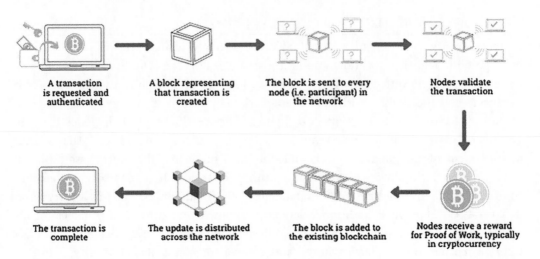

FIGURE 6.1 How does a transaction get into the Blockchain?

Source: From [29].

A transaction represents a change in an asset's ownership, thus a confirmed transaction registered on a Blockchain is simply a change in the ownership of an asset. Now for a transaction to be added to the blockchain, it passes through determined processing indicated in figure 6.1. Primarily, for a person to transfer the ownership of an asset to another person, it is mandatory to assure that the first person has the rightful owner of that asset. This can be performed by checking the past transactions in the Blockchain and finding that the first person acquired the asset at a point and has not yet sold it. Once the ownership of the asset is confirmed, the two persons agree to the transaction. Next, the system creates a block including the details of the agreement, and then both parties confirm the contract by adding their unique digital signature. After both persons have digitally signed the contract, the system calculates a string of characters called a "cryptographic hash" that is used to link the new transaction to the chain of previous transactions [30]. Each block with time-stamped digital data; enclosing at least one transaction; is then associated with a cryptographic hash that is easy to verify but difficult to calculate, and protected with a unique identifier or public key infrastructure (PKI). The cryptographic hash includes the contract details, the digital signatures of the contract's parties, and the previous block or transaction's details. Thus, it is easy to verify a legitimate transaction or a block but difficult to design and add an illegal transaction or block to the chain. At this point arrives the role of the consensus mechanism that confirms the transaction and adds it to a new or a block with recent transactions. It is worth noting that the consensus mechanism requires substantial computing resources to confirm the validity of the transactions. The updated Blockchain is then transmitted to all users of the network so that every participant has an updated and identical copy of the master ledger. The immutable and undone transactions and blocks are then accessible by all the members of the Blockchain network (figure 6.2).

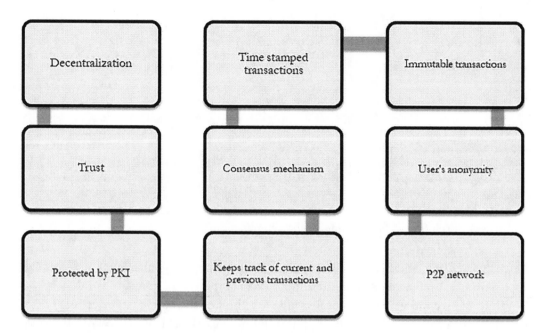

FIGURE 6.2   Key characteristics of blockchain, author's compilation.

Based on the above discussion, the Blockchain enjoys many characteristics. Firstly, the DLT provides a technology of decentralized data management and storage and eliminates the requirements of a centralized authority [31]. Consequently, the decentralized aspect removes the necessity to trust any party to confirm, record, and secure transactions. Furthermore, the security of the data in a Blockchain comes from many protocols such as the public key infrastructure PKI, the time-stamped transactions, the consensus mechanism, and the immutability of transactions. The Blockchain allows also us to visualize all confirmed transactions in the ledger. Moreover, the Blockchain is a P2P network that allows for transactions between addresses. The address is comprised of alphabets and numbers and represents an operator in the network. The operator can share or keep secret his address; thus preserving the user's anonymity and private data are no longer saved by a central authority [32]. However, some blockchain constraints prevent total privacy protection.

6.2.2 The Evolution of Blockchain

The development of Blockchain is marked by three technological generations: Blockchain 1.0, Blockchain 2.0, and Blockchain 3.0 [33]. The first generation of Blockchain was used to develop the first and most prominent digital currency, Bitcoin. Apart from Bitcoin, Blockchain technology is used to develop thousands of digital currencies and tokens known as altcoins such as Ethereum, Ripple, Cardano, and Monero (figure 6.3).

Generation 2.0 goes beyond the development of digital currencies and transactions to include bonds, smart contracts, futures, and other financial instruments and applications. This stage is marked by the integration of smart contracts in the Blockchain process.

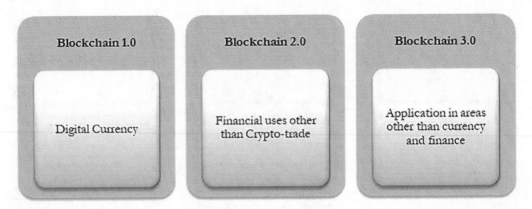

FIGURE 6.3   Evolution of blockchain, author's compilation.

Blockchain 2.0 includes also decentralized autonomous organizations, decentralized applications as well as decentralized autonomous corporations [34].

While the second generation deals only with the financial application of Blockchain, the third generation extends the application of the Blockchain to other industries. Blockchain in this stage is being used as a universal platform by different sectors such as governmental, medical, and cultural. By way of illustration, this technology is could be used in preserving individual credit records in banks, maintaining medical data in hospitals, and tracing the flow of products in manufacturing [35]. Blockchain 3.0 is also the back-end technology of a new era, the integration of tokens. Tokens represent evidence of a right to a unique digital asset such as academic diplomas, event tickets, and personal identity. The non-fungible tokens (NFTs) represent an important evolution of this era, each NFT represents a unique digital asset like a piece of art or digital content. The most admired Blockchain for NFTs is currently Ethereum and its standard ERC20 [7].

6.2.3 Permissionless and Permissioned Blockchain

The first use of the Blockchain application was in 2009 with the implementation of the famous digital currency "Bitcoin" [36] and expanded later to include varied industries [37]. The Blockchain used in developing Bitcoin is an illustration of a public network that is open to all users wishing to transact and any member of the network can see all the blockchain's transactions. In this meaning, this type of Blockchain is called permissionless because transactions are added to the Blockchain through the consensus mechanism explained earlier without the need for a central authority's confirmation or denial. Because every member on the Bitcoin Blockchain has access to see all the transactions recorded on the ledger, users can confirm the validity of the transaction by assuring that the member who spent the Bitcoin has received it earlier and not yet spent it [32]. Thus, the accuracy of the ledger is secured by the automated consensus mechanism where all transactions are recorded on a master ledger and every user has an identical copy of it leaving no way for failure or a need for further reconciliation. As a result, the Blockchain gained its immutable character [38]. The Blocks are chained together with a "cryptographic hash" making it difficult for fraudulent activity to change a block of a transaction [39]. Moreover, the older a block is, the more it becomes difficult to manipulate it. For instance, changing a block on a Blockchain requires replacing that block with a new one and reproducing all the subsequent blocks with their complete information. Thus changing a block requires time and energy to regenerate the same chain of subsequent blocks while overcoming the oversight of the consensus mechanism. Thus, the older a block is, the more confident a user will have that it will not be fraudulently changed.

However, the use of Blockchain technology in the financial markets requires special attention. The permissionless aspect of the Blockchain contradicts some peculiarities of the financial markets such as the existence of intermediaries, the sometimes-undesirable transparency, and the need to comply with regulations [6]. Thus, private and permissioned Blockchain is used instead in the financial markets. A permissioned Blockchain is only accessible by the member of the network who met the membership's criteria to join. The confirmation of transactions in a private Blockchain is controlled by certain members who are provided with a certain level of control depending on the network's design. These members called also consensus authorities may have the authority to explicitly approve or reject a transaction. They may also be the sole users who have the access to participate in a consensus mechanism. Consequently, the trust in transactions in such a network is maintained due to the trust in the permissioning members. The permissioned Blockchain may have lost a key advantage of a Blockchain technology that allows the creation of a decentralized "peer-to-peer" network with no control of authority such as a government or a central bank [22]. However, it still enjoys the benefits of decentralized storage of the ledger with the timely assured reconciliation of all users' copies of the master database. Furthermore, the private Blockchain may present some solutions to problems encountered by permissionless Blockchain such as the need for large computing power to confirm transactions. Along the same line, a permissionless Blockchain that is open and anonymous fails to comply with some regulatory requirements such as know your customer (KYC) which requires pre-approval and trust in those who participate in a network. Nevertheless, private networks allow different levels of access to the information on the Blockchain. By way of illustration, controlling authorities may have access to view all transactions without permission to add any while other users may have access to view specific information depending on their role.

6.3 BLOCKCHAIN TECHNOLOGY APPLICATIONS

Blockchain is a promising technology that has the potential to provide many benefits and gains if applied in the financial markets. Reducing intermediation and reconciliation costs due to this technology are among many efficiency gains in the financial markets. This innovation has ignited a lot of interest in the FinTech industry [40]. The application of Blockchain in the financial markets refers to applying this technology in the different functions and operations in this sector. Blockchain applications are, for example, considered in the insurance industry to improve fan of internal operations. [33], discusses the role of the Blockchain and smart contracts in insurance to prevent fraudulent claims from beneficiaries. They also add that the DLT contributes to eliminating the requirement for brokers or other intermediaries, streamlining payments, and optimizing other functionalities. Thus, the following discussion illustrates three important applications of the DLT in the financial industry: digital currencies, financial markets, and the banking sector.

6.3.1 Cryptocurrencies

Satoshi Nakamoto, a pseudonym, created Bitcoin in 2008, the first digital and leading currency predicated on Blockchain technology with a limited supply of 21 million units [41]. The Bitcoin Blockchain uses cryptography for its creation and proof of work mechanism to confirm transactions away from the control of central authority [42]. Blockchain uses a decentralized technology that keeps records for every single transaction and the transactions are confirmed by all nodes in the network through the consensus mechanism. Individuals known as "miners" accumulate these transactions into blocks. The miners confirm the validity of the transaction and race to solve complicated computer work [43]. The first miner who comes to solve the problem adds the transaction to the Blockchain and gets rewarded with a certain number of Bitcoin in return. Scalability is the major concern for Bitcoin due to the size of each block (1 MB per block) and the number of transactions that can be accommodated by this block [44]. The Bitcoin system can provide only seven transactions per second compared to more than 12 transactions per second for Ethereum.

Since the launch of Bitcoin, thousands of digital currencies are issued and many have been adopted for real-world transactions [45]. For instance, the Ethereum project that was launched in 2013 using Blockchain technology is considered the second most important digital currency after Bitcoin and the most prominent altcoin [46]. An altcoin is any cryptocurrency other than Bitcoin. Ethereum addresses different limitations of the Bitcoin system and allows for the integration of smart contracts in the Blockchain. Ethereum is considered also the most popular system for tokens, especially for NFTs [7]. Dash is another digital currency that shares some similar properties with Bitcoin. However, Bitcoin faces critics that its value is unfounded since no one overlooks the whole system. In contrast, Dash is a permissioned Blockchain that is controlled by a decentralized network of nodes referred to as Masternodes [42]. Therefore, Dash Blockchain has the advantage of real-time confirmation of transactions since the Masternodes are separate from miners with no overlapping functions between both parties. In the same line, many other digital currencies were created based on the Bitcoin system with adjustments made to overcome some discrepancies. Lite coin, for example, is similar to the Bitcoin system but enjoys a higher speed of transaction confirmation, the same goes for Dogecoin, Ripple, Monero, MadeSafeCoin, and many other currencies [42]. Cryptocurrencies use Blockchain technology and are free of any central bank oversight (permissionless). However, many central banks are studying the issuance of a digital currency, called fiat currency that is backed and monitored by the government/ central bank (permissioned) [6].

Digital currencies can be stored in an electronic wallet that can only be accessed using a private key. The key feature of Cryptocurrencies is that they can be utilized to transfer value between two persons without the interference of a third party with the necessity of using the private key [47]. They can be traded on electronic platforms such as Coinbase, WazirX, Unocoin, and Binance. The acceptance of Cryptocurrencies as a payment method for purchases is still very limited. Some stores started to accept payment using Cryptocurrencies, they can be used to buy ice cream from Baskin Robbins or pizza from Dominos. On the other hand, the price of a digital currency is highly volatile, it can spike very high and rapidly can crash very low. Speculation is the main reason for prices' dizziness in the crypto market. Another problem related to Cryptocurrencies is the weak regulations in the field allowing crypto exchange for criminal purposes such as money laundering.

Individuals involved in the Cryptocurrency market are of four types according to [48]. The first type is the fortune hunter who invests for capital gain and seeks speculation. The second type is the freshman depicting the general public with little knowledge whereas the third type is the idealist that invests in knowledge gain. Lastly, the last type is the trailblazer which illustrates the professionals and experts in the field. The Cryptocurrencies market is marked by instability and legal uncertainty [49]. However, this market with all its complexities is progressively going to resemble the traditional financial markets as Cryptocurrencies are starting to be new alternatives for investment and portfolio diversification [50].

6.3.2 Financial Markets

The financial markets are divided according to their functions into primary and secondary markets [51]. The primary market refers to selling new shares and bonds for the first time to the public such as in the initial public offering (IPO) whereas the trading of shares after the IPO happens in the secondary market. At present, trading securities in both markets are still guaranteed and controlled by a centralized authority [52]. However, the application of Blockchain in exchange markets is timidly adopted with a focus on over-the-counter market securities. IBM for example developed a trading system based on Blockchain technology for the London Stock Exchange market LSE [53]. In the same line, the Australian securities exchange is planning with the Hong Kong exchange to implement Blockchain to ease some services similar to post-trade services and clearing [54].

The implementation of Blockchain in the financial industry has resulted in the rise of decentralized finance known also as DeFi [1]. Blockchain utility in the financial markets is a current and rich subject for scholars. For instance, [55] explained that the first use of Blockchain in the financial sector was to handle back-office tasks. NASDAQ has used Blockchain technology in issuing and transferring shares for non-listed companies through the launch of a securities trading platform named Linq [56]. The examples in this context are many, Korean stock exchange uses DLT to develop over the counter-trading system for non-listed companies [53]. In the same line, reference [57] discussed the usage of this technology in the capital markets for the payments of notes and bonds, they also illustrate its use in stock issuance in the primary and the trade in the secondary market. Another great application of the Blockchain is the use of smart contracts. Smart contracts are digital computer-coded contracts that execute automatically once the agreed-upon conditions specified in the contract are met such as stop-buy or stop-loss orders. When added to a Blockchain, smart contracts allow for the automation of many transactions and processes, thus reducing manual intervention and the time and cost of execution [1]. Digital assets are also other results of the application of Blockchain. The trade-in of physical assets such as real estate requires many verifications for each transaction, thus prolonging the execution of the transaction and its settlement. However, Blockchain technology has the potential to digitalize these assets for recordkeeping and transactional purposes [6]. Thus, DLT serves to safeguard or change the ownership of this asset. Furthermore, reference [58] points out that the Blockchain characteristics greatly fit the infrastructure of the financial market and will have a remarkable impact on several functions such as the payment system and securities settlement. Reference [52] explains that Blockchain technology can be applied to securities trading in three ways. It can be applied before the transaction to fulfil the requirements of KYC for example. It also might be applied during the transaction to store all related information. Lastly, its application can extend after the transaction for purposes of registration, settlement, data sharing, dividend payment, and so on.

Similar to the secondary market, the integration of Blockchain in clearing houses brought the attention of scholars and has also many applications [52]. A clearing house is an intermediary in a financial market that ensures that the buyer and seller honour their contractual requirements for a given transaction. Reference [58] explains that the key features of Blockchain can resolve the limitations of the traditional clearing house such as complicated workflow, low speed of information transfer, and asymmetry of information between exchanges and or banks. In the same context, reference [59] reveals that the use of Blockchain in clearing houses enlarges the volume of transactions. For instance, a clearing house named Guangdong performed experimentation using this model for 2 months, and the findings reveal that these 2 months are equivalent to 16 months of trading at NASDAQ. Also for illustration, the American Securities Depository and Clearing Corporation (DTCC) has recently implemented a Blockchain project in the name of Project Whitney to increase the transaction volume. This project permits to perform 115 million transactions per day which is equivalent to 6300 transactions per second. This speed represents more than dozens of times the speed of the original process [60].

The primary market, compared to the secondary market and clearing house also has many limitations that can be resolved with the use of Blockchain technology [7]. The use of Blockchain in primary markets has many practical cases. The SEC approved for Overstock.com to issue its newly listed stock using the Blockchain [52]. Similarly, the World Bank used for the first time the Blockchain to issue bonds under the name of "Bondi" in 2018 [61]. Reference [62] states that the application of Blockchain in the primary market can eliminate the need for a third party which can result in more accurate tracking, reduced costs, increased speed of issuance, and as result improved liquidity. Relatedly, the use of Blockchain also reduces information asymmetry and thus decreases the risk of fraud [63].

6.3.3 Banking Sector

The application of Blockchain technology in the banking sector is very auspicious. Garg et al. (2020) explain that Blockchain technology can be used to maintain bank-end utilities. Furthermore, they argue that this technology is efficient in performing fund transfers and registration as well as advancing clients' experiences. Reference [64] revealed that the application of Blockchain in the banking sector could help in eliminating some tiring protocols and requirements inherent in the banking sector just like know your customer (KYC). Furthermore, they argue that Blockchain will contribute to reducing transaction costs while at the same time speeding them up. They add that this technology increases security and leads to the automation of some processes using smart contracts, thus saving labour review. Furthermore, the incorporation of Blockchain in banks helps to understand financial movements such as transferring money and credit swaps, it also improves small businesses' experience in receiving and sending money [65]. Reference [38] argues that the implementation of Blockchain technology in local and international banks is driven by cost efficiency and value transfers, effective control of risk, the development of new services for innovative profit, and reducing duplication of audit work. They also explain that the Blockchain is applied in different services in banks such as supply chain finance and bill settlement. Furthermore, Blockchain technology is found to be an effective tool when it comes to fighting anti-money laundering, the application of DLT allows the tracking of suspicious transactions and customers' fraudulent activities in real time [66].

6.4 BENEFITS AND CHALLENGES

Blockchain technology enjoys great potential but many challenges are still stopping the wide utilization of Blockchain. The decentralization and P2P aspects are the foundation of this technology, which may have limited the utilization of Blockchain [67].

6.4.1 Benefits of Blockchain

One of the key benefits of a DLT is the creation of immutable records. Immutability is a main key feature of the DLT, a confirmed transaction is permanent and immutable. Another benefit is the traceability of transactions, the Blockchain keeps detailed information for each transaction and gives the users easy accessibility to see all the transactions in a chain [68]. Furthermore, Blockchain technology allows for time efficiencies in the transaction itself and the settlement period post-transaction [69]. The settlement period is the time between the execution of a transaction and the fulfilment of the transaction's requirements towards all parties in the contract (change of ownership and payment). The transaction on a blockchain can happen at any time or on any date in a few seconds and is a certain legal finality [57]. However, trade-in of most financial assets can happen only when financial markets and banks are open. Thus, the use of Blockchain in trading fosters liquidity availability in the hands of investors which may result in better

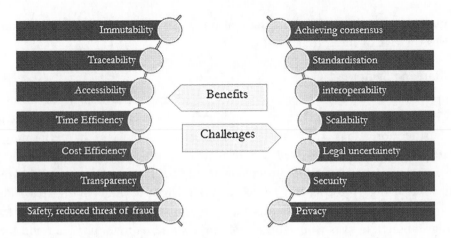

FIGURE 6.4 Benefits and challenges, author's compilation.

capital usage and return. In the same line, Blockchain usage in settling the transactions may shorten settlement times for many types of trades, especially in intermediated markets such as the foreign exchange industry which requires long settlement cycles and the involvement of many banks. Relatedly, reference [68] conducted a systematic literature review on the state of play the Blockchain in the financial sector. The results revealed that the benefits are many such as increased transparency, traceability and speed of transactions, cost efficiency, and increased safety. These results are aligned with those of reference [70] who found that the use of the Blockchain in the banking sector improves customer experience, enhances transparency, increases traceability, and reduces cost and probability of fraud (figure 6.4).

6.4.2 Challenges Faced by Blockchain

On the other hand, the implementation of a good-quality Blockchain is quite challenging. For instance, achieving the consensus mechanism requires the approval of all network members for any change in the ledger, especially in permissionless networks [6]. Moreover, the Blockchain designs differ among developers, thus the lack of standardization causes major challenges in implementing the Blockchain for businesses and organizations [64]. The different designs, as well as the discrepancies between the Blockchain structures and the existing internal systems within organizations, makes it challenging to implement the Blockchain [6]. Such a problem can also arise in external aspects such as the interoperability between a firm's Blockchain and other businesses' existing systems or with their different Blockchain designs [26]. Another challenge that may face Blockchain implementation, especially permissionless networks is scalability [38]. The DLT requires vast computing power to solve to confirm a transaction, resulting in lowering the speed of transactions' confirmation [71]. Furthermore, permissioned and permissionless networks require a large volume of storage resources as each user in the network is keeping an identical copy of the whole ledger [6]. Nonetheless, the Blockchain is still in its developing stage, making some ambiguity in the applications of the laws and regulations in cases of disputes such as bankruptcy [72], fraud, or other technical problems, a problem that is bigger for firms operating in multiple jurisdictions. Relatedly, the security of data provided by the distributed ledger is faced with another security concern [73], the more users in a Blockchain network, the more points there are for hackers to attack [31]. Another concern for some users is the lack of confidentiality and privacy of a network's participants and their transactions as all members can see the whole ledger [74]. Consequently, some organizations may be reluctant to participate in a DLT to avoid leakage of information that may affect their competitive advantage for example [6]. However, reference [38] conducted a qualitative study based on professional interviews and concluded many critical factors to overcome the challenges of adopting the Blockchain in the financial industry such as having enough capital availability, sufficient energy, reliable computational power, and well-trained personnel.

6.5 CONCLUSION, RECOMMENDATIONS, AND FUTURE WORK

While much effort remains to be done, DLT bestows a promising technology for future innovation. If implemented in the right way, the Blockchain possesses the potential to improve the efficiency and security of operations in the financial markets [6]. Thus, the purpose of this chapter is to conceptualize Blockchain technology and its implication in the financial markets. The study provides enough description of this technology and its working mechanisms. It also illustrates its evolution from being only used as digital currency (Bitcoin) to its applications in finance and many other industries. This research provides also an important differentiation between permissionless and permissioned blockchain technologies. Furthermore, the chapter outlines the primary applications of Blockchain technology in finance. The literature revealed many implementations of this technology, for example, Cryptocurrencies, digital assets, smart contracts, the baking sector, financial markets, and the insurance sector. The Blockchain is found to have many benefits as it is an efficient technology that reduces the time and cost of transactions. The unique technical characteristics of Blockchain have the potential to safeguard the records, increase traceability and transparency and reduce the threat of fraudulent manipulations. However, the Blockchain is still in its early stages with various challenges to overcome [38]. For instance, achieving consensus is technically a challenging process to confirm transactions. Additionally, the lack of standardization that results in interoperability problems is another problem facing firms willing to implement the technology. Furthermore, scalability, legal uncertainty, security, and privacy are also challenges to address when implementing Blockchain technology.

The design of the Blockchain technology lacks standardization, leaving different designs and protocols for developing the network. Thus, it is recommended to develop and establish generally accepted technical standards such as those imposed by the European Union regarding C-type USB chargers for mobile. In the same line, the developers in this industry are increasingly patenting DLT-related technologies. Thus making the firms working in this field vulnerable to legal disputes and preventing other firms from entering the market and resulting in limiting innovation. Therefore, existing regulating authorities must work together with firms involved in Blockchain research as they are working on improving or developing this technology. Nonetheless, the mining activities that are related to Cryptocurrencies result in huge energy consumption and carbon emission [75]. Thus, with the increased motivation to mine, developing appropriate regulations to reduce the impact of mining on the environment appears to be a necessity. This could be done by dictating laws to induce reliance on renewable sources of energy such as solar or wind power. Additionally, to overcome the challenges of achieving the consensus mechanism, it is recommended to allow trusted network members the authority to make protocol changes such as in permissioned Blockchain networks. For illustration, the permissionless network requires huge computational and storage power to confirm and store the transactions as each node in the chain has to confirm each transaction and maintain a copy of the ledger. However, permissioned networks are more efficient in this context with the consensus mechanism entrusted to a trusted permissioning authority. The DLT is also promising in developing the relationship between the public sector and the private sector [6]. Thus, it is recommended to develop specific applications of Blockchain to enable better cooperation between both sectors through improved transparency and information sharing. Moreover, these applications increase the trust between both parties and allow for improved audit trials especially, for example, tax filing. In the same context, regulatory bodies should work to prohibit the use of Blockchain for criminal objectives such as the transfer of assets and money for terrorism.

The economics and financial benefits of the DLT have been widely investigated in previous literature [7]. However, future research can be conducted to explore the key success factors in implementing Blockchain in the financial industry. In the same line, it would be interesting to assess the utility of this technology in specific services such as the initial public offering, bond issuance, or stock trading or in reducing the information asymmetry in the financial markets. Additionally, further research can look at the adoption of Blockchain technology along with artificial intelligence in certain areas such as the insurance sector. Moreover, it is salient to study the effect of Blockchain implementation on the organizational structure or managerial efficiency of firms. Finally, understanding the influence of the Blockchain on businesses and finances will require further academic investigations.

REFERENCES

[1] S. Trivedi, K. Mehta, and R. Sharma, "Systematic Literature Review on Application of Blockchain Technology in E-Finance and Financial Services," *Journal of Technology Management & Innovation*, vol. 16, no. 3, pp. 89–102, 2021.

[2] S. T. Kong and N. Loubere, "Digitally Down to the Countryside: Fintech and Rural Development in China," *The Journal of Development Studies*, vol. 57, no. 10, pp. 1739–1754, 2021.

[3] R. Hendrikse, M. Van Meeteren, and D. Bassens, "Strategic Coupling Between Finance, Technology, and the State: Cultivating a Fintech Ecosystem for Incumbent Finance," *Environment and Planning A: Economy and Space*, vol. 52, no. 8, pp. 1516–1538, 2020.

[4] S. Claessens, D. Klingebiel, and T. Glaessner, "E-Finance: A New Approach to Financial Sector Development?," *Financial Markets, Institutions and Instruments*, vol. 11, pp. 1–97, 2002.

[5] Y. Tang, "How Fintech Changes Our Life?," 2018. [Online]. Available: [Online] Available from: https://mp.weixin.qq.com/s/1RdTkI9q4NlMrdxNqQFO2w [Accessed 5 May 2022].

[6] R. Lewis, J. McPartland, and R. Ranjan, "Blockchain and Financial Market Innovation," *Economic Perspectives, Federal Reserve Bank of Chicago*, vol. 7, pp. 1–13, 2017.

[7] M. Xu, X. Chen, and G. Kou, "A Systematic Review of Blockchain," *Financial Innovation*, vol. 5, no. 27, pp. 1–14, 2019.

[8] M. Janssen, V. Weerakkody, E. Ismagilova, U. Sivarajah, and Z. Irani, "A Framework for Analyzing Blockchain Technology Adoption: Integrating Institutional, Market and Technical Factors," *International Journal of Information Management*, vol. 50, pp. 302–309, 2020.

[9] J. Huang, L. Kong, G. Chen, M. Wu, X. Liu, and P. Zeng, "Towards Secure Industrial IoT: Blockchain System with Credit-based Consensus Mechanism," *IEEE Transactions on Industrial Informatics*, vol. 15, no. 6, pp. 3680–3689, 2019.

[10] A. N. Islam, M. Mäntymäki, and M. Turunen, "Why Do Blockchains Split? An Actor-Network Perspective on Bitcoin Splits," *Technological Forecasting and Social Change*, vol. 148, no. 119743, 2019.

[11] M. Antonio and J. DiNizo, "From Alice to Bob: The Patent Eligibility of Blockchain in a Post-CLS Bank World," *Case W. Res. J.L. Tech. & Internet 1 (2nd)*, vol. 9, no. 1, 2018.

[12] J. Abou Jaoude and R. Saade, "Blockchain Applications – Usage in Different Domains," *IEEE Access*, vol. 7, pp. 45360–45381, 2019.

[13] M. Engelhardt, "Hitching Healthcare to the Chain: An Introduction to Blockchain Technology in the Healthcare Sector," *Technology Innovation Management Review*, vol. 7, no. 10, pp. 22–34, 2017.

[14] M. Iansiti and K. Lakhani, "Do Not Copy or Post," *HBR*, vol. R1701J, pp. 1–11, 2017.

[15] Grand View Research, "Blockchain Technology Market Size, Share & Trends Analysis Report by Type (Public, Private, Hybrid), by Application (Financial Services, Consumer Products, Technology, Telecom), and Segment Forecasts, 2019–2025," 2019.

[16] R. Böhme, N. Christin, B. Edelman, and T. Moore, "Bitcoin: Economics, Technology, and Governance," *Journal of Economic Perspectives*, vol. 29, no. 2, pp. 213–238, 2015.

[17] J. Cruz, Y. Kaji, and N. Yanai, "RBAC-SC: Role-Based Access Control Using a Smart Contract," *IEEE Access*, vol. 6, pp. 2240–12251, 2018.

[18] D. Zetzsche, R. Buckley, D. Arner, and J. Barberis, "From FinTech to TechFin: The Regulatory Challenges of Data-Driven Finance," *SSRN Electronic Journal*, vol. 6, pp. 1–36, 2017.

[19] T. Dhanabalan and A. Sathish, "Transforming Indian Industries Through Artificial Intelligence and Robotics in Industry 4.0.," *International Journal of Mechanical Engineering and Technology*, vol. 9, no. 10, pp. 835–845, 2018.

[20] A. B. Brem, V. Bilgram, and A. Marchuk, "How Crowdfunding Platforms Change the Nature of User Innovation From Problem-Solving to Entrepreneurship," *Technological Forecasting and Social Change*, vol. 144, pp. 348–360, 2017.

[21] M. Stanley, "Global Insight: Blockchain in Banking: Disruptive Threat or Tool? Global Financials/FinTech," *Morgan Stanley Global Insight*, pp. 1–31, 2016.

[22] S. Meunier, "Blockchain Technology—A Very Special Kind of Distributed Database," *Saatavissa*, Hakupäivä, 4, 2018, 2016. https://medium.com/@sbmeunier/blockchain-technology-a-very-special-kind-of-distributed-database-e63d00781118

[23] M. Ertz and É. Boily, "The Rise of the Digital Economy: Thoughts on Blockchain Technology and Cryptocurrencies for the Collaborative Economy," *International Journal of Innovation Studies*, vol. 3, no. 4, pp. 84–93, 2019.

[24] Z. Church, "Blockchain, Explained," 2017. [Online]. Available: https://mitsloan.mit.edu/ideas-made-to-matter/blockchain-explained [Accessed 6 May 2022].

[25] W. Rashideh, "Blockchain Technology Framework: Current and Future Perspectives for the Tourism Industry," *Tourism Management*, vol. 80, no. 104125, 2020.

[26] M. Zachariadis, G. Hileman, and S. Scott, "Governance and Control in Distributed Ledgers: Understanding the Challenges Facing Blockchain Technology in Financial Services," *Information and Organization*, vol. 29, no. 2, pp. 105–117, 2019.

[27] S. Yoo, "Blockchain-Based Financial Case Analysis and Its Implications," *Asia Pacific Journal of Innovation and Entrepreneurship*, vol. 11, no. 3, pp. 312–321, 2017.

[28] H. Lycklama à Nijeholt, J. Oudejans, and Z. Erkin, "A Framework for Preventing Double-financing Using Blockchain Technology," *Proceedings of the ACM Workshop on Blockchain, Cryptocurrencies and Contracts*, pp. 29–34, 2017.

[29] Euromoney Learning, "Euromoney Learning," 2022. [Online]. Available: https://www.euromoney.com/learning/blockchain-explained/how-transactions-get-into-the-blockchain [Accessed 1 June 2022].

[30] C. Lin, N. Ma, X. Wang, and J. Chen, "Rapido: Scaling Blockchain With Multi-path Payment Channels," *Neurocomputing*, vol. 406, pp. 322–332, 2020.

[31] Z. Zheng, S. Xie, H. Dai, X. Chen, and H. Wang, "Blockchain Challenges and Opportunities: A Survey," *International Journal of Web and Grid Services*, vol. 14, no. 4, pp. 352–375, 2018.

[32] A. Tapscott and D. Tapscott, "How Blockchain Is Changing Finance," *Harvard Business Review*, vol. 1, no. 9, pp. 2–5, 2017.

[33] A. K. Kar and L. Navin, "Diffusion of Blockchain in Insurance Industry: An Analysis Through the Review of Academic and Trade Literature," *Telematics and Informatics*, vol. 58, no. 101532, 2021.

[34] M. Swan, "Blockchain: Blueprint for a New Economy," *O'Reilly Media*, p. 152, 2015.

[35] I. Milic, "Blockchain Statistics and Facts That Will Make You Think: The Dawn of Hyper-capitalism," 2019. [Online]. Available: https://fortunly.com/statistics/blockchain-statistics/#gref

[36] M. V. M. Silva and M. A. Simplicio Jr., "Secure Protocol for Exchanging Cards in P2P Trading Card Games Based on Transferable e-cash," *Journal of Information Security And Cryptography (Enigma)*, vol. 3, no. 1, p. 26, 2016.

[37] A. Reyna, C. Martín, J. Chen, E. Soler, and M. Díaz, "On Blockchain and Its Integration with IoT. Challenges and Opportunities," *Future Generation Computer Systems*, vol. 88, pp. 173–190, 2018.

[38] V. Chang, P. Baudier, H. Zhang, Q. Xu, J. Zhang, and M. Arami, "How Blockchain Can Impact Financial Services–The Overview, Challenges, and Recommendations From Expert Interviewees," *Technological Forecasting and Social Change*, vol. 158, no. 120166, 2020.

[39] M.-J. Rennock, A. Cohn, and J. Butcher, "Blockchain Technology and Regulatory Investigations," *The Journal*, vol. 1, pp. 35–44, 2018.

[40] Y. Guo and C. Liang, " Blockchain Application and Outlook in the Banking Industry," *Financial Innovation*, vol. 2, no. 1, pp. 1–12, 2016.

[41] L. Luu, V. Narayanan, C. Zheng, K. Baweja, S. Gilbert, and P. Saxena, "October. A Secure Sharding Protocol for Open Blockchains," *In Proceedings of the 2016 ACM SIGSAC Conference on Computer and Communications Security*, pp. 17–30, 2016.

[42] S. Chan, J. Chu, S. Nadarajah, and J. Osterrieder, "A Statistical Analysis of Cryptocurrencies," *Journal of Risk and Financial Management*, vol. 10, no. 12, pp. 1–23, 2017.

[43] H. Vranken, "Sustainability of Bitcoin and Blockchains," *Current Opinion in Environmental Sustainability*, vol. 28, pp. 1–9, 2017.

[44] J. Poon and T. Dryja, "The Bitcoin Lightning Network: Scalable Off-chain Instant Payments", vol. 1, pp. 1–59, 2016.

[45] A. Ghosh, S. Gupta, A. Dua, and N. Kumar, "Security of Cryptocurrencies in Blockchain Technology: State-of-Art, Challenges and Future Prospects," *Journal of Network and Computer Applications*, vol. 163, p. 102635, 2020.

[46] V. Buterin, "A Next-generation Smart Contract and Decentralized Application Platform," *White Paper*, vol. 3, no. 37, pp. 2–1, 2014.

[47] M. Fauzi, N. Paiman, and Z. Othman, "Bitcoin and Cryptocurrency: Challenges, Opportunities, and Future Works," *The Journal of Asian Finance, Economics and Business*, vol. 7, no. 8, p. 695–704, 2022.

[48] C. F. Breidbach and S. Tana, "Betting on Bitcoin: How Social Collectives Shape Cryptocurrency Markets," *Journal of Business Research*, vol. 122, pp. 311–320, 2021.

[49] A. Klarin, "The Decade-Long Cryptocurrencies and the Blockchain Rollercoaster: Mapping the Intellectual Structure and Charting Future Directions," *Research in International Business and Finance*, vol. 51, p. 101067, 2020.

[50] M. Wątorek, S. Drożdż, J. Kwapień, L. Minati, P. Oświęcimka, and M. Stanuszek, "Multiscale Characteristics of the Emerging Global Cryptocurrency Market," *Physics Reports*, vol. 901, pp. 1–8, 2021.

[51] N. Szabo, "Smart Contracts: Building Blocks for Digital Markets," *EXTROPY: The Journal of Transhumanist Thought*, vol. 16, no. 18.2, 1996.

[52] J. Liu, Z. Xu, R. Li, H. Zhao, H. Jiang, J. Yao, D. Yuan, and S. Chen, "Applying Blockchain for the Primary Financial Market: A Survey," *IET Blockchain*, vol. 1, pp. 65–81, 2021.

[53] S. Jacobs, "The ASX Says Its New Blockchain Platform Will Be Ready by the End of 2020," 2018. [Online]. Available: https://www.businessinsider.com.au/asx-blockchain-distributed-ledger-technology-chess-replacement-2018-4 [Accessed 2 May 2022].

[54] E. Dunkley, "HKEX Working with ASX on Blockchain," *Financial Times*, 2018.

[55] K. Fanning and D. P. Centers, "Blockchain and Its Coming Impact on Financial Services," *Journal of Corporate Accounting & Finance*, vol. 27, no. 5, pp. 53–57, 2016.

[56] S. Schuetz and V. Venkatesh, "Blockchain, Adoption, and Financial Inclusion in India: Research Opportunities," *International Journal of Information Management*, vol. 52, p. 101936, 2020.

[57] D. Kimani, K. Adams, R. Attah-Boakye, S. Ullah, J. Frecknall-Hughes, and J. Kim, "Blockchain, Business and the Fourth Industrial Revolution: Whence, Whither, Wherefore and How?," *Technological Forecasting and Social Change*, vol. 161, p. 120254, 2020.

[58] T. Wu and X. Liang, "Exploration and Practice of Inter-bank Application based on Blockchain," *In 2017 12th International Conference on Computer Science and Education (ICCSE)*, pp. 219–224, 2017.

[59] F. Mvula, J. Phiri, and S. Tembo, "A Conceptual Secure Blockchain Based Settlement," *Proceedings of the International Conference INICT (ICIC2019)*, 2019.

[60] DTCC, "Project Whitney: Case Study. Depository Trust & Clearing Corporation," 2020. [Online]. Available: https://perspectives.dtcc.com/articles/project-whitney [Accessed 25 May 2022].

[61] WorldBank, "World Bank Prices First Global Blockchain Bond, Raising A$110 million," 2018. [Online]. Available: https://www.worldbank.org/en/news/press-release/2018/08/23/ [Accessed 4 June 2022].

[62] T. Halevi, F. Benhamouda, A. De Caro, S. Halevi, C. Jutla, Y. Manevich, and Q. Zhang, "Initial Public Offering (IPO) on Permissioned Blockchain Using Secure Multiparty Computation," *In 2019 IEEE International Conference on Blockchain (Blockchain)*, vol. IEEE (2019), pp. 91–98, 2019.

[63] D. Mills, K. Wang, B. Malone, A. Ravi, J. Marquardt, A. Badev, T. Brezinski, L. Fahy, K. Liao, V. Kargenian, and M. Ellithorpe, "Distributed Ledger Technology in Payments, Clearing, and Settlement (2016-12)". FEDS Working Paper No. 2016-095. 2016. Available at SSRN: https://ssrn.com/abstract=2881204

[64] H. Hassani, X. Huang, and E. Silva, "Banking With Blockchained Big Data," *Journal of Management Analytics*, vol. 5, no. 4, pp. 256–275, 2018.

[65] Q. K. Nguyen, "Blockchain-a Financial Technology for Future Sustainable Development," *In 2016 3rd International Conference on Green Technology and Sustainable Development (GTSD)*, pp. 51–54, 2016.

[66] K. Lai, "Blockchain as AML Tool: A Work in Progress," *International Financial Law Review*, 2018.

[67] D. Drescher, "Blockchain Basics: A Non-technical Introduction in 25 Steps," *Apress, Frankfurt-am-Mein*, vol. 978, no. 1, 2017.

[68] O. Ali, M. Ally, and Y. Dwivedi, "The State of Play of Blockchain Technology in the Financial Services Sector: A Systematic Literature Review," *International Journal of Information Management*, vol. 54, p. 102199, 2020.

[69] J. Mendling, I. Weber, W. Aalst, J. Brocke, C. Cabanillas, F. Daniel, S. Debois, C. Ciccio, M. Dumas, S. Dustdar, and A. Gal, "Blockchains for Business Process Management-Challenges and Opportunities," *ACM Transactions on Management Information Systems (TMIS)*, vol. 9, no. 1, pp. 1–16, 2018.

[70] P. Garg, B. Gupta, A. K. Chauhan, U. Sivarajah, S. Gupta, and S. Modgil, "Measuring the Perceived Benefits of Implementing Blockchain Technology in the Banking Sector," *Technological Forecasting and Social Change*, vol. 163, p. 120407, 2021.

[71] B. Marr, "The 5 Big Problems with Blockchain Everyone Should Be Aware Of," *Forbes*, vol. 19, 2018.

[72] L. Cong, "Blockchain Disruption and Smart Contracts," *The Review of Financial Studies*, vol. 32, no. 5, pp. 1754–1797, 2019.

[73] K. Werbach, "Trust, But Verify: Why the Blockchain Needs the Law," *Berkeley Technology Law Journal*, vol. 33, no. 2, pp. 487–550, 2018.

[74] G. Hileman and M. Rauchs, "A Global Blockchain Benchmarking Study," *Rochester, NY: Social Science Research Network*, 2017.

[75] J. Truby, "Decarbonizing Bitcoin: Law and Policy Choices for Reducing the Energy Consumption of Blockchain Technologies and Digital Currencies," *Energy Research & Social Science*, vol. 44, pp. 399–410, 2018.

CHAPTER 7

Machine Learning and the Optimal Choice of Asset Pricing Model

Aleksander Bielinski and Daniel Broby

CONTENTS

DOI: 10.1201/9781003327745-7

7.1 INTRODUCTION

Asset pricing is a major area of interest within the field of quantitative finance. The forecasting of the asset price is one of the main fundamental challenges for quantitative finance practitioners and academics alike. With the rapid development of technology, the computing power increased, thus making more investment firms and managers point their attention to machine learning techniques. Data are central to the modern digital economy and with humans generating and capturing more and more of it each year, there was a need to apply modern computer science techniques to deal with such a large volume of this resource.

Machine learning is defined as a mechanism used to train machines to perform a specific task while handling the data in the most efficient way. Machine learning techniques are designed to handle highly dimensional, large volumes of data, which make them a great tool for estimating asset prices. While traditional asset pricing models are largely linear, machine learning techniques allow to utilize the new data sources and incorporate non-linear interactions among variables in making the predictions. With a large body of documented stock-level factors (Green, Hand and Zhang, 2013; Harvey, Liu and Zhu, 2016), the question remains which ones to use and how to best capture the ongoing relationships between them and expected return. Furthermore, Harvey and Liu (2021) argue that traditional statistical techniques used in evaluating the explanatory power of these factors are redundant given the multiplicity issues arising from such methods. Machine learning techniques offer a wide range of approaches to deal with the evaluation of the predictive power of factors, which were proven to be more effective compared to traditional statistics methods.

In this chapter, we will discuss the issues with traditional factor models and identify the main constraints when designing an asset pricing model. From explaining the main principles of machine learning methods described to showing their practical application in the asset pricing field, we will show the disruptive potential of machine learning techniques in finance. Moreover, the discussion will also highlight the role of neural networks (NNs) in asset pricing as they have been one of the fastest-growing sub-fields of machine learning recently. NNs have been successfully applied in many fields of study and their ability to capture complicated non-linear relationships in a variable-rich environment makes them a perfect tool for designing an asset-pricing factor model.

7.2 EMPIRICAL ASSET PRICING MODELS

In this section, we will focus on examining the most popular empirical asset pricing models in financial markets. These models are the Capital Asset Pricing Model (CAPM), the Arbitrage Pricing Theory (APT) model and Fama-French 3 and 5 factor model.

7.2.1 Overview and Rationale

Traditionally, investors were referring to income statements, balance sheets and other publicly available information on a company to perform their investment choices. With the increased access to high-quality fundamental data, investors and academics have begun employing statistical, behavioural and machine learning techniques to facilitate the asset pricing methods, which gave birth to systematic value investing, first mentioned by Graham and Dodd (1951). The fundamental property of empirical asset pricing models is that not all risks should affect the performance of an asset; therefore, it is important to distinguish key factors influencing asset price (Pástor and Stambaugh, 2000). Investors all over the world continue to use such models to aid their investment decisions.

7.2.2 The CAPM

Developed independently by Treynor (1961), Sharpe (1964), Lintner (1965) and Mossin (1966), CAPM is considered the first comprehensible asset pricing model (Perold, 2004). CAPM builds directly on Markowitz's Modern Portfolio Theory (MPT) in which achieving higher yields is possible only though taking on more risky investments (Markowitz, 1952), which is addressed by including market risk premium in the model's equation. According to MPT, the risk of an asset consists of systematic (market) and unsystematic risk (company-specific). Since non-systematic risk can be fully diversified away, though reducing correlation between returns of the assets, CAPM assumes that the only relevant metric in determining the expected return on the asset is market risk, commonly referred to as beta. Therefore, the CAPM can be described as follows:

$$R_i = R_f + \beta_i * (R_m - R_f) + e_{it} \qquad (7.1)$$

where

R_i = the expected return on the investment

R_f = the risk-free rate

β_i = the market risk of the investment

R_m = the expected return on the market

e_{it} = the standard error of the linear regression.

7.2.2.1 CAPM Limitations

Although CAPM is one of the most widely taught theories on MBA (Master of Business Administration) (Womack and Zhang, 2005) and financial economics courses (Dempsey, 2013), the model has its limitations, mostly resulting from its unrealistic assumptions and difficulties in beta estimation. Roll (1977) argued that the CAPM model cannot be tested as creating a market portfolio would require collecting all of the information about the market from many different industries and sectors which in practice is impossible. Moreover, Banz (1981) found that the average yields are contingent on the size capitalization of the companies, which is especially visible among small-cap stocks with higher average returns than large-cap ones, further highlighting the ineffectiveness of CAPM. However, surveys such as that conducted by Partington et al. (2013) have shown that empirical test performed on CAPM has not so much proved its validity but rather highlighted the important correlations among variables with respect to the cross-section of realized returns.

7.2.3 Multifactor Models

7.2.3.1 APT

Developed by Ross (1977), APT was created as an alternative to CAPM. It is a multifactor model that builds on the existence of a linear relationship between an asset's expected return and multiple possible factors influencing systematic risk. In APT, the return of an asset is influenced by a range of macroeconomic factors such as unemployment, GDP growth, inflation or interest rates. If the APT holds, there would be no arbitrage opportunities (i.e., creation of riskless profits by taking positions that are based on security "mispricing"). The more efficient market is, the quicker the arbitrage opportunities will disappear. The model, due to its simplicity and flexibility, is commonly used in asset management, cost of capital estimation, portfolio diversification as well as evaluation of collective investment schemes (e.g., ETFs, mutual funds, hedge funds) performance (Huberman, 2005). The mathematical representation of the model is

$$r_i = \alpha_j + b_{i1}F_1 + b_{i2}F_2 + \ldots + b_{in}F_n + e_{it} \qquad (7.2)$$

where

r_i = the total return of individual asset i

F_s = the factors affecting the asset's return

b_{ik} = the sensitivity of the ith asset to the factor k

e_{it} = the standard error of the linear regression.

7.2.3.1.1 The Limitations of APT The main weakness with this theory is the fact that it does not specify what factors should be chosen. However, the analyst can decide on what factors to choose by regressing historical portfolio returns against the chosen range of macroeconomic factors. By doing so, they can identify the statistical significance of any of these factors, thus tailor the model to the specific asset or group of assets. Nevertheless, Dhrymes, Friend and Gultekin (1984) found that with the increasing number of securities, the number of determining factors increases making it gruelling to distinguish between "priced" and "non-priced" risk factors.

7.2.3.2 Fama-French 3 and 5 Factor Models

Following Roll's and Banz's critique of CAPM, Eugene and French (1992) developed a new asset pricing model, which introduced two new variables in explaining the expected asset returns. The *size factor* adapted from Banz and *book equity/market equity* (*BE/ME*) ratio building on Chan, Hamao and Laonishok (1991) who found that book-to-market (BE/ME) plays a huge role in explaining the cross-section of average returns. The formula for Fama-French 3 factor model can be described as follows:

$$R_{it} - R_{Ft} = \alpha_i + \beta_i(R_{Mt} - R_{Ft}) + \beta_s SMB_t + \beta_h HML_t + e_{it} \qquad (7.3)$$

where

R_{it} = the total return of individual asset i

R_{Ft} = the risk-free rate

R_{Mt} = the total market portfolio return

$R_{it} - R_{Ft}$ = the expected excess return

$R_{it} - R_{Ft}$ = the excess return on a market portfolio index

SMB_t = the difference between the return of a diversified portfolio of small and big stocks (size premium)

HML_t = the difference between the returns on a diversified portfolios of high and low BE/ME stocks (value premium)

$\beta_{i,s,h}$ = factors' coefficients

α_i = Fama-French three-factor alpha

e_{it} = the standard error of the linear regression.

To evaluate the effectiveness of their model, Fama and French used a sample of monthly stock returns from July 1963 until December 1991. Using the data from the Center for Research in Security Prices (CRSP), they have created 25 separate equity portfolios based on the size (i.e., Small, 2, 3, 4 and BIG) and BE/ME (i.e., Low, 2, 3, 4 and High) factors with Treasury Bill rate as the risk-free rate. The results have shown the negative correlation between size factor and average yields as well as a positive relationship between BE/ME indicator and average returns, with the latter being persistent in all 25 portfolios. Their research showed that this three-factor model was capable of explaining a significant portion of stock return variation, eventually becoming a basis for evaluation of other asset classes and different markets.

In 2015, having investigated the profitability and investments of the companies, Fama and French developed their model by adding two more factors:

$$R_{it} - R_{Ft} = \alpha_i + b_i(R_{Mt} - R_{Ft}) + \beta_s SMB_t + \beta_h HML_t + \beta_r RMW_t + \beta_c CMA_t + e_{it} \ (7.4)$$

where

R_{it} = the total return of individual asset i

R_{Ft} = the risk-free rate

R_{Mt} = the total market portfolio return

$R_{it} - R_{Ft}$ = the expected excess return

$R_{Mt} - R_{Ft}$ = the excess return on a market portfolio index

SMB_t = the difference between the returns on a diversified portfolio of small and big stocks (size premium)

HML_t = the difference between the returns on a diversified portfolio of high and low BE/ME stocks (value premium)

RMW_t = the difference in returns between the most and least profitable companies (profitability risk factor)

CMA_t = the difference in returns between conservatively and aggressively investing firms (investment factor)

$\beta_{i,s,h,r,c}$ = factors' coefficients

α_i = Fama-French five-factor alpha

e_{it} = the standard error of the linear regression

Similar tests were performed to evaluate the effectiveness of the model, with additional 22 years of return data from the same source. Although the five-factor model was superior to the three-factor model when it comes to forecasting asset prices, the researchers have highlighted the redundancy of *value premium* factor as it was largely explained by *profitability risk* and *investment* factors (Fama and French, 2015). Additionally, their study showed that, within the sample used, small-cap stocks showed performance similar to low profitable but highly investing firms.

7.2.3.3 Fama-French 3 and 5 Models Limitations

Despite satisfactory results of Fama and French models in their research and the wide adaptation of them among both academics and investment professionals, according to Blitz et al. (2016), the models fail to account for low-volatility and momentum premiums and do not attempt to address robustness issues. Even though Fama and French claim that in long run, the low beta anomaly is addressed by their five-factor model (Fama and French, 2016), there is a lack of significant evidence confirming that higher market beta exposure is rewarded with increased returns. Moreover, later studies by Dichev (1998) and Campbell, Hilscher and Szilagyi (2008) have demonstrated the negative relationship between distress risk and return, confirming the existence of low-risk premium. Fama-French models do not attempt to account for the momentum premium and with momentum profits becoming increasingly more important in asset pricing, many researchers began adding momentum factors resulting in four- (Carhart, 1997) and six-factor variants (Roy and Shijin, 2018). In addition to the lack of robustness of two newly added factors, the economic rationale for their addition to the updated model is also unclear. While size and value factors in the three-factor model were justified from the risk-based perspective (Fama and French, 2021), in the five-factor model it is unclear whether the observed return premiums are associated with systematic risk or behavioural anomalies.

7.2.4 Discussion

Although multifactor models are commonly used by investment managers, there is a discussion regarding their performance with respect to machine learning methods. Despite multifactor models being able to explain the historical correlation matrix relatively well (Chan, Karceski and Lakonishok, 1999), they deliver poor predictions (Simin, 2008). Understanding the behaviour of risk premium is crucial in asset pricing. Traditionally, differences in expected returns were estimated using cross-sectional regressions, which in addition to the Ordinary Least Squares (OLS) method involved sorting assets into individual portfolios based on their underlying characteristics (Lewellen, 2014). However, time-series forecasts of returns were obtained using time-series regressions of entire portfolio returns, with few macroeconomic predictors tested (Rapach and Zhou, 2013). While such methods are relatively simple and easy to implement, they pose substantial limitations in contrast to modern machine learning solutions. Evidence suggests that the main weakness of such methods is their inability to handle a large number of predictors (Gu, Kelly and Xiu, 2018), which considering the large body of currently documented possible predictor variables is not desirable.

7.3 MACHINE LEARNING IN ASSET PRICING

In this section, we will explore the potential use of machine learning techniques in asset price forecasting. We will show the rationale behind the application of machine learning techniques in asset price forecasting. By synthesizing the machine learning methods with modern empirical asset pricing research, we will show why this particular financial field has the potential for a successful machine learning application.

7.3.1 Machine Learning: Overview

Although the definition of machine learning can vary from one scientific field to another, according to Dey (2016), machine learning is generally used to train machines to perform a specific task while handling the data in the most efficient way. Regardless of the definition used, the fundamental property of machine learning is its high-dimensional nature, which is the main reason why its suitable for asset pricing. Machine learning techniques provide more flexibility compared to traditional econometric methods, thus allowing to better capture the complexity of the asset pricing problem. However, the increased flexibility offered by machine learning comes at the cost of a higher probability of overfitting (Mullainathan and Spiess, 2017). Therefore, it is important to perform adequate refinements while applying machine learning that would reduce the chance of overfitting (Cawley and Talbot, 2010).

The machine learning algorithms work by extracting the patterns from historical data, in the process known as "training" and therefore applying these findings to accurately predict new data. After the process is completed, the created predictions need to be tested, allowing for their performance evaluation.

7.3.2 The Case for Machine Learning in Asset Pricing

As shown in the first chapter, the prevailing question in forecasting a future price of an asset was to predict the risk premium. The tests performed by Fama-French on their 5 factor model showed the R^2 ranging from 0.91 to 0.93 (Fama and French, 2015). However, even when the model can almost perfectly observe the expected results, the remaining issue is how well it explains its behaviour, which requires additional testing. Additionally, with market efficiency making the risk premium estimation limited to news headlines response, there is a need to update traditional asset pricing methods by exploring new predictor variables. Nevertheless, calculating the risk premium remains the conditional function of future expected excess return. Therefore, thanks to its predictive capabilities resulting from combining forces of statistics and computer science (Das and Behera, 2017), machine learning makes a perfect tool for this task. If applied correctly, it has the chance to revolutionize the asset pricing (Arnott, Harvey and Markowitz, 2019).

Another issue with traditional approaches to factor models, as highlighted by Harvey, Liu and Zhu (2016), is the way the explanatory power of the factors is evaluated. Typically, the statistical significance of the factor explanatory power is reported as the t-statistics, with factors scoring t-statistics of at least 2.0 considered significant. Although when testing a single factor it is unlikely for the t-statistics of 2.0 or greater to occur by chance, with the number of factors and therefore the number of tests increasing, the probability of t-statistics achieving such levels by chance is significantly higher. The issue has been also investigated by Harvey and Liu (2014) and Bailey et al. (2015), both raising concerns regarding the use of traditional significance criteria for newly discovered factors. Harvey and Liu (2021) argue that given the test statistic multiplicity in a numerous factors environment, some of the factors found to be significant have only be deemed so because of luck rather than their actual predictive power (i.e., "Lucky Factors"). The authors of the paper suggest that to evaluate the significance of the factor it is important to perform the out-of-sample testing procedure which will prove whether the examined factor or group of factors are explaining the risk premium well enough to be included in the asset pricing model. Moreover, they propose a new method for evaluating the significance of tested factors based on the number of the variables that have been tested.

Moreover, since the creation of CAPM, researchers and academics alike were testing various financial and economic predictors that show forecasting capabilities, with more than 300 stock level factors used to describe return on the asset (Green, Hand and Zhang, 2013; Harvey, Liu and Zhu, 2016). Although identifying the whole array of factors with high predictive power is relatively simple, traditional methods break down when the number of predictors is close to or higher, compared to the number of observations. Additionally, such models are also subject to failure resulting from high multicollinearity, which considering the similar nature of many possible predictors is inevitable. Thanks to the broad availability of dimension reduction tools (i.e., Principle Component Analysis, Random Forest, Factor Analysis), machine learning offers degrees of freedom optimization and condenses the variance among predictors (Fodor, 2002).

As mentioned before, in traditional asset pricing models the interactions among the predictors were linear, more precisely modelled using the OLS method, possibly due to its simplicity of application. However, the relationship among the independent variables can be also non-linear. The lack of documented guidance regarding the functional form of the predictors poses a huge problem when designing an asset pricing model. Luckily, machine learning offers a broad range of unique techniques from generalized linear methods, through regression trees to NNs, offering high diversity in creating the model (i.e., high number of functional forms). Together with highly controllable parameter penalization and strict criteria for model selection, the created models are less likely to overfit or be subject to false discovery. Moreover, some of the machine learning algorithms can help to eliminate unnecessary factors from the model and extracting the underlying relationships that are likely to be true in the future, thus reducing the estimation error.

To summarize, there are four main challenges when it comes to designing a factor model:

- Predicting the Risk Premium

- Determining the Functional Form

- Variable Selection

- Managing the Estimation Error.

7.3.2.1 Machine Learning and MPT

According to MPT, it is possible to construct an "efficient frontier" that would consist of optimal portfolios, offering the maximum possible expected return for a given level of risk. To determine optimal weights for the portfolio, MPT suggests using mean-variance analysis. However, the main issue with using this approach is the large numbers of estimates required even for a smaller portfolio (Hirschberger, Qi and Steuer, 2010). The high number of estimates leads to high estimation error, effectively making it impossible to compute 100% accurate efficient frontier. While multi-factor models such as these described in section 2 address some of the MPT issues by including multiple sources of risk, thus in theory reducing the estimation error and improving the quality of the estimates. Nevertheless, as mentioned in the previous section, traditional approaches to factor models pose some limitations as well. We believe that by applying machine learning techniques, it is possible to design an effective factor model that, by solving the issues highlighted in section 3.2, would more accurately estimate the risk premium. With the quality of the estimates improved, investors could make better investment decisions (i.e., superior portfolio allocation, better stocks picks etc.), hence moving the efficient frontier above the optimal level (figure 7.1). The final result would be the portfolio with a higher Sharpe ratio (3.1) (i.e., figure 7.1):

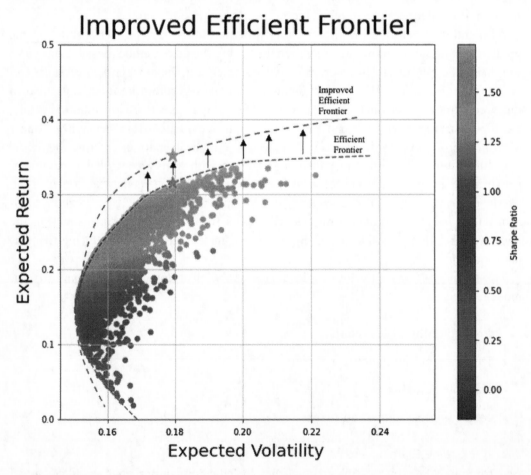

FIGURE 7.1 The improved efficient frontier. We believe that incorporating machine learning techniques into the portfolio creation process would shift the efficient frontier up and improve the Sharpe ratio.

$$SharpeRatio = \frac{E[Ri - Rf]}{\sigma_a} \tag{7.5}$$

where

R_i = the expected return on the asset i

R_f = the risk-free return

σ_i = standard deviation of an asset i

$R_i - R_f$ = the risk premium.

7.4 MACHINE LEARNING METHODS IN ASSET PRICING

There is a growing body of literature that recognizes the importance of machine learning in asset pricing (Ayodele, 2010). This results in a wide assortment of machine learning algorithms that can be applied to the asset pricing problem, which we will further explore in this section. Due to the nature of an asset pricing problem, most academics classify it as a supervised learning problem (Henrique, Sobreiro and Kimura, 2019; Krollner, Vanstone and Finnie, 2010). In supervised learning, parameters used for prediction need to be user-defined (i.e., labelled data), with both input and output data provided for training, whereas unsupervised learning requires only input data with the purpose of finding the unknown patterns.

This chapter will describe the possible machine learning methods that are best suited to address issues from section 3.2 in two fundamental areas. From providing a statistical background for each of the machine learning methods that can be used in risk premium estimation to discussing its possible application in the financial field through real-world applications.

7.4.1 Penalized Linear Regression

7.4.1.1 Statistical Overview

Although a simple linear model becomes inefficient when the number of predictors is close to or larger than the number of observations, by using penalization techniques the number of parameters can be limited. Considering that a large percentage of stock data consist of noise, an unmodified linear model with a large number of parameters will often overfit such noise rather than extracting valuable information. To avoid such a situation, machine learning proposes the introduction of a regularization parameter that will adequately penalize each factor by reducing the variance of the estimated regression parameters (Bruce, Bruce and Gedeck, 2020). However, while this solution minimizes the error term, it also reduces the complexity of the model eventually adding the bias to the final estimation. The OLS regression finds the optimal value of the coefficients by minimizing the residual sum of squares (RSS) through finding the adequate coefficients:

$$RSS(\beta) = \sum_{i=1}^{N} (Y_i - \beta_0 - \beta_1 X_{i1} - \cdots - \beta_p X_{ip})^2 \tag{7.6}$$

where

$RSS(\beta)$ = residual sum of squares for coeffcient β

Y_i = the response variable

X_{is} = the predictor variables

β_s = coefficients.

To prevent less contributive variables from impacting the forecast, penalizing methods reduce the coefficients' values towards zero, hence excluding such variables from the final model. There are several regularization methods that can be applied to the linear models. The general form of the penalization methods for linear models can be described as

$$\bar{\beta} = arg\ min_\beta \left(\sum_{i=1}^{N} (y_i - (X\beta)_i)^2 + \lambda P(\beta) \right) \tag{7.7}$$

The solution for the vector of the regression coefficient, $\bar{\beta}$, is calculated through minimizing the RSS function based on the established penalty on the regression coefficients ($\lambda P(\beta)$). The parameter λ, known as the shrinkage parameter, sets the shrinkage on the regression coefficients. It is a non-negative number and the bigger it gets the more penalty is applied to the regression coefficients. However, current academic research proposes a wealth of penalization methods; the most popular ones are LASSO (Tibshirani, 1996), Elastic net (Zou and Hastie, 2005) and Adaptive LASSO (Zou, 2006). The main difference between these methods lies in the form that penalty takes (table 7.1).

7.4.1.2 Application in Asset Pricing

In their paper, Kelly and Pruitt (2015) propose a method called three-pass regression filter (3PRF) in asset price forecasting using many predictors. By applying regularization techniques to OLS regression, 3PRF separates the factors that highly influence the target variable, while discarding irrelevant ones. While high percentage of methods dealing with problems involving many predictors relied on Principal Component Regression (PCR) (Stock and Watson, 2012; Bai and Ng, 2006; Boivin and Ng, 2006), Kelly and Pruitt (2015) argue that 3PRF method delivers better performance. The main difference between 3PRF and PCR is that the former condenses the cross-section size in accordance with covariance with the forecast target, while the latter does it using covariance within the predictors. As a result, the 3PRF process estimates only relevant factors, hence making it more efficient while dealing with a large number of predictors. The superiority of 3PRF compared to other regularization methods is especially noticeable when dealing

TABLE 7.1   Popular Regularization Methods

Regression Regularization Methods		
Method	**Penalty Equation**	**Description**
LASSO	$\Sigma_{j=1}^{p}\,|\beta_j| < \lambda$	The penalty is placed on the L1 norm of the regression coefficient, indicating it reduces overfitting by estimating the median of the data. Each factor is adequately penalized.
Elastic net	$\Sigma_{j=1}^{p}\,|\beta_j| < \lambda_1$ and $\Sigma_{j=1}^{p}\,\beta_j^2 < \lambda_2$	It combines the L1 penalty with the L2. The L2 penalty tries to estimate the mean instead of the median of the data to avoid overfitting. The method uses two shrinkage parameters (i.e., λ_1 and λ_2), which allows for more flexibility compared to the LASSO method.
Adaptive LASSO	$\Sigma_{j=1}^{p}\left(|\beta_j|/|\widehat{\beta_j}|\right) < \lambda$	Similar to the LASSO, the penalty is placed on the L1 norm of the regression coefficient; however, in the adaptive LASSO, the user can assign different penalty weights to different coefficients.

with small samples. Moreover, Kelly and Pruitt (2015) provide empirical results that prove superiority of 3PRF estimating market returns compared to PCR from Stock and Watson (2002), Lest Absolute Residuals (LAR) proposed by De Mol, Giannone and Reichlin (2008) as well as Quasi–Maximum Likelihood Approach developed by Doz, Giannone and Reichlin (2012). It is important to mention that all of the tests, evaluating the effectiveness of their method, were performed out of sample, demonstrating the competitive forecasting performance compared to other method tested.

Regarding the issues stated in section 3.2, the 3PRF method effectively addresses four issues with the designing factor model listed in section 3.2. Apart from being an effective tool for risk premium estimation, it allows to improve models of a linear functional form, helps to isolate the most influential variables which translate to fewer estimations required, thus decreases the estimation error. Furthermore, as the model is evaluated using out-of-sample forecasting, the probability of tested factors being "lucky" is relatively small. However, Kelly and Pruitt (2015) have applied 3PRF only to linear models; therefore, its performance when dealing with non-linear models is yet to be tested.

7.4.2 Regression Trees

7.4.2.1 Statistical Overview

Although we previously showed how regularization techniques can improve the linear forecasting models, parameters penalization fails to deliver desirable results when the number of estimators is larger than the sample size. Considering a large number of documented possible predictors as highlighted in section 3.2, the issue lies not only in choosing the most appropriate factors but also to account for interactions among them. In statistics, the interaction effect refers to a situation in which the effect of the predictor on the dependent variable is subject to changes in one or more other regressands. Traditional statistics methods offer variance analysis (i.e., one-way and two-way ANOVA) to capture interaction effects among independent variables. However, creating a model using ANOVA methods, considering a large body of available factors, would be infeasible as all combinations of parameters would have to be tested. The machine learning alternative to incorporate multi-way predictor interactions are regression trees. Given their intelligibility and simplicity, they become one of the most popular machine learning techniques in data mining[1] (Wu et al., 2008). The regression tree starts by identifying the groups of observations that show some similarities to each other. Therefore, through a process of binary recursive partition, that splits the data into partitions (i.e., branches), the tree is built until the split that further reduces impurity cannot be found. In the Classification and Regression Tree (CART) algorithm, proposed by Breiman et al. (1984), when it comes to regression trees the impurity methods that can be used are:

- Mean Square Error (MSE) where the split is based on the minimized value of the RSS between the observation and the mean in each node.

- Least Absolute Deviation (LAD) in which the mean absolute deviation is minimized from the median within a node.

Figure 7.2 shows the basic regression tree example with two variables (i.e., size and investment factor) in accordance with the CART algorithm. The yellow rectangles are the factors used in the regression tree, with different rectangles representing the terminal nodes (i.e., leafs) of the tree. In this case, the sample of individual stocks is divided into three categories based on the value of only two characteristics. Each terminal node is defined as a simple average of all observations within the subset. Before each split the algorithm would minimize the impurity, using the equation that can be written as

$$minimise: J(k, t_k) = \frac{m_{left}}{m} G_{left} + \frac{m_{right}}{m} G_{right} \qquad (7.8)$$

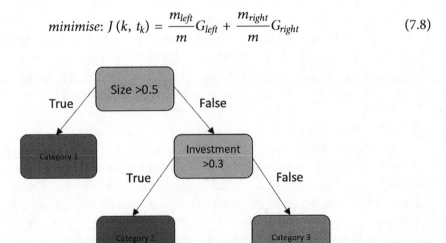

FIGURE 7.2 The diagram of the regression tree using two variables. The categories 1, 2 and 3 rectaFngles are the terminal nodes (i.e., leafs). In this case, the algorithm divided the sample of stock data into three categories based on the values of size and investment factors.

where

k = the feature in a subset

t_k = the threshold for a split

G_s = the impurity of a subset s

m_s = the number of instances in each subset.

Note that k and t_k are chosen as to produce the purest subsets.

Ideally, we would grow the tree until the best predictor variable and its value is found so that the forecast error is minimized. However, as Bramer (2007) points out, the decision trees are prone to overfitting, as excessive growing could lead to each of the leafs containing only one instance. For that reason, regression trees need to be highly regularized so that the final model will also be optimal, apart from being accurate. As Wolpert (1996) suggests without assumptions about the data, there is no reason to prefer one model from another. Instead of relying on the results of one algorithm, it is desirable to aggregate the results of multiple models in the technique known as Ensemble Learning.

7.4.2.1.1 Regression Tree Boosting   First proposed by Schapire (1990), as a way to improve the performance of weak learners for the classification problem, boosting techniques were extended to the concept of gradient boosted regression tree by Friedman (2001). The operating principle behind "boosting" is to combine forecast from multiple over-simplified trees. In theory that should lead to the creation of a "strong-learner" that would not only be superior to the single complex tree in terms of predictive power but also will be characterized by greater stability and less computational cost. The algorithm starts by fitting the shallow tree with only two branches. Therefore, the second shallow tree is used but this time to fit the residuals from the first regression tree. The procedure is repeated by adding other trees fitting the residuals from previous models, however, at each step the estimated values from the new tree are penalized by a tuning parameter to prevent overfitting the residuals. The algorithm stops when the pre-specified number of trees is reached. The final model can be described as

$$\widehat{g_B}(B, v, L, z) = \sum_{b=1}^{B} v\widehat{f_b}(\cdot) \tag{7.9}$$

where

$\widehat{g_B}$ = the final ensemble predictor

b = the step of the algorithm

z = data used for the regression

B = the total number of trees in a ensemble

L = the depth of each tree

v = the tuning parameter

$\widehat{f_b}$ = the single over-simplified regression tree function.

7.4.2.1.2 Random Forest Regression   Similar to regression tree boosting, random forest is an ensemble method used to improve the accuracy of the model by aggregating the forecasts from many different trees. However, unlike the boosting, the random forest method builds on bootstrap aggregating, commonly known as bagging. In bagging, the regression tree is trained on various subsets of data, which are sampled with replacement (i.e., multiple subsets can include the same instance). Random forests build on bagging, however, instead of searching for the best feature when splitting a node it tries to find among the random subset of features (Breiman, 2001). By doing so, it addresses the limitations of simple bagging by producing more diverse trees with weaker correlation among bootstrap samples. Moreover, the method trades higher bias for a lower variance (figure 7.3), which addresses the biggest drawback of regression trees which is overfitting. Bias refers to errors resulting from simplifying assumptions made by the model to make the target function easier to approximate (i.e., underfitting). Variance error comes from too much sensitivity to the fluctuations in data (i.e., overfitting). The bias-variance trade-off refers to the inability to reduce both variance and bias at the same time, hence the most optimal solution is to minimize the total error, which is roughly at the intersection of bias and variance (Von Luxburg and Schölkopf, 2011).

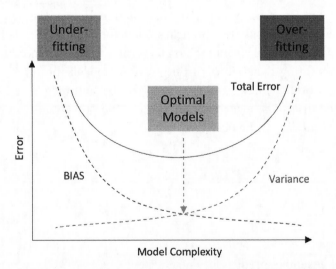

FIGURE 7.3   This figure is the graphical representation of the bias-variance trade-off. The optimal model will be the one that minimizes the bias error (i.e., underfitting) and at the same time minimizes the variance error (i.e., overfitting). At that point, further minimization of either bias or variance errors will cause one of them to increase significantly as they are negatively correlated.

The final output of random forest is the average output of all trees used for the ensemble, which can be described as

$$\widehat{g_B} (L, B, z) = \frac{1}{B} \sum_{b=1}^{B} \widehat{f_b} (\cdot) \tag{7.10}$$

where

g_B = the final ensemble predictor

b = the current number of bootstrap sample

B = the total number of trees in a ensemble

z = the data for the regression

L = the depth of each tree

$\widehat{f_b}$ = the single regression tree.

7.4.2.2 Application in Asset Pricing

Fama and MacBeth (1973) introduced the multivariate regressions to address the issue of cross-predictor interactions. Their model allows exploring the marginal effect on each predictor by controlling other variables. However, the issue arises when variables are considered jointly (i.e., multi-way interactions). For example, even in a 50-variable model, accounting for only two-way interactions would result in 1275 regression coefficients, which is significantly larger than sample sizes splits proposed by Fama and French (2008). Moreover, the results from their model can be extremely vulnerable to outliers (i.e., extreme returns) in the data. To address these issues, Moritz and Zimmermann (2016) proposed the random forest regression approach to establish portfolio sorts and therefore combined all estimates from each tree into final prediction. As shown in section 4.2.1, random forests allow producing de-correlated trees, which in that respect allow spotting many different, yet related predictors. Additionally, the problem of overfitting is addressed as each tree is trained only on the subset of data. Apart from classic accounting variables (i.e., book-to-market ratio), they also test their framework using return-based variables, arguing for the importance of momentum factors. By testing 126 return-based factors from many different time horizons on various company sizes (i.e., large, small and micro firms according to Fama and French, 2008), they conclude that more recent past returns are more relevant than intermediate past returns in return forecasting. Therefore, they combine the most influential return-based indicators into the one model using random forest method with a total of 200 independent trees (i.e., 200 different portfolio sorts) each using 8 out of 25 possible regressors (roughly 30%) as suggested by Breiman (2001). To test their method, they employ a simple strategy of going long on the stocks with the highest decile of predicted returns and shorting the lowest decile of predicted returns, using the CRSP data from 1963 to

2012. To test the out-of-sample performance of their model they employ a pseudo-out-of-sample procedure, which works by training the model using the data only available at a given time t and then computing all of the forecasts outside of the training set (i.e., $t + 1$, $t + 2, \cdots, t + n$). Additionally to confirm the importance of momentum factors they supplement their model with 86 different accounting factors such as book-to-market, leverage, gross profitability, etc. with the momentum factors continuing to be the most influential. Their result shows that, when applied to the tested data, their strategy would deliver a positive annual return for the past 45 years from 1967 to 2012 (figure 7.4). Moreover, despite most of the momentum strategies delivering negative returns during the Global Financial Crisis (GFC), their strategy would not lose money in that period either. Their algorithm was able to detect the reversal in momentum factors soon enough, thus avoid the drawdown in 2009. Overall their strategy delivered a superior information ratio[2] compared to the standard Fama-Macbeth framework (2.9 vs 1.3 per month). However, its performance begins to deteriorate from early 2000, suggesting that the algorithm was not able to capture momentum movements soon enough to match its previous performance.

With respect to the issues highlighted in section 3.2, Moritz and Zimmermann (2016) model does generally a good job at predicting the risk premium and managing the estimation error. Furthermore, the effectiveness of their method is supported by the out-of-sample testing, limiting the probability of "lucky factors". However, as regression trees are non-linear models, the issue of functional form remains as the model cannot be simply summarized in a linear equation, thus complicating the interpretation of the results. Additionally considering the decrease in performance of the model from the early

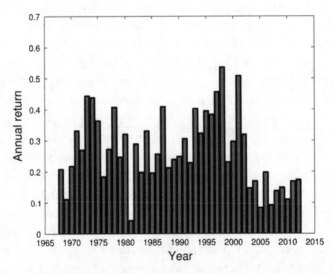

FIGURE 7.4   The annual percentage return of researchers strategy. The algorithm used to create an investing strategy was random forests based on momentum factors. It delivered positive returns, even during the 1980s crisis. However, its performance deteriorated noticeably from the beginning of the 21st century and failed to match the previous performance in a given time period.

Source: Moritz and Zimmermann (2016).

2000s onward, the question remains whether the momentum factors proposed by them will continue to have high predictive power in the future. Nevertheless, with the framework constructed around tree-based conditional portfolio sorts, they hope for an increased level of scientific discovery regarding asset pricing in the years to come.

7.4.3 Support Vector Regression

7.4.3.1 Statistical Overview

According to Efficient Market Hypothesis (EMH), it is impossible to consistently achieve above-market returns. However, the theory has been questioned since its introduction (Malkiel, 2003). Moreover, considering the computational advancements over the past decade, the use of machine learning techniques in asset pricing is constantly growing (Gerlein et al., 2016). Studies by Ballings et al. (2015) or Nayak, Mishra and Rath (2015) show the successful application of support vector machines (SVMs) in asset pricing. However, as SVM are primarily used for classification problems, the methods above were focusing on determining only the direction of asset prices, rather than estimating their exact value. The goal of support vector regression (SVR) algorithm is to find function $f(x)$, with at most ϵ-*deviation* from the target y. The problem can be written as

$$min \ \frac{1}{2}\|w\|^2$$
$$s.t. : y_i - w_1 * x_i - b \leq \epsilon;$$
$$w_1 * x_i + b - y_i \leq \epsilon$$

(7.11)

where

y_i = the target variable

w_s = the weighted coefficients

b = the intercept

x_i = the factor used for the regression

ϵ = the precision (tolerance) level.

The graphical representation of linear SVR in a two-variable environment can be seen in figure 7.5. The SVR tries to fit as many instances within the decision boundaries, as possible, while limiting the number of margin violations. The middle line is the final equation used to predict continuous output (i.e., hyperplane). Errors are ignored as long as they are within the earlier set decision boundaries. The decision margin can be either soft or hard. While the soft decision boundaries allow for some margin violations, hard margins strictly impose that all instances have to be within decision boundaries. The hard decision boundaries are infeasible where data consist of a large number of outliers.

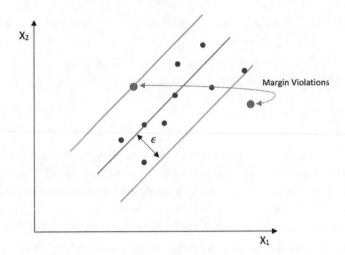

FIGURE 7.5 This figure is the graphical representation of how support vector regression works. The dots are the data points and the algorithm tries to find the optimal hyperplane that will predict the final output while keeping the number of margin violations outside of the decision boundaries to the minimum.

However, SVRs are not only limited to describe linear relationships. Using the so-called kernel trick allows for the data to be transformed into a higher dimensional space without the need for data transformations. By doing so, the explicit mapping needed for linear algorithms to capture non-linear interactions is avoided. Kernels allow finding a hyperplane in the higher dimensional space without a huge increase in computational cost. Table 7.2 shows three most commonly used kernels along with their mathematical functions and brief descriptions.

7.4.3.2 Application in Asset Pricing

According to Awad and Khanna (2015), one of the main advantages of SVR is that its computational complexity does not depend on the dimensionality of the data. Thanks to the earlier described kernel trick, SVRs can easily deal with a large number of variables, maintaining high prediction accuracy. Henrique, Sobreiro and Kimura (2018) used SVR to predict stock prices for firms of various sizes coming from different markets. Similar to the methods described in section 4.2.2, the authors focus on momentum-based factors. Using the SVR's ability to capture high-dimensional non-linear interactions among the variables, they evaluate the significance of technical analysis (TA) indicators including Simple Moving Average (SMA), Weighted Moving Average (WMA), Relative Strength Index (RSI), the Accumulation/Distribution Oscillator (ADO) and the Average True Range (ATR). They employed their model on Brazilian, American and Chinese stocks with three bluechip and three small-cap stocks for each country, resulting in 18 assets total. The model was tested in three different scenarios. The first one considered daily price changes over 15-year period (2002–2017). Second used up-to-the-minute price changes from three months (03/2017–05/2017). Lastly as three-month period is unlikely to include all possible market conditions, they evaluated their model using two-year up-

TABLE 7.2   Popular SVR Kernels

Types of Kernels for SVR		
Kernel	Mathematical Function	Description
Linear Kernel	$K(x, y) = (x^T y)$	With x and y as the vectors computed from training the model
Polynomial Kernel	$K(x, y) = (x^T y + 1)^d$	With d being the degree of the polynomials. In addition to examining the features of the given sample, the polynomial kernel allows for exploring their combinations, known as interaction features.
Radial Basis Function (RBF) Kernel	$K(x, y) = \exp(-\lambda \|x - y\|^2)$	With λ being a free parameter, that cannot be calculated precisely and must be estimated and $\|x - y\|^2$ being the squared euclidean distance between the two feature vectors. The RBF kernel works by transforming the data in accordance with the similarity between instances in the range from 0 (far away) to 1 (identical).

to-the-minute prices, this time using solely Brazilian stocks. Although the second environment might seem too short to determine the effectiveness of any asset pricing model, note that as the test considered one-minute price data, there are over 33,000 observations, making it computationally expensive even for SVR. For the up-to-the-minute data sets, the prediction model starts 10 minutes after the beginning of the trading session. First, they run multiple SVRs using normalized TA indicators to determine the optimal degree of polynomials for the polynomial kernel as well as the optimal λ parameter for the radial kernel. Therefore, by applying the optimal parameters, they run the test in each of the earlier defined environments using three different kernels (i.e., linear, polynomial and radial). To determine test and training sample they used k-fold cross-validation. This process differs from boot-strapping as resampling is done without replacement; hence, surrogate data sets are smaller than the original. One of their key findings was that the linear kernel performed the best across all three tests with the smallest Mean Absolute Percentage Error (MAPE). They compared their method with the random walk theory of Fama and Malkiel (1970). Although in a fixed training period their SVR model delivered worse predictions than random walk model, when periodically updated[3] up-to-the-minute models predictions, using the linear kernel, were more accurate than random walk model ones for the majority of the stocks. They claim that missing data were the main obstacle to their models achieving better results, especially in the one-minute data sets.

Considering the issues listed in section 3.2, the models proposed by Henrique, Sobreiro and Kimura (2018) do not address any of the four issues well enough. Although the authors showed their models have some predictive power, considering the small sample period it is impossible to validate that claim. Moreover, the variables proposed were strictly momentum-based and the fact that their model failed to deliver consistent outcomes across all of the stocks remains a huge issue especially if the model was to be used by other investors. Finally, the fact that their model uses TA indicators in estimating asset price poses the concern as TA methods lack substantial empirical evidence. Overall, while SVRs have the potential to be utilized in asset pricing, thanks to their numerous advantages; in this case, it is impossible to determine whether the models discussed are indeed good asset pricing tools.

7.4.4 Markov Switching Models

7.4.4.1 Statistical Overview

Traditional factor models assume that the comovement among the variables is constant over time. In other words, regardless of the state of the economy or business cycle, factors within these models are assumed to have the same effect on the estimated asset price. However, in reality, markets fluctuate between regimes of growth characterized by low volatility as well as periods of economic downturn often accompanied by high volatility and negative returns. Therefore, it is crucial to not only be able to identify these regime changes but also be able to adequately adjust the asset pricing models to exploit such events. Clarke and Silva (1998) showed that by adjusting the investment exposure in accordance to the present regime, investors can improve their efficient frontier. To model these state changes, the Markov model assumes that the future state depends solely on the current state (Gagniuc, 2017). Following that assumption, one can estimate the probability distributions of future shifts in non-stationary predictor variables and adequately update their coefficients with respect to the regime identified. In 1989, Hamilton introduced Markov switching model (MSM) of regime change in which he recognized the presence of periods of faster and slow economic growth in the US economy. Therefore, using autoregressive process 1 (AR1), he modelled long-term economic trends incorporating the transition between the states. The transition between the states is governed using a first-order Markov chain in which the probability of a subsequent state (S_{t+1}) is based only on the immediately preceding state (S_t) (section 4.7). Note that there are higher order Markov chains in which the probability of the transition depends on more than one preceding states.

$$P(S_{t+1}, |S_0, \ldots, S_t) = P(S_{t+1}|S_t) \tag{7.12}$$

The Markov chains own their popularity mainly thanks to their simplicity. Apart from providing a model that is easy to specify, they also allow for network extension. Each of the modelled future states can be used to perform the additional test in data considering various environments.

7.4.4.2 Application in Asset Pricing

Building on the model of Hamilton (1989), Chen and Kawaguchi (2018) applied Markov Regime Switches on multi-factor asset pricing models. The two states they recognized were bull and bear market and they used Hamilton's framework to model the transition between these states. The rationale for their model was the fact that as size factor (SMB) and value factor (HML) originate for the stocks in the market and return series come from the market itself, it is sensible that these factors may vary over time. Therefore, they extend the Fama-French three-factor model shown in section 2.3.2 with Markov Switching, creating the MR-FF3 Model. They assume that the betas for the three factors in the model are regime-dependent and adequately estimate them for bull and bear markets using Markov chains. To test their model, they use Chinese stock market data from 1995 to 2015. One of their key findings was that in the bear market the risk premiums of SMB and HML factors are higher than in the bull market. Such phenomenon is possible since, during bear periods, investors seek a higher return on size- and value-related risks (Cochrane, 2009). Additionally, they found that in a bear market, betas for SMB and HML[4] factors increased. It not only highlights the ability of the size factor to capture the risk-return relationship but also the capacity of the value factor to explain the return dispersions between low and high BE/ME stocks in a bear market. Furthermore, their tests using time-series regression on stocks proved the presence of the regime-dependent risk exposure pattern in the data. Finally, to confirm their findings, they performed one-step-ahead out-of-sample forecasting on all of the tested portfolios. The average root means squared error (RMSE) in out-of-sample tests was 0.0188, indicating the high predictive ability of the MR-FF3 model across the Chinese stock market.

This particular model not only explains risk premiums well but also is clear on its functional form and the variables required. By building on the already existing Fama-French three-factor model, MR-FF3 creates a powerful and relatively simple to implement method for asset price forecasting. It allows capturing bull and bear cycles effects on asset price while providing the explanation between investigated relationships. Moreover, by keeping the number of factors low, the estimation error is kept at an acceptable level. However, to ultimately confirm the predictive ability of the model, further tests are required. Possibly testing it on different markets and using bootstrapping procedure would allow to test its effectiveness and also highlight other regime-dependent relationships between the variables.

7.5 ARTIFICIAL NEURAL NETWORKS IN ASSET PRICING

While NNs are an indispensable part of machine learning, their extraordinary ability to deal with a large number of variables makes NNs potentially very useful in asset pricing. There are many types of NNs; however, in this section, we will discuss what we believe are the two most prominent types when it comes to asset price forecasting.

7.5.1 ANNs: Overview

The main idea behind artificial neural networks (ANNs) is to teach computers to process data the way humans do. Traditionally, potential predictors in a factor model were tested on the basis of the hypotheses, which results determined whether to include given variables in the final model. In contrast, the ANNs' output is algorithmically engineered, meaning that thousands of different combinations of trainable parameters are tested to finally maximize the explanatory power of the network. Thanks to their ability to model non-linear processes, NNs[5] have been successfully applied in medical diagnosis (Jiang,

Trundle and Ren, 2010; Sengupta, Sahidullah and Saha, 2016), automated trading (Azzini and Tettamanzi, 2008), speech (Abdel-Hamid et al., 2014) and handwritten text (Maitra, Bhattacharya and Parui, 2015), recognition as well as finance (French, 2017), to name a few. According to Hornik, Stinchcombe and White (1989), NNs are one of the most powerful modelling techniques in machine learning.

There are four main components of every ANN:

- **Neurons** – The main component of all NNs. Neurons are divided into input and output neurons. The former consists of either feature from the training set or outputs from the previous layer of neurons, while the latter is simply a successor of input neurons.

- **Connections and Weights** – Each NN consists of connections that connect input with output neurons. Every connection will have assigned weight based on the algorithm's learning.

- **Propagation Function** – It is used to compute the input of a neuron based on its predecessor neurons. It establishes the initial connections' weights by minimizing the observed errors considering sample observations.

- **Learning Rule** – It is used to adjust the connections' weights, by compensating for each error found during the learning process. It uses stochastic gradient descent or other optimization methods to compute gradient descent with respect to weights, thus improves the accuracy of the NN.

The ANN consists of input and output neurons, connected by weighted synapses. Figure 7.6 shows the simple ANN with only one output layer (i.e., one-layer NN). NNs

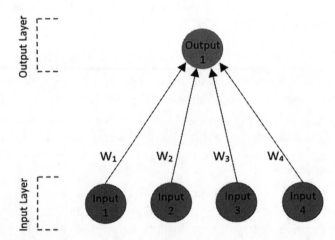

FIGURE 7.6 This figure is the graphical representation of a simple neural network in which the inputs are transformed into the outputs in accordance with weights, (W_s), associated with each neuron.

are usually divided into shallow networks with 1–3 layers and deep networks with more than three layers. The learning process involves adjusting the weights of the synapses in accordance to minimized observed errors. Usually the more data available (i.e., bigger data sets), the better NN will learn, thus more accurate predictions. The learning process starts from forward propagation in which data are transformed from the input to the output layer, with each of the neurons adequately processing the input data. The next step is backpropagation in which the weights of the connections are adjusted so that the errors will be minimized.

7.5.2 Feed-Forward Neural Networks

The feed-forward neural networks (FFNs) are considered one of the simplest type of NNs. In addition to the input layer of raw predictors, they also have one or more hidden layers that interact with each other and perform non-linear transformations of the data. The output layer in FNNs is aggregating hidden layers into the final pre-diction, hence capturing more predictive associations within the data set. Figure 7.7 shows a simple FNN with only one hidden layer between inputs and outputs. The hidden layer consists of additional neurons that take the set of weighted inputs and returns the output through the activation function. For example, the second neuron from the hidden layer in figure 7.7, (S_2), is the weighted sum of all of its input neurons:

$$X_{S2} = w_1 * x_1 + w_2 * x_2 + w_3 * x_3 + w_4 * x_4 \tag{7.13}$$

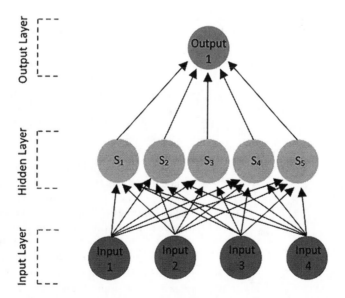

FIGURE 7.7   The neural network with a single hidden layer. Each of the hidden layer's neurons has an activation function upon which the algorithm decides whether to activate the neuron. The final output is the weighted sum of all active neurons.

where

X_{S2} = the output variable for S_2

w_{is} = the weight for each of the input neurons

x_{is} = the inputs from input neurons.

Therefore, the final output forecast consists of results from aggregated neurons, similar to formula (5.1), however, this time using all active neurons. Using the example from figure 7.7 there are a total of $31 = (4 + 1) * 5 + 6$ parameters, with five parameters to reach each neuron and six different weights used to aggregate the neurons into the single forecast.

The person responsible for structuring the FNN has to decide the number of hidden layers, the number of neurons within each layer and finally how the neurons are connected. The results from Eldan and Shamir (2016) show that deepening the FNNs (i.e., more hidden layers) is more valuable than increasing width (i.e., adding more neurons in the layer), with algorithms achieving similar accuracy using fewer parameters. It is important to mention that each of the hidden layer's neurons is subject to the activation function which determines whether it is used for the final prediction or not. If the activation function is not applied, the output would be a linear function, thus the more complex non-linear interactions would not be captured. Table 7.3 shows three main activation functions along with their mathematical functions and brief descriptions.

TABLE 7.3   Popular Activation Functions for FNNs

Penalized Regression Methods		
Activation Function	**Mathematical Function**	**Description**
Rectified Linear Activation Function (ReLU)	$max\,(0.0, x)$	If the input value x is negative the value 0.0 is returned (i.e., dead neuron) if not, the value x is returned. The main advantage of ReLU is that it does not activate all neurons at the same time being more computationally efficient. However, during the backpropagation process, the weights of such neurons will not be updated, resulting in never activated neurons.
Sigmoid Hidden Layer Activation Function	$\dfrac{1.0}{(1.0 + e^{-x})}$	The e is the mathematical constant, which is the base of the natural logarithm. The sigmoid activation function returns the output between 0 and 1; therefore, it is especially useful when predicting probability. However, for large negative or positive numbers, the function flattens, resulting in a small gradient. If the local gradient becomes too small, the backpropagation process will not work properly.
TanH Hidden Layer Activation Function (TanH)	$\dfrac{(e^x - e^{-x})}{e^x + e^{-x}}$	The function takes and real value and returns the output value between −1 and 1. The main advantages of TanH are that strongly negative inputs will be mapped strongly negative and near-zero inputs will be mapped near zero. However, similar to the sigmoid function, it is subject to the vanishing gradient problem.

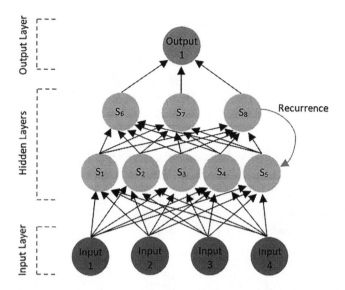

FIGURE 7.8 The recurrent neural network with two hidden layers. In RNNs, the signal can travel in both directions, therefore allows for the network to capture underlying relationships over time. This allows for the NN to build up memory which can affect the activation of other neurons, thus the final output.

The choice of activation function is data specific and will determine the learning rate of FNN. The higher the learning rate, the shorter the training time, however, at the cost of diminished accuracy (Bai, Zhang and Hao, 2009).

7.5.3 Recurrent Neural Networks

While FNNs allows for the signals to travel only one way (i.e., from input to output), recurrent neural networks (RNNs) can have signals travelling in both directions. It is possible through the introduction of loops in the network. The main assumption of forward NNs is that the input and outputs are independent of each other. By introducing self-loops, the RNNs have the capability to memorize the data. The memorized data are affecting the activation of other neurons within the hidden layer, therefore affecting the ultimate forecast. Figure 7.8 shows the simple RNN, with the recurrence process highlighted. Note that recurrence can involve all neurons from the hidden layer.

RNNs can be viewed as multiple copies of the same network, each time with the signal passed onto the successor. To define values of hidden units, RNNs often use the following equation:

$$h^t = f(h^{(t-1)}, x^t; \theta) \tag{7.14}$$

where

h^t = the state of current neuron in a hidden layer at the time step t

x^t = the variable value at time step t

θ = the weight parameter for current synapse determined by the activation function and learning process.

As explained in section 4.4, many macroeconomic variables are non-stationary. Thanks to its ability to recognize past sequences of data, RNNs can find the adequate stationary transformation of the variables so that their dynamics can explain asset prices (Chen, Pelger and Zhu, 2020). In contrast to Markov model, RNNs can learn important variable interactions across different states using information from both current and past states. Additionally, RNNs can detect changes over time, which is impossible with FNN (Gencay and Liu, 1997). Nevertheless, all that extra information used in RNNs makes them more computationally expensive and often complicates the training as such NNs are prone to problems of gradient vanishing (Li et al., 2018).

7.5.4 Ensemble Neural Networks

One of the major drawbacks of NNs, similar to other non-linear models, is that they are prone to high variance. Recall section 4.2 in which we discussed the use of ensemble methods to deal with excessive over-fitting. Such methods can also be applied to NNs. By combining the predictions from numerous NNs, the variance can be reduced, thus a smaller chance of over-fitting. Table 7.4 shows the three main ensemble types used in ANNs. However, the choice of ensemble method is problem dependent. Usually, the constants of the problem can help in determining the optimal ensemble method. For example, if we were dealing with low amounts of data, the varying models or combinations methods would be probably a better choice than varying training data.

TABLE 7.4   Popular Ensemble Methods for Neural Networks

Neural Network's Ensemble Methods		
Ensemble Type	**Popular Methods**	**Description**
Varying Training Data	Bootstrap Aggregation (bagging), K-fold Cross-Validation, Random Training Subset	Varying Training Data ensembles, as the name suggests, use different techniques to divide the data into different subsets and then use these subsets to train the model. The final output is the weighted sum of all the single networks' forecasts.
Varying Models	Multiple Training Run, Snapshot, Horizontal Epochs, Hyperparameter Tuning	This group of ensembles is used to train the same data set using different variations of the neural network. Everything from the activation function to the number of neurons in the hidden layer.
Varying Combinations	Model Averaging, Stacked Generalization (Stacking), Boosting, Weighted Average	In this family of ensemble methods, the way the forecasts from single models are combined is altered. These methods are used to update the weights from each prediction model.

7.5.5 NNs in Asset Pricing

In traditional factor models, each factor is tested in terms of its explanatory power of the target variable (i.e., expected return). When it comes to NNs, especially the ones with an extensive amount of hidden layers (i.e., deep NNs), the trainable parameters used are adjusted through the learning process to maximize the explanatory power of the network's forecast. Constructing a factor model requires testing various combinations of variables, NNs are effectively performing multiple hypotheses at the same time, thus facilitating the entire process. NNs allow the discovery of the important relationships within the data, without the need for extensive feature engineering. Moreover, recurrent NNs allow to model these relationships using the data from various points in time or even incorporate the changes in the structure of the specific variables over time. In other words, NNs are capable of finding qualities and sequences of a company's data that have the most predictive power.

The factor model can be used to construct portfolios, sort stocks and produce a cross-section of return analysis. Messmer (2017) uses a deep feed-forward neural network (DFN) to predict the US cross-section of stock returns. Using the data from the CRSP database from 1970 to 2014, he tested 68 individual firm characteristics, which are believed to possess information to explain differences in expected cross-sectional returns as suggested by Harvey, Liu and Zhu (2016) or Green, Hand and Zhang (2017). He recognizes the problem of over-fitting as the main concern when training the NN to predict excess returns. To deal with the excessive variance, he employs various regularization techniques such as bagging[6] or early stopping.[7] Additionally, he performs stochastic gradient descent on mini-batch of data which decreases computational cost and proved to have regularization benefit (Wilson and Martinez, 2003). On the other hand, to control under-fitting he evaluates the created model on independent data sets, derived using k-fold cross-validation, similar to methods shown in section 4.3.2, however, given the large time period of data, k-fold splits are more likely to bring desirable outcome. To find optimal hyper-parameters for his network, such as number of neurons per layer, number of hidden layers, activation algorithm, etc. he employs random-search in which the hyper-parameters are drawn randomly. To determine which hyper-parameters to choose, he tested them on a sub-sample of data from 1970 to 1981 and therefore combines the random set of 75 predictions (from 150 available) as well as all 150 predictions for each stock to construct value-weighted portfolios for mid- and large-cap stocks separately. The performance of the value-weighted portfolio is compared to the equally weighted one, Fama-French 5 factor model and Fama-French 5 factor model plus momentum factor, using the remaining time period (from 1981 to 2014). Finally, Messmer (2017) tests his strategy results in terms of the Sharpe ratio using a linearly computed benchmark. Overall, 16 different median, max, min, linear, value-weighted and equally weighted portfolios are compared. Figure 7.9 shows the results from his tests across large- and mid-cap stocks.

The difference between the best- and worst-performing DFN portfolio reflects the uncertainty arising from model estimation. Although the DFN used delivered a higher

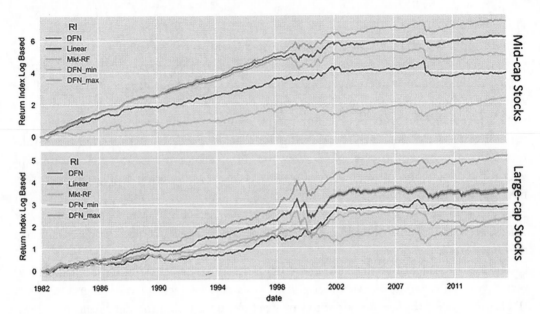

FIGURE 7.9 The return from mid- and large-cap stocks using the strategy based on a deep forward network. The results are compared with the linear benchmark and the Fama-French 5 factor model with a momentum factor. The DFNs-based strategy delivers on average superior returns compared to other methods. However, the fact that there is a significant difference between the best- and worst-performing DFN portfolios represents the uncertainty arising from the model estimation.

Source: Messmer (2017).

return than linear-based benchmark and other tested methods, the fact that there is a huge difference between worst- and best-performing DFN model's deciles highlights the uncertainty arising from model estimation. Additionally, when testing the impact of trading cost on strategies' return, he found that every month rebalancing prevents any of the DFD's strategies from achieving a positive mean return. Reducing the rebalancing frequency to every five months yields the best results when accounting for transaction costs. Nevertheless, the superior performance of DFN compared to the linear benchmark highlights the importance of non-linear relationships between firm characteristics and expected return. Furthermore, Messmer (2017) identifies the short-term reversal and the twelve-month momentum factors as the main drivers of expected return.

The model created by Messmer (2017) performs well, considering the issues stated in section 3.2. It is not only in line with finance theory but also showed high explanatory capability in estimating excess returns of the stocks. It clearly specifies what factors, along with their predictive power, are to be implemented to the model and employ modern regularization techniques to ensure the most optimal structure of his network. As the model is still being improved, we expect that in the near future it could become a useful tool that will aid investment professionals in portfolio creation.

7.6 LIMITATIONS

7.6.1 Limitations of Machine Learning

In this chapter, we showed multiple applications of machine learning in asset price forecasting. Although some of the methods discussed showed promising results in practical application, designing an asset pricing model requires more than accurate predictions. The machine learning algorithms are designed to improve the way the model can fit the data; however, they do not disclose underlying economic mechanisms or equilibria. In addition to the data scientist responsible for designing and adjusting the model, there is a need for economists who can provide an underlying structure for the estimation problem. Only that way the created models can be implemented into the finance theory and further contribute to the asset pricing field.

7.6.1.1 Machine Learning and Regulatory Environment

Apart from concerns regarding the model's predictive power and constraints coming from traditional econometric and financial theory, investors have to also consider the legal implications while using machine learning in asset pricing. Although algorithmic forecasts are on average 10% more accurate than human forecasters, across numerous domains, people continue to have a very low tolerance to machine learning's errors (i.e., algorithm aversion) (Dietvorst, Simmons and Massey, 2014). Since the 2008-GFC, regulators undertook a more proactive approach when designing a financial regulation. For example, 2018s E.U. General Data Protection Regulation (GDPR) grants investors the right to ask companies about their machine learning practices. Such a decision prompted private institutions to make their machine learning algorithms more transparent as well as ensure they are in line with finance theory (Kou et al., 2019). Furthermore, the Markets in Financial Instruments Directive (MiFID) II, also introduced in 2018, allows regularity authorities to have detailed information about the machine learning algorithm company uses, including the details of trading strategies or limits of the systems employed (Sheridan, 2017).

7.6.2 Limitations of This Study

The main purpose of this chapter was to explain the potential use of machine learning techniques in asset pricing. Although the results from individual studies were discussed, it is impossible to determine the effectiveness of any of the models presented in sections 4 and 5, without performing additional tests. Possibly all of the discussed methods would have to be evaluated over the same time period using the same data set. Only such test would allow evaluating the predictive power of each model in comparison to the other methods including traditional factor models discussed in section 2.

Moreover, some of the investigated models such as these described in section 4.2.2 or 4.3.2 diverge from traditional finance theory by leaving the estimation of the stock prices only to the momentum-based factors. However, more recently, finance practitioners and academics have focused on making the loss functions of machine learning algorithms more in line with the finance theory. For example, modern machine learning techniques are being used to reduce the number of features in the model (Feng, Giglio and Xiu, 2020; Kelly and Pruitt, 2015). Additionally, the implementation techniques used for model explainability, such as LIME (Ribeiro, Singh and Guestrin, 2016) or SHAP (Lundberg and Lee, 2017) into the programming languages, allow researchers to explain their algorithms better.

7.7 CONCLUSIONS

In conclusion, this chapter first provided the theoretical framework for traditional asset pricing methods and highlighted their limitations, which we believe can be addressed by machine learning techniques. The current machine learning techniques show promising results in dealing with high dimensional data of large volumes, such as today's financial data. Although in this chapter we have not performed any tests that would allow for evaluation of machine learning models described, identifying main obstacles in designing a factor model served as the main discussion point in the assessment of the models. From showing the statistical overview of each examined methods, to discussing their current application in asset pricing, we were able to show the disruptive power of machine learning in the financial field. Machine learning methods such as penalized linear models, regression trees, SVR or MSM can be used to model expected return with respect to finance theory but also aid its development thanks to innovative solutions they provide. Traditionally, the modelling process involved testing numerous predictor variables in terms of their t-statistics and therefore combine findings into the linear regression model. Machine learning techniques can handle large amounts of data relatively easily, thus allowing for more possible factors to be tested. Moreover, they also introduce more appropriate evaluation methods such as bootstrapping or cross-validation, which let researchers assess their models more deeply without the significant increase in computational cost. Additionally, some of the methods that are able to capture non-linear interactions among variables are yet to be fully documented when it comes to financial data. Furthermore, we believe that as one of the most rapidly developing subsets of machine learning, NNs are especially fit for the asset pricing problem. Thanks to their ability to deal with a massive amount of variables and highly adjustable properties, NNs make a great tool for estimating excess returns of stocks. NNs can learn from data and use the knowledge to adjust their structure. In that respect, the output from the ANNs can be viewed as a factor itself, mainly because of the fact that it can be used to construct portfolios, sort the stocks or perform a cross-section of return analysis. The issue remains with carefully constructing a network itself, deciding on its width and depth as well as other hyperparameters. It is crucial for the network effectiveness to structure it the best way possible. However, the task is highly problem dependent, thus calls for experts from the desired field to contribute. Luckily, the recent developments in the open-source software community open doors for many researchers outside of the data science field to exploit the use of NNs in other disciplines. The finance theory has not yet confirmed whether the NNs are indeed a good tool in estimating asset price. Nevertheless, increasing availability of NN frameworks will help to address this question.

NOTES

1 Data mining – the process of finding anomalies, patterns and correlations within large data sets to predict outcomes.
2 Information ratio is the metric used to compare excess active return (i.e., above the benchmark) of the investment, considering the overall volatility of those returns in a given time period.
3 Each of the tested models was updated in accordance to the periodicity of its data, e.g., for up-to-the-minute observations the model was updated every minute, every time with next minute's closing price serving as a test observation.
4 Only for the high BE/ME firms.
5 For the purpose of this chapter, the terms neural networks (NNs) and artificial neural networks (ANNs) will be used interchangeably.
6 Bagging is the ensemble method that aggregates the multiple predictions from various models to provide a final weighted forecast.
7 Early stopping is another regularization strategy that stops the training process after the validation error is not improved for a certain amount of iterations.

BIBLIOGRAPHY

Abdel-Hamid, Ossama et al. (2014). "Convolutional neural networks for speech recognition". In: *IEEE/ACM Transactions on Audio, Speech, and Language Processing* 22.10, pp. 1533–1545.
Arnott, Rob, Campbell R Harvey, and Harry Markowitz (2019). "A backtesting protocol in the era of machine learning". In: *The Journal of Financial Data Science* 1.1, pp. 64–74.
Awad, Mariette and Rahul Khanna (2015). "Support vector regression". In: *Efficient Learning Machines*. Springer, pp. 67–80.
Ayodele, Taiwo Oladipupo (2010). "Types of machine learning algorithms". In: *New Advances in Machine Learning* 3, pp. 19–48.
Azzini, Antonia and Andrea GB Tettamanzi (2008). "Evolving neural networks for static single-position automated trading". *Journal of Artificial Evolution and Applications*, vol. 2008, pp. 1–17.
Bai, Jushan and Serena Ng (2006). "Confidence intervals for diffusion index forecasts and inference for factor-augmented regressions". In: *Econometrica* 74.4, pp. 1133–1150.
Bai, Yanping, Haixia Zhang, and Yilong Hao (2009). "The performance of the backpropagation algorithm with varying slope of the activation function". In: *Chaos, Solitons & Fractals* 40.1, pp. 69–77.
Bailey, David H. et al. (2015). "Mathematical appendices to: 'The probability of backtest overfitting'". In: *Journal of Computational Finance (Risk Journals)*.
Ballings, Michel et al. (2015). "Evaluating multiple classifiers for stock price direction prediction". In: *Expert Systems with Applications* 42.20, pp. 7046–7056.
Banz, Rolf W (1981). "The relationship between return and market value of common stocks". In: *Journal of Financial Economics* 9.1, pp. 3–18.
Blitz, David et al. (2016). "Five concerns with the five-factor model". Available at SSRN 2862317.
Boivin, Jean and Serena Ng (2006). "Are more data always better for factor analysis?" In: *Journal of Econometrics* 132.1, pp. 169–194.
Bramer, Max (2007). "Avoiding overfitting of decision trees". In: *Principles of Data Mining*, Springer, pp. 119–134.
Breiman, Leo (2001). "Random forests". In: *Machine Learning* 45.1, pp. 5–32.
Breiman, Leo et al. (1984). *Classification and Regression Trees*. CRC Press.
Bruce, Peter, Andrew Bruce, and Peter Gedeck (2020). *Practical Statistics for Data Scientists: 50+ Essential Concepts Using R and Python*. O'Reilly Media.

Campbell, John Y, Jens Hilscher, and Jan Szilagyi (2008). "In search of distress risk". In: *The Journal of Finance* 63.6, pp. 2899–2939.

Carhart, Mark M (1997). "On persistence in mutual fund performance". In: *The Journal of Finance* 52.1, pp. 57–82.

Cawley, Gavin C and Nicola LC Talbot (2010). "On over-fitting in model selection and subsequent selection bias in performance evaluation". In: *The Journal of Machine Learning Research* 11, pp. 2079–2107.

Chan, Louis KC, Yasushi Hamao, and Josef Lakonishok (1991). "Fundamentals and stock returns in Japan". In: *The Journal of Finance* 46.5, pp. 1739–1764.

Chan, Louis KC, Jason Karceski, and Josef Lakonishok (1999). "On portfolio optimization: Forecasting covariances and choosing the risk model". In: *The Review of Financial Studies* 12.5, pp. 937–974.

Chen, Jieting and Yuichiro Kawaguchi (2018). "Multi-factor asset-pricing models under Markov regime switches: Evidence from the Chinese stock market". In: *International Journal of Financial Studies* 6.2, p. 54.

Chen, Luyang, Markus Pelger, and Jason Zhu (2020). "Deep learning in asset pricing". Available at SSRN 3350138.

Clarke, Roger G and Harindra de Silva (1998). "State-dependent asset allocation". In: *Journal of Portfolio Management* 24.2, p. 57.

Cochrane, John H (2009). *Asset Pricing: Revised Edition*. Princeton University Press.

Das, Kajaree and Rabi Narayan Behera (2017). "A survey on machine learning: Concept, algorithms and applications". In: *International Journal of Innovative Research in Computer and Communication Engineering* 5.2, pp. 1301–1309.

De Mol, Christine, Domenico Giannone, and Lucrezia Reichlin (2008). "Forecasting using a large number of predictors: Is Bayesian shrinkage a valid alternative to principal components?" In: *Journal of Econometrics* 146.2, pp. 318–328.

Dempsey, Mike (2013). "The capital asset pricing model (CAPM): The history of a failed revolutionary idea in finance?" In: *Abacus* 49, pp. 7–23.

Dey, Ayon (2016). "Machine learning algorithms: A review". In: *International Journal of Computer Science and Information Technologies* 7.3, pp. 1174–1179.

Dhrymes, Phoebus J, Irwin Friend, and N Bulent Gultekin (1984). "A critical reexamination of the empirical evidence on the arbitrage pricing theory". In: *The Journal of Finance* 39.2, pp. 323–346.

Dichev, Ilia D (1998). "Is the risk of bankruptcy a systematic risk?" In: *The Journal of Finance* 53.3, pp. 1131–1147.

Dietvorst, Berkeley J, Joseph Simmons, and Cade Massey (2014). "Understanding algorithm aversion: Forecasters erroneously avoid algorithms after seeing them err". In: *Academy of Management Proceedings* 2014. 1. Academy of Management Briarcliff Manor, NY, p. 12227.

Doz, Catherine, Domenico Giannone, and Lucrezia Reichlin (2012). "A quasi–maximum likelihood approach for large, approximate dynamic factor models". In: *Review of Economics and Statistics* 94.4, pp. 1014–1024.

Eldan, Ronen and Ohad Shamir (2016). "The power of depth for feedforward neural networks". In: *Conference on Learning Theory*. PMLR, pp. 907–940.

Eugene, Fama and Kenneth French (1992). "The cross-section of expected stock returns". In: *Journal of Finance* 47.2, pp. 427–465.

Fama, Eugene and James MacBeth (1973). "ARisk, return and equilibrium: Empirical tests". In: *Journal of Political Economy* 81.3, p. 607.

Fama, Eugene F and Kenneth R French (2008). "Dissecting anomalies". In: *The Journal of Finance* 63.4, pp. 1653–1678.

Fama, Eugene F and Kenneth R French (2015). "A five-factor asset pricing model". In: *Journal of Financial Economics* 116.1, pp. 1–22.

Fama, Eugene F and Kenneth R French (2016). "Dissecting anomalies with a five-factor model". In: *The Review of Financial Studies* 29.1, pp. 69–103.

Fama, Eugene F and Kenneth R French (2021). *Common Risk Factors in the Returns on Stocks and Bonds*. University of Chicago Press.

Fama, Eugene F and Burton G Malkiel (1970). "Efficient capital markets: A review of theory and empirical work". In: *The Journal of Finance* 25.2, pp. 383–417.

Feng, Guanhao, Stefano Giglio, and Dacheng Xiu (2020). "Taming the factor zoo: A test of new factors". In: *The Journal of Finance* 75.3, pp. 1327–1370.

Fodor, Imola K (2002). *A Survey of Dimension Reduction Techniques*. Tech. Rep. Citeseer.

French, Jordan (2017). "The time traveller's CAPM". In: *Investment Analysts Journal* 46.2, pp. 81–96.

Friedman, Jerome H (2001). "Greedy function approximation: A gradient boosting machine". In: *Annals of Statistics*, pp. 1189–1232.

Gagniuc, Paul A (2017). *Markov Chains: From Theory to Implementation and Experimentation*. John Wiley & Sons.

Gencay, Ramazan and Tung Liu (1997). "Nonlinear modelling and prediction with feedforward and recurrent networks". In: *Physica D: Nonlinear Phenomena* 108.1–2, pp. 119–134.

Gerlein, Eduardo A et al. (2016). "Evaluating machine learning classification for financial trading: An empirical approach". In: *Expert Systems with Applications* 54, pp. 193–207.

Graham, Benjamin and D Dodd (1951). *Security Analysis: Principles and Technique*. New York, NY: McGraw-Hill.

Green, Jeremiah, John RM Hand, and X Frank Zhang (2013). "The supraview of return predictive signals". In: *Review of Accounting Studies* 18.3, pp. 692–730.

Green, Jeremiah, John RM Hand, and X Frank Zhang (2017). "The characteristics that provide independent information about average US monthly stock returns". In: *The Review of Financial Studies* 30.12, pp. 4389–4436.

Gu, Shihao, Bryan Kelly, and Dacheng Xiu (2018). *Empirical Asset Pricing Via Machine Learning*. Tech. Rep. National Bureau of Economic Research.

Hamilton, James D (1989). "A new approach to the economic analysis of nonstationary time series and the business cycle". In: *Econometrica: Journal of the Econometric Society*, vol. 57.2, pp. 357–384.

Harvey, Campbell R and Yan Liu (2014). "Evaluating trading strategies". In: *The Journal of Portfolio Management* 40.5, pp. 108–118.

Harvey, Campbell R and Yan Liu (2021). "Lucky factors". In: *Journal of Financial Economics*.

Harvey, Campbell R, Yan Liu, and Heqing Zhu (2016). "… and the cross-section of expected returns". In: *The Review of Financial Studies* 29.1, pp. 5–68.

Henrique, Bruno Miranda, Vinicius Amorim Sobreiro, and Herbert Kimura (2018). "Stock price prediction using support vector regression on daily and up to the minute prices". In: *The Journal of Finance and Data Science* 4.3, pp. 183–201.

Henrique, Bruno Miranda, Vinicius Amorim Sobreiro, and Herbert Kimura (2019). "Literature review: Machine learning techniques applied to financial market prediction". In: *Expert Systems with Applications* 124, pp. 226–251.

Hirschberger, Markus, Yue Qi, and Ralph E Steuer (2010). "Large-scale MV efficient frontier computation via a procedure of parametric quadratic programming". In: *European Journal of Operational Research* 204.3, pp. 581–588.

Hornik, Kurt, Maxwell Stinchcombe, and Halbert White (1989). "Multilayer feedforward networks are universal approximators". In: *Neural networks* 2.5, pp. 359–366.

Huberman, Gur (2005). *Arbitrage Pricing Theory*. Tech. Rep. Staff Report.

Jiang, Jianmin, P Trundle, and Jinchang Ren (2010). "Medical image analysis with artificial neural networks". In: *Computerized Medical Imaging and Graphics* 34.8, pp. 617–631.

Kelly, Bryan and Seth Pruitt (2015). "The three-pass regression filter: A new approach to forecasting using many predictors". In: *Journal of Econometrics* 186.2, pp. 294–316.

Kou, Gang et al. (2019). "Machine learning methods for systemic risk analysis in financial sectors". In: *Technological and Economic Development of Economy* 25.5, pp. 716–742.

Krollner, Bjoern, Bruce J Vanstone, and Gavin R Finnie (2010). "Financial time series forecasting with machine learning techniques: A survey." In: *ESANN*.

Lewellen, Jonathan (2014). "The cross section of expected stock returns". In: *Forthcoming in Critical Finance Review, Tuck School of Business Working Paper* 2511246.

Li, Shuai et al. (2018). "Independently recurrent neural network (indrnn): Building a longer and deeper RNN". In: *Proceedings of the IEEE Conference on Computer Vision and Pattern Recognition*, pp. 5457–5466.

Lintner, John (1965). "Security prices, risk, and maximal gains from diversification". In: *The Journal of Finance* 20.4, pp. 587–615.

Lundberg, Scott and Su-In Lee (2017). "A unified approach to interpreting model predictions". arXiv preprint, arXiv:1705.07874.

Maitra, Durjoy Sen, Ujjwal Bhattacharya, and Swapan K Parui (2015). "CNN based common approach to handwritten character recognition of multiple scripts". In: *2015 13th International Conference on Document Analysis and Recognition (ICDAR)*. IEEE, pp. 1021–1025.

Malkiel, Burton G (2003). "The efficient market hypothesis and its critics". In: *Journal of Economic Perspectives* 17.1, pp. 59–82.

Markowitz, Harry (1952). "The utility of wealth". In: *Journal of Political Economy* 60.2, pp. 151–158.

Messmer, Marcial (2017). "Deep learning and the cross-section of expected returns". Available at SSRN 3081555.

Moritz, Benjamin and Tom Zimmermann (2016). "Tree-based conditional portfolio sorts: The relation between past and future stock returns". Available at SSRN 2740751.

Mossin, Jan (1966). "Equilibrium in a capital asset market". In: *Econometrica: Journal of the Econometric Society*, pp. 768–783.Vol. 34, No. 4

Mullainathan, Sendhil and Jann Spiess (2017). "Machine learning: An applied econometric approach". In: *Journal of Economic Perspectives* 31.2, pp. 87–106.

Nayak, Rudra Kalyan, Debahuti Mishra, and Amiya Kumar Rath (2015). "A naıve SVM-KNN based stock market trend reversal analysis for Indian benchmark indices". In: *Applied Soft Computing* 35, pp. 670–680.

Partington, Graham et al. (2013). "Death where is thy sting? A response to Dempsey's despatching of the CAPM". In: *Abacus* 49.1, pp. 69–72.

Pástor, L'uboš and Robert F Stambaugh (2000). "Comparing asset pricing models: An investment perspective". In: *Journal of Financial Economics* 56.3, pp. 335–381.

Perold, André F (2004). "The capital asset pricing model". In: *Journal of Economic Perspectives* 18.3, pp. 3–24.

Rapach, David and Guofu Zhou (2013). "Forecasting stock returns". In: *Handbook of Economic Forecasting*. Vol. 2. Elsevier, pp. 328–383.

Ribeiro, Marco Tulio, Sameer Singh, and Carlos Guestrin (2016). ""Why should I trust you?" Explaining the predictions of any classifier". In: *Proceedings of the 22nd ACM SIGKDD International Conference on Knowledge Discovery qnd Data Mining*, pp. 1135–1144.

Roll, Richard (1977). "A critique of the asset pricing theory's tests. Part I: On past and potential testability of the theory". In: *Journal of Financial Economics* 4.2, pp. 129–176.

Ross, Stephen (1977). "Risk, return and arbitrage". In: *Risk and Return in Finance* 1, pp. 189–218.

Roy, Rahul and Santhakumar Shijin (2018). "A six-factor asset pricing model". In: *Borsa Istanbul Review* 18.3, pp. 205–217.

Schapire, Robert E (1990). "The strength of weak learnability". In: *Machine Learning* 5.2, pp. 197–227.

Sengupta, Nandini, Md Sahidullah, and Goutam Saha (2016). "Lung sound classification using cepstral-based statistical features". In: *Computers in Biology and Medicine* 75, pp. 118–129.

Sharpe, William F (1964). "Capital asset prices: A theory of market equilibrium under conditions of risk". In: *The Journal of Finance* 19.3, pp. 425–442.

Sheridan, Iain (2017). "MiFID II in the context of financial technology and regulatory technology". In: *Capital Markets Law Journal* 12.4, pp. 417–427.

Simin, Timothy (2008). "The poor predictive performance of asset pricing models". In: *Journal of Financial and Quantitative Analysis*, pp. 355–380.

Stock, James H and Mark W Watson (2002). "Forecasting using principal components from a large number of predictors". In: *Journal of the American Statistical Association* 97.460, pp. 1167–1179.

Stock, James H and Mark W Watson (2012). "Generalized shrinkage methods for forecasting using many predictors". In: *Journal of Business & Economic Statistics* 30.4, pp. 481–493.

Tibshirani, Robert (1996). "Regression shrinkage and selection via the lasso". In: *Journal of the Royal Statistical Society: Series B (Methodological)* 58.1, pp. 267–288.

Treynor, Jack L (1961). "Market value, time, and risk". In: *Time, and Risk.*

Von Luxburg, Ulrike and Bernhard Schölkopf (2011). "Statistical learning theory: Models, concepts, and results". In: *Handbook of the History of Logic*. Vol. 10. Elsevier, pp. 651–706.

Wilson, D Randall and Tony R Martinez (2003). "The general inefficiency of batch training for gradient descent learning". In: *Neural Networks* 16.10, pp. 1429–1451.

Wolpert, David H (1996). "The lack of a priori distinctions between learning algorithms". In: *Neural Computation* 8.7, pp. 1341–1390.

Womack, Kent L and Ying Zhang (2005). "Core finance trends in the top MBA programs in 2005". Available at SSRN 760604.

Wu, Xindong et al. (2008). "Top 10 algorithms in data mining". In: *Knowledge and Information Systems* 14.1, pp. 1–37.

Zou, Hui (2006). "The adaptive lasso and its oracle properties". In: *Journal of the American Statistical Association* 101.476, pp. 1418–1429.

Zou, Hui and Trevor Hastie (2005). "Regularization and variable selection via the elastic net". In: *Journal of the Royal Statistical Society: Series B (Statistical Methodology)* 67.2, pp. 301–320.

CHAPTER 8

Testing for Market Efficiency Using News-Driven Sentiment: Evidence from Select NYSE Stocks

S Rangapriya and Madhavi Lokhande

CONTENTS

8.1 INTRODUCTION

The advent of data analytics has enabled the financial industry to ascertain, understand and establish market characteristics and dynamics comprehensively. This study attempts to determine if the classical market efficiency theory continues to hold ground when superimposed by sentiment analysis which falls within the realm of behavioural finance. The Efficient Market Hypothesis (EMH) establishes that the share prices always reflect all publicly available information, making it impossible to generate alpha consistently. The other central tenet of this theory is that the stock trades at fair value at all periods, thus negating the ability of individuals to invest in undervalued stocks or short stocks which are trading at inflated valuations. The theory rejects the entire effort of expert stock selection or market timing and suggests that they are futile. It is also imperative to note that this theory considers the investors' community or market

DOI: 10.1201/9781003327745-8

participants to be rational beings. This theory establishes that market dynamics drive the prices and investors have no role to play in determining the stock price hence, market stochasticity is purely market-driven [1,2]. This theory has stood the test of time and academic works continue to draw upon this classic theory in their works. Despite revolutionizing the investment world and bringing rigour to the system, the theory failed to address the many lacunae that continue to exist in the capital markets. The growing dissent among academicians towards standard finance paved the way for behavioural finance, a diametrically opposite postulate which puts the investor sentiment and their psychological biases to the forefront. Behavioural finance is the interaction of psychology with financial decision-making and the actions of market participants. The premise of behavioural finance normalizes the irrational behaviour of investors and behavioural biases and perceptions to justify bouts of market inefficiencies. According to Statman (1995) psychology, behaviour and semantics market participants, particularly risk assessment and processing of available information, hence, have a telling impact on the market dynamics. There is no cohesive theory for behavioural finance as yet; however, there have been many academic works acknowledging the essence of investor psychology influencing financial decision-making. Industry practitioners are also in a constant endeavour to build investment strategies and financial products which include and align with the heuristics of investors [3,4].

AI as a tool is enabling market participants to make informed decisions by providing both qualitative and quantitative insights about the market. From the perspective of information accessibility and processing, AI tools facilitate uniform access across varied sources, reducing biases, and increasing informational efficiency. A study that evaluated the approach towards information between machines and humans observed that both looked for timely and complex information. The research work also pointed to the human tendency to be more susceptible to negative sentiment [5,6]. There has been an increased interest in sentiment analysis over the past few years, the earlier techniques of research in this area of evaluation of sentiment were based on the frequency of terminology, and usage of phrases for semantic orientation. The AI techniques involved today are of the finest grade where the research is granular, the sentiment polarity is assessed at the word level within each sentence, and word disambiguation is also processed effectively using Natural Language Processing (NLP).

This study intends to evaluate the sentiment of news headlines for select stocks from the NYSE and assess the correlation and causality of such sentiment with returns generated by the stocks. Python 3.10, an open-source data analytics tool, has been used to conduct the analysis. The rest of the study covers a literature review in section 8.2, research methodology in section 8.3, findings and discussion in section 8.4, implications in section 8.5 and conclusion in section 8.6.

8.2 LITERATURE REVIEW

Many literary works evaluate sentiment around financial news, specific stock-related news, press releases and earnings updates. The intent is to enable ascertainment of their impact on investor psychology and risk perception. Identifying the trend or pattern between factors affecting investor behaviour and the k prices enables better risk evaluation and mitigation. One such study evaluated the predictability of investor buying behaviour in the futures market using supervised sentiment analysis. The study uses net buying pressure to ascertain the market sentiment, real-time news events are automatically captured and labelled as interesting market events. A certain lag was assumed between market information and the impact of news on the buying behaviour of traders. The study concluded that news had a significant impact on buying behaviour of S&P NIFTY index futures with a lag of 5 minutes [7].

The existence of sentiment makes the prices waver from equilibrium, which is otherwise justifiable by fundamental valuation. To ascertain the impact of sentiment on stock returns, many proxies for the sentiment were studied. Based on literary evidence the following were used as proxies for sentiment analysis: VIX, share turnover, number of IPOs, first-day IPO returns, closed-end fund discount rate, dividend premiums, consumer attitudes and expectations, the future outlook of stock and motive for holding the stock. Based on causality tests that were undertaken it was deduced that there was evidence of a strong relationship between sentiment and stock returns, VIX was identified as the favoured measure of sentiment that demonstrated better explanatory power. It was also observed that the sentiment and stock return relationship was heavily influenced by macro-environmental factors, particularly recessionary trends [8].

Amidst the claims that stock market boards can move markets, a study analysed over 1.5 million messages from Yahoo! Finance and the Raging Bull platform across 45 stocks listed on DJIA and DJII. Basing the analysis of the computational linguistics method and using news stories published in *Wall Street Journal* as control measures, it was empirically established that stock volatility can be predicted using messages. Although the effect on stock returns was statistically significant, the economic effect was insignificant. However, this study observed that there was no basis for related trading volumes to stock messages [9].

To ascertain the premise of under-reaction and over-reaction to news, a database of headlines about individual companies, the dataset spans 1980–2000 and the stocks analysed ranged from 766 to 1500 from the CRSP index over the horizon under consideration. The objective of this research work was to identify the movement in returns of stocks consequent to any prominent news item and juxtapose such movement in returns with other stocks which have moved in a similar direction despite no prominent news. The findings established that stocks with bad news exhibit a strong drift, the authors conclude that this is evidence of under-reaction and slow absorption of information. Extreme fluctuations observed in stocks which have no prominent news show signs of mean reversal. The paper concludes that some of the integrated market theories were established using this study [10].

Another study suggested a sentiment analysis model inferring the polarity of news items related to specific companies with the intent to predict the stock market. The dataset constituted the news items from *Wall Street Journal* and stock data from

NASDAQ. Five companies were selected from the DJIA, these were the top gainers on the day the data collection was initiated; the analysis was conducted for 30 days. The stock market predictability under the test runs using the logistic regression indicated that the ability to predict stock market volatility was weak, thus aligning with the EMH tenet which iterates that all publicly available information is factored into the stock prices [11].

Based on the literature review that was conducted, there is a need to evaluate sentiment around stock-specific news concerning stock returns movement within the premise of EMH. This theory emphasizes the utility of stock price prediction and the non-existence of the impact of public news (including sentiment) on stock market fluctuations. To ascertain this, here the attempt is to assess the correlation between stock-specific news-related sentiment and stock returns and evaluate its statistical significance. Causality subsumes prediction, most predictive models have the premise of consistent behaviour in the future; however, in the real world, the constant evolution of the environment and human interactions is apparent. There is a need to build causal models to address the ever-changing perspectives of investors and the volatility of markets. This should be done with a relevant established causal relationship between independent variables and the dependent variables [12,13]. Approaching the stock market risk-return paradox with an etiological perspective will facilitate answering 'what if' questions and enable better risk mitigation.

8.3 RESEARCH METHODOLOGY

To conduct this study, the top 25 stocks from S&P500 based on the market capitalization were selected. The stocks within the Universe of the S&P 500 remain the benchmark for the depth of the market which is measured by the frequency and volume of transactions. A stock's liquidity is a leading factor that is indicative of its ability to absorb intermittent volatilities without excessive price disruptions from the fair value. The daily transaction volume of stocks correlates positively with the frequency of the number of mentions in financial news, liquidity of stocks increases the informational content for share prices [14–16]. The period of study was for a window of 6 months (31 December 2021 to 31 May 2022) which includes one round of quarterly earnings-related news articles. Headline news feeds are important and the earliest form of communication to industry practitioners and market participants. The headline is considered the most important aspect of the news article using headlines alone provides good data analytics results. The usage of headlines improves the results, especially while considering analysis using NLP tools [7,17]. The news headlines were web scraped from the Finnhub website alongside manual extraction from Seeking Alpha based on data availability across stocks, and the prices of the stocks understudy for the corresponding period were scraped from Yahoo! Finance. The scraped data was converted into a pandas data frame to facilitate analysis. The analysis was conducted on Python 3.10, an open-source analytical software.

For analysing the headline data from the perspective of drawing insights, we use the NLTK (Natural Language ToolKit) considered a go-to API for NLP in Python. This tool offers a bouquet of programs and libraries for statistical NLP, the toolkit is considered a prominent tool in computational linguistics in Python. The VADER (Valence Aware Dictionary and sEntiment Reasoner) sentiment analysis enables computational determination of the polarity of the news headlines. This is a rule-based, lexicon tool meant for sentiment analysis specifically attuned to sentiment conveyed on public platforms including, but not limited to stock-specific news aggregators. VADER not only classifies the sentiment based on their semantic orientation into Positive, Neutral and Negative, but it also provides a score for such positivity or negativity which ranges between −1 (extremely negative) and +1 (extremely positive). Neutral sentiment is when the compound sentiment score falls between − 0.05 and + 0.05 [18–20]. The daily stock returns are arrived at based on log returns, it has been a standard practice to model stock prices using 'log returns'. Log returns are preferred in financial calculations due to their assumption of log-normal distribution and the property of time-additive. From the perspective of computation of correlation, log returns are used, as it ensures that the higher moments are negligible [21].

The sentiment scores and daily stock price returns are converted to a data frame in pandas for further analysis. In case, there is no stock-specific news on any date, then the previous day's sentiment score is passed forward. The sentiment scores for any news during non-trading days are carried forward to the subsequent trading day, unless there is stock-specific news for that day, in which case the most recent sentiment score has been retained. This rule is aligned to the recency bias which is one of the prominent information processing behavioural biases found in investors. Recency bias is the predisposition of investors to weigh in on the experiences that are freshest in their memory [22].

8.3.1 Correlation Coefficient

The correlation coefficient is used to ascertain the existence and strength of the relationship between the two variables, namely sentiment score from news articles and daily returns of the specific stock. Pearson's correlation coefficient is commonly used for linear regression, the value returned lies between −1 and +1 indicating the strength of the relationship. The statistical significance of the test has also been ascertained. The correlation coefficient is given by:

$$r_{xy} = \frac{S_{xy}}{S_x S_y}$$

where r_{xy} is the correlation coefficient, S_x S_y is the sample standard deviations of variables x and y, S_{xy} is the covariance of variables x and y.

Source: [23].

8.3.2 Granger Causality Test

The Granger Causality test is a statistical hypothesis test for assessing if one time series enables the prediction of the other. This test remains neutral to instantaneous and non-linear causal relationships. For this test, the lag has been considered at 1 day, as the news is likely to have an extreme reaction within a 24-hour timeframe. Below is the depiction of X_1 & X_2 variables where $y(t)$ Granger-causes $x(t)$:

$$X1(t) \;=\; \Sigma_{j=1}^{p} A11, \; jX1(t-j) + \Sigma_{j=1}^{p} A12, \; jX2(t-j) + E1(t)$$
$$X2(t) \;=\; \Sigma_{j=1}^{p} A21, \; jX1(t-j) + \Sigma_{j=1}^{p} A22, \; jX2(t-j) + E2(t)$$

where j is the lag being considered for each iteration, p is the maximum number of lagged observations, matrix A contains the coefficients of the model, E_1 and E_2 are residuals for each time series. This test has two important assumptions about the time series: (1) stationarity of the time series; (2) described adequately by a linear model. As required, the Augmented Dickey-Fuller test is conducted prior to the implementation of the Granger Causality test. ADF tests the existence of unit root in a time series.

Source: [24,25].

8.4 FINDINGS AND DISCUSSION

The descriptive summary of the data used is as mentioned in table 8.1, the overall mean daily returns across the 25 stocks are – 0.03% for the period under study. The average standard deviation for the dataset is 2.21% with a maximum standard deviation, a measure of risk being apparent in stocks including Tesla Inc, NVIDIA Corp and Meta Platforms Inc, with greater than 4.2% standard deviation. Kurtosis and Skewness are important descriptive statistical data, Skewness measures the symmetry of the distribution and Kurtosis measures the heaviness of the distribution towards the tails. Kurtosis is considered a pseudo measure for financial risk, stocks with higher Kurtosis are often considered highly volatile, so it is best to study Kurtosis in conjunction with standard deviation. Kurtosis, a measure of the distribution of the dataset, when greater than +1, is considered to be too peaked and when lower than −1, distribution is considered too flat [26,27]. Meta Platforms Inc. and Walmart indicate that the observations have heavy tails or outliers. The skewness that assesses the extent of variability of distribution from being symmetrical, for the below dataset, was notably negatively skewed for Meta Platforms, Walmart and Costco Wholesale Corp and positively (and prominently) skewed for Eli Lilly and Co.

As a next step, the sentiment scores based on the news for each scrip are assessed using the SentimentIntensityAnalyzer framework within the NLTK Vader module. The sentiment scores across dates are populated to align with the daily returns of the stock. The necessary adjustments are made for those fields without a sentiment score or with multiple sentiment scores as indicated in the research methodology section. The date, daily returns and sentiment scores are converted to a data frame to facilitate correlation

TABLE 8.1   Descriptive Summary

Stock Ticker	Name	Count	Mean	Standard Deviation	Kurtosis	Skewness
AAPL	Apple Inc	123	(0.0008)	0.0219	0.2201	0.0358
ABBV	AbbVie Inc	123	0.0021	0.0138	4.2856	(1.3319)
AMZN	Amazon.com, Inc.	123	(0.0033)	0.0315	5.0960	(0.4642)
AVGO	Broadcom Inc	123	0.0004	0.0257	(0.1441)	0.1622
BAC	Bank of America Corp	123	(0.0014)	0.0208	0.6581	0.2379
BRK	Berkshire Hathaway	123	(0.0003)	0.0086	(0.2246)	0.1130
COST	Costco Wholesale Corp	123	(0.0010)	0.0221	9.7072	(1.5631)
CVX	Chevron Corporation	123	0.0038	0.0190	1.5974	(0.7240)
FB	Meta Platforms Inc	123	(0.0038)	0.0422	21.3367	(2.5925)
GOOG	Alphabet Inc Class C	123	(0.0018)	0.0221	0.2302	0.1295
HD	Home Depot Inc	123	(0.0021)	0.0203	2.2771	(0.9152)
JNJ	Johnson & Johnson	123	0.0011	0.0116	1.5770	0.6628
JPM	JPMorgan Chase & Co	123	(0.0015)	0.0193	0.7220	(0.0582)
KO	Coca-Cola Co	123	0.0017	0.0134	7.2038	(1.3815)
LLY	Eli Lilly And Co	123	0.0021	0.0187	4.9188	1.2255
MA	Mastercard Inc	123	0.0013	0.0226	1.1993	0.3033
MSFT	Microsoft Corporation	123	(0.0015)	0.0217	(0.5382)	(0.0876)
NVDA	NVIDIA Corporation	123	(0.0042)	0.0426	(0.5905)	0.2614
PFE	Pfizer Inc.	123	(0.0001)	0.0199	0.0098	0.1844
PG	Procter & Gamble Co	123	0.0001	0.0142	3.1496	(0.6139)
TSLA	Tesla Inc	123	(0.0030)	0.0450	0.1935	(0.1100)
UNH	UnitedHealth Group Inc	123	0.0011	0.0150	0.4005	(0.4527)
V	Visa Inc	123	0.0009	0.0219	2.9659	0.6922
WMT	Walmart Inc	123	(0.0005)	0.0179	16.4936	(2.8190)
XOM	Exxon Mobil Corp	123	0.0040	0.0209	2.4146	(0.7584)

analysis and further tests. In table 8.2, the correlation value and their statistical significance have been indicated. In this study, the null hypothesis for the correlation test and the alternate hypothesis are as stated below:

H_0: No correlation exists between sentiment scores and daily returns of stock
H_1: Correlation exists between sentiment scores and daily returns of stock

Only in two instances, namely, Coca-Cola Inc and Mastercard, the correlation between the sentiment scores and daily returns of the stock were statistically significant. In all other instances, it was established that there was no statistically significant correlation. Interestingly, the correlation between the sentiment scores and daily returns of specific stocks ranges from −0.09 to 0.19 with an average of 0.046, this also iterates that there is no strong correlation between news-based sentiment scores and daily returns of the stock. The results align with the earlier studies where content analysis to quantify the document tone was conducted to ascertain correlation and predictability of IPO pricing, the study concluded that the correlation was negative and very low. A such low

TABLE 8.2   Correlation Test

Stock Ticker	Correlation	P-value	Conclusion
AAPL	0.0077	0.9325	*Not enough evidence to reject the Null Hypothesis*
ABBV	0.0584	0.5212	*Not enough evidence to reject the Null Hypothesis*
AMZN	0.0358	0.6943	*Not enough evidence to reject the Null Hypothesis*
AVGO	0.1017	0.2628	*Not enough evidence to reject the Null Hypothesis*
BAC	0.0568	0.5323	*Not enough evidence to reject the Null Hypothesis*
BRK	0.1346	0.1378	*Not enough evidence to reject the Null Hypothesis*
COST	0.0017	0.9849	*Not enough evidence to reject the Null Hypothesis*
CVX	(0.0047)	0.9591	*Not enough evidence to reject the Null Hypothesis*
FB	0.0712	0.4338	*Not enough evidence to reject the Null Hypothesis*
GOOG	(0.0222)	0.8072	*Not enough evidence to reject the Null Hypothesis*
HD	(0.0622)	0.4945	*Not enough evidence to reject the Null Hypothesis*
JNJ	0.0714	0.4323	*Not enough evidence to reject the Null Hypothesis*
JPM	(0.0640)	0.4821	*Not enough evidence to reject the Null Hypothesis*
KO	0.1883	0.0370	*Enough evidence to reject the Null Hypothesis*
LLY	0.0386	0.6713	*Not enough evidence to reject the Null Hypothesis*
MA	0.1876	0.0377	*Enough evidence to reject the Null Hypothesis*
MSFT	0.0024	0.9790	*Not enough evidence to reject the Null Hypothesis*
NVDA	(0.0253)	0.7811	*Not enough evidence to reject the Null Hypothesis*
PFE	0.0779	0.3916	*Not enough evidence to reject the Null Hypothesis*
PG	0.1582	0.0805	*Not enough evidence to reject the Null Hypothesis*
TSLA	0.0501	0.5820	*Not enough evidence to reject the Null Hypothesis*
UNH	(0.0710)	0.4350	*Not enough evidence to reject the Null Hypothesis*
V	0.1697	0.0606	*Not enough evidence to reject the Null Hypothesis*
WMT	(0.0927)	0.3077	*Not enough evidence to reject the Null Hypothesis*
XOM	0.0839	0.3563	*Not enough evidence to reject the Null Hypothesis*

correlation could not potentially assist in the predictability of IPO pricing. Another study indicates that there is specific news such as earnings announcements which have better predictive value and garner deeper investor reactions than generic stock-specific news articles [28,29].

As a pre-amble to conducting the Granger causality test, to establish stationarity of the time series the ADF test is conducted, and the results are tabulated in table 8.3. The null hypothesis being tested and the alternative hypothesis is as stated below:

H_0: Unit Root exists in time series or time series is non-stationary

H_1: Unit Root does not exist in time series or time series is stationary

The check for stationarity must be conducted for both the time series at hand, namely the sentiment analysis and daily returns of each specific stock.

Having established the stationarity of both time series across stocks, the Granger Causality test is initiated. The results which are tabulated in table 8.4, the null and alternative hypotheses for this test is as indicated below:

TABLE 8.3   ADF Test

| | Time Series | | | | |
| | Daily Returns | | Sentiment Scores | | |
Stock Ticker	ADF Test Statistic	P-value	ADF Test Statistic	P-value	Conclusion
AAPL	−10.966	–	−11.206	–	*Both time series are stationary*
ABBV	−10.294	–	−5.113	–	*Both time series are stationary*
AMZN	−12.137	–	−8.698	–	*Both time series are stationary*
AVGO	−12.3	–	−10.373	–	*Both time series are stationary*
BAC	−10.761	–	−6.979	–	*Both time series are stationary*
BRK	−11.968	–	−4.045	–	*Both time series are stationary*
COST	−10.019	–	−5.166	–	*Both time series are stationary*
CVX	−6.672	–	−10.684	–	*Both time series are stationary*
FB	−11.584	–	−5.406	–	*Both time series are stationary*
GOOG	−11.715	–	−8.446	–	*Both time series are stationary*
HD	−10.837	–	−4.096	–	*Both time series are stationary*
JNJ	−12.165	–	−8.876	–	*Both time series are stationary*
JPM	−9.689	–	−12.231	–	*Both time series are stationary*
KO	−7.659	–	−4.892	–	*Both time series are stationary*
LLY	−9.657	–	−8.586	–	*Both time series are stationary*
MA	−10.142	–	−5.06	–	*Both time series are stationary*
MSFT	−12.758	–	−8.557	–	*Both time series are stationary*
NVDA	−11.903	–	−5.927	–	*Both time series are stationary*
PFE	−10.773	–	−8.282	–	*Both time series are stationary*
PG	−8.533	–	−3.816	0.003	*Both time series are stationary*
TSLA	−3.811	–	−8.294	–	*Both time series are stationary*
UNH	−10.947	–	−4.38	–	*Both time series are stationary*
V	−11.087	–	−14.992	–	*Both time series are stationary*
WMT	−7.865	–	−4.02	0.001	*Both time series are stationary*
XOM	−10.781	–	−10.444	–	*Both time series are stationary*

H_0: News-led sentiment does not cause daily returns in stocks and fluctuations thereof (change in price)

H_1: News-led sentiment causes daily returns in stocks and fluctuations thereof (change in price)

Granger causality test cannot be conducted with zero lags, hence, a T+1 lag has been considered in line with other literary works which establish that the recall indicators of news have the highest probability on T+1 day [30].

Except for Broadcom Inc., there is no evidence of news-led sentiment causing the quantum of daily returns in stocks or fluctuations thereof. This aligns not only with the basic premise of market efficiency, one of the works which evaluate the extent of variance in aggregate stock returns that can be attributed to various kinds of news, evaluated the impact of macro-economic news, other stock-specific news, major political and world events on stock returns. The study evidenced that despite major news releases,

TABLE 8.4   Granger Causality Test

Stock Ticker	F-Test statistic	*P-value*	Conclusion
AAPL	0.3973	0.5297	*Not enough evidence to reject the Null Hypothesis*
ABBV	0.1027	0.7492	*Not enough evidence to reject the Null Hypothesis*
AMZN	1.3752	0.2433	*Not enough evidence to reject the Null Hypothesis*
AVGO	4.3979	0.0381	*Enough evidence to reject the Null Hypothesis*
BAC	0.0030	0.9566	*Not enough evidence to reject the Null Hypothesis*
BRK	0.7790	0.3792	*Not enough evidence to reject the Null Hypothesis*
COST	0.4194	0.5185	*Not enough evidence to reject the Null Hypothesis*
CVX	0.0120	0.9128	*Not enough evidence to reject the Null Hypothesis*
FB	0.0528	0.8187	*Not enough evidence to reject the Null Hypothesis*
GOOG	1.3691	0.2443	*Not enough evidence to reject the Null Hypothesis*
HD	2.3132	0.1309	*Not enough evidence to reject the Null Hypothesis*
JNJ	0.1648	0.6855	*Not enough evidence to reject the Null Hypothesis*
JPM	1.2596	0.2640	*Not enough evidence to reject the Null Hypothesis*
KO	1.4735	0.2272	*Not enough evidence to reject the Null Hypothesis*
LLY	0.9276	0.3374	*Not enough evidence to reject the Null Hypothesis*
MA	0.9211	0.3391	*Not enough evidence to reject the Null Hypothesis*
MSFT	0.0020	0.9643	*Not enough evidence to reject the Null Hypothesis*
NVDA	–	0.9956	*Not enough evidence to reject the Null Hypothesis*
PFE	0.6732	0.4136	*Not enough evidence to reject the Null Hypothesis*
PG	0.1279	0.7213	*Not enough evidence to reject the Null Hypothesis*
TSLA	0.0327	0.8568	*Not enough evidence to reject the Null Hypothesis*
UNH	0.4272	0.5146	*Not enough evidence to reject the Null Hypothesis*
V	0.4279	0.5143	*Not enough evidence to reject the Null Hypothesis*
WMT	3.4656	0.0651	*Not enough evidence to reject the Null Hypothesis*
XOM	0.1720	0.6791	*Not enough evidence to reject the Null Hypothesis*

there were relatively insignificant market responses and on days with large market moves, there was no identifiable key news pertaining to the stock, economy or world events in general. The work concluded that stock price volatility was inexplicable by the news and future cashflows/discount rates pertaining to stock prices were not related to publicly available news articles [1,31].

8.5 IMPLICATIONS AND FUTURE RESEARCH

This study iterates through evidence of the authenticity of the EMH, that all public information is already factored in the price of the stock and hence, does not lead to any untoward volatility. The study superimposes investor sentiment upon such publicly available information, which forms a part of the behavioural finance framework. The findings are imperative from the perspective of building a holistic asset pricing model, to acknowledge the factors within the environment of the capital markets assessing their influence is critical to building a realistic and accurate pricing model. The study is also significant, for it highlights, albeit subtly that attempting to decipher market dynamics by considering one factor as a silo may not provide optimal insight. As a future research activity, the study should include multiple factors including sectoral news, regulatory framework changes and social media discussion points apart from macro indicators to study the influence of these aspects on investor sentiment and subsequently on market returns.

8.6 CONCLUSION

This research work evaluates the impact of stock-specific news-led sentiment on stock market movement. While the study tests the market efficiency hypothesis, it super-imposes sentiment analysis which falls within the realm of behavioural finance. The study leverages sophisticated tools available within data analytics and uses AI-led techniques to assess the sentiment score for stock-specific news. The sentiment scores are juxtaposed with daily returns from the stocks to ascertain the correlation if any and their statistical significance. While there is a subtle correlation between the sentiment score and daily returns, it remains unanimously and statistically insignificant. This work further con-ducts the Granger Causality to assess the popular belief that 'news causes reaction'; however, on most counts, it is evidenced that news-led sentiment does not cause market movement. Thus, establishing the market efficiency principle yet again, the publicly available information in the form of stock-specific news has already been factored into the prices, hence, there is no untoward/irrational market movement observed within the dataset studied. The findings facilitate a better understanding of the market dynamics and provide deeper insight into the influence of this factor on asset pricing. The research can be deepened by studying the intra-day movement of stocks and their reaction to stock-specific news [32,33].

REFERENCES

[1] E. F. Fama, "Efficient Capital Markets: A Review of Theory and Empirical Work," *The Journal of Finance*, pp. 383–417, 1970.

[2] B. G. Malkiel, "Efficient Market Hypothesis," *Journal of Economic Perspectives*, pp. 59–82, 2003.

[3] H. Shefrin and M. Statman, "Behavioral Portfolio Theory," *The Journal of Financial and Quantitative Analysis*, pp. 127–151, 2000.

[4] V. Ricciardi and H. K. Simon, "What Is Behavioral Finance?," *Business, Education and Technology Journal Fall*, pp. 26–34, 2000.

[5] L. G. Barbopoulos, R. Dai, T. J. Putniņš and A. Saunders, "Market Efficiency in the Age of Machine Learning," *SSRN Electronic Journal*, 2021.

[6] K. Wegner, "Business Insider," Business Insider, 26 June 2019. [Online]. Available: https://www.businessinsider.in/finance/responsible-use-of-artificial-intelligence-can-make-our-financial-markets-even-stronger/articleshow/69963155.cms. [Accessed 29 May 2022].

[7] R. Yadav, V. A. Kumar and A. Kumar, "Behaviour, News-Based Supervised Sentiment Analysis for Prediction of Futures Buying," *IIMB Management Review*, vol. 31, no. 2, pp. 157–166, 2019.

[8] H. Bourezk, A. Raji, N. Acha and H. Barka, "Analyzing Moroccan Stock Market Using Machine Learning and Sentiment Analysis," in *International Conference on Innovative Research in Applied Science, Engineering and Technology (IRASET)*, Morocco, 2020.

[9] W. Antweiler and M. Z. Frank, "Is All That Talk Just Noise? The Information Content of Internet Stock Message Boards," *The Journal of Finance*, vol. 59, no. 3, pp. 1259–1294, 2005.

[10] W. S. Chan, "Stock Price Reaction to News and No-News: Drift and Reversal After Headlines," *Journal of Financial Economics*, vol. 70, no. 2, pp. 223–260, 2003.

[11] M. Sorto, C. Aasheim, and H. Wimmer, "Feeling the Stock Market: A Study in the Prediction of Financial Markets Based on News Sentiment," in *SAIS*, Georgia, 2017.

[12] J. Pearl, "An Introduction to Causal Inference," *The International Journal of Biostatistics*, vol. 6, no. 2, pp. 1–59, 2010.

[13] S. Acharya, "Causal Modeling and Prediction over Event Streams," University of Vermont, Vermont, 2014.

[14] V. W. Fang, T. H. Noe and S. Tice, "Stock Market Liquidity and Firm Value," *Journal of Financial Economics*, vol. 94, no. 1, pp. 150–169, 2009.

[15] M. Alanyali, H. S. Moat and T. Preis, "Quantifying the Relationship between Financial News and the Stock Market," *Scientific Reports*, vol. 3, no. 3578, pp. 1–6, 2013.

[16] P. Spirtes, C. Glymour, R. Scheines and D. Heckerman, *Causation, Prediction, and Search*. Cambridge: MIT Press, 2000.

[17] A. H. V. Bunningen, "Augmented Trading - From news articles to stock price predictions using syntactic analysis (Master's Thesis)," University of Twente, Enschede (Netherlands), 2004.

[18] S. Bird, "Readthedocs," 28 September 2017. [Online]. Available: https://buildmedia. readthedocs.org/media/pdf/nltk/latest/nltk.pdf. [Accessed 02 June 2022].

[19] S. Saha, "Intro to NLTK for NLP with Python," *Towards Data Science*, 24 November 2020.

[20] C. Hutto and E. Gilbert, "VADER: A Parsimonious Rule-based Model for Sentiment Analysis of Social Media Text," in *Eighth International Conference on Weblogs and Social Media (ICWSM-14)*, MI, 2014.

[21] C. Smith and E. Kammers, "Cointegration, Correlation, and Log Returns," *Quantoisseur*, 6 November 2017.

[22] M. M. Pompian, "Risk Tolerance and Behavioural Finance," *Investments and Wealth Monitor*, vol. 20, no. 31, pp. 34–45, 2017.

[23] E. S. Pearson, "The Test of Significance for the Correlation Coefficient," *Journal of the American Statistical Association*, vol. 26, no. 174, pp. 128–134, 1931.

[24] C. W. J. Granger, "Investigating Causal Relations by Econometric Models and Cross-Spectral Methods," *Econometrica*, vol. 37, pp. 424–438, 1969.

[25] Seif Eldawlatly and K. Oweiss, "Graphical Models of Functional and Effective Neuronal Connectivity," in *Statistical Signal Processing for Neuroscience and Neurotechnology*, NY, Academic Press, 2010, pp. 129–174.

[26] J. F. Hai Jr., G. T. Hult, C. Ringle and M. Sarstedt, *A Primer on Partial Least Squares Structural Equation Modeling (PLS-SEM)*. Los Angeles: SAGE Publications, Inc, 2016.

[27] Corporate Finance Institute, "Corporate Finance Institute," Corporate Finance Institute, 07 May 2022. [Online]. Available: https://corporatefinanceinstitute.com/resources/knowledge/ other/kurtosis/. [Accessed 13 June 2022].

[28] N. Jegadeesha and D. Wu, "Word Power: A New Approach for Content Analysis," *Journal of Financial Economics*, vol. 110, no. 3, pp. 712–729, 2013.

[29] S. L. Heston and N. R. Sinha, "News vs. Sentiment: Predicting Stock Returns from News Stories," *Financial Analysts Journal*, vol. 73, no. 3, pp. 67–83, 2017.

[30] M. Ormos and M. Vázsonyi, "Impacts of Public News on Stock Market Prices: Evidence from S&P500," *Interdisciplinary Journal of Research in Business*, vol. 1, no. 2, pp. 1–17, 2011.

[31] D. M. Cutler, J. M. Poterba and L. H. Summers, "What Moves Stock Prices?," *The Journal of Portfolio Management*, vol. 15, no. 3, pp. 4–12, 1989.

[32] M. Statman, "Behavioral Finance versus Standard Finance," in *AIMR Conference Proceedings*, NY, 1995.

[33] S. Krishnamoorthy, "Sentiment Analysis of Financial News Articles Using Performance Indicators," *Knowledge and Information Systems*, vol. 56, pp. 373–394, 2018.

CHAPTER 9

Comparing Statistical, Deep Learning, and Additive Models for Forecasting in the Indian Stock Market

Vaibhav Shastri

CONTENTS

9.1 INTRODUCTION

Proponents of the efficient market hypothesis (EMH) believe that it is impossible to systematically predict the movement of stock prices in the long run [1]. However, the presence of counter-arguments in the literature [2] and success of many hedge funds challenges this basic premise. Regardless of the position of researchers on the EMH, financial asset forecasting remains one of the most researched topics in finance.

DOI: 10.1201/9781003327745-9

Classical efforts to predict future values of stocks revolved around two types of analyses: fundamental as well as technical analyses. Fundamental analysis seeks to evaluate a stock determined upon its intrinsic fair or book value, while technical analysis relies on historical price movements using charts and trends. Technical analysis has seen resurgence lately as many studies in recent years have used technical indicators derived from historical chart analysis as input features for AI models.

After the saturation of fundamental and technical analyses, more math-savvy researchers began using statistical time-series models to study and predict price movements, giving rise to popular models which include the ARIMA (autoregressive integrated moving average) [3] and the GARCH (generalized autoregressive conditional heteroskedasticity) models [4].

In recent years, driven by a seismic growth of computational power and the easy availability of data, researchers and investment firms have shifted their focus on techniques found in the field of Machine Learning (ML) which is inspired by the quest to create intelligent software or Artificial Intelligence (AI). ML and its sub area Deep Learning (DL) contain models which have been specifically developed to deal with unstructured and high volume, large dimensional data making them ideal for solving problems encountered in numerous fields [5]. In finance especially, in contrast with the (mostly linear) traditional models, AI algorithms (if adapted properly) may generate accurate predictions utilizing not only the traditional data sources but also previously unavailable "alternative data" sources [6].

For asset price forecasting, many research papers in literature report notable empirical performance demonstrated by ML algorithms when compared with traditional models [7–11]. Although the classical methods of time series such as ARIMA have been used for many decades, they have certain limitations, such as not being able to deal with missing or corrupt data, only able to map linear relationships, and focus on univariate data [12,13]. The latest innovation in the field of AI, deep neural networks have a strong capacity to learn the non-linear relationships between input features and prediction targets and have shown improved performance over both linear statistical and traditional supervised ML models on many tasks including stock market prediction. DL algorithms can be applied to large datasets and are able to learn arbitrary non-linear mapping functions. Moreover, they do not require scaling of inputs and can support multiple inputs and outputs. RNNs (recurrent neural networks) and CNNs (convolutional neural networks) are two most fundamental types of deep learning algorithms used in literature. CNNs are more suited to the task of modeling cross-sectional dependence whereas RNNs have been designed to deal with tasks requiring modeling of temporal characteristics [14]. LSTM (long-short term memory) neural networks, a type of RNN, have shown tremendous promise in the field of financial asset price forecasting [15–18].

Another class of ML models, called the additive models, have been gaining traction in recent years. A prime example of the additive models is the FbProphet algorithm developed by Meta for performing time-series analysis at scale. The FbProphet algorithm has been applied to many domains which require forecasting. This study uses the additive FbProphet algorithm as the third model for forecasting.

The main goal of this study is to compare the efficacy of both ARIMA and LSTM-based time-series models for making predictions on real data. For additional comparison, the study also employs the FbProphet model as the third forecasting model. Though some previous studies have compared the performance of these models either individually or in pairs, this study employs all three models for the same dataset over same time period. For empirical testing, a dataset containing daily closing prices of an ETF based on the NIFTY 50 Index has been chosen since ETFs are able to mimic the performance of its underlying almost perfectly and have the liquidity of common stocks. This provides a sense of realism to the study as a practitioner intending to trade in the market would follow a similar procedure for testing trading strategies. As representative fundamental techniques all three models, ARIMA, LSTM, and FbProphet show good performance for the dataset used; however, the results indicate that both LSTM and FbProphet far outperforms ARIMA in terms of out-of-sample forecasting. Among LSTM and Prophet, LSTM still shows superior results, demonstrating the power of AI models over other techniques.

The rest of this chapter is structured as follows. First, the literature review where recently published previous years' studies which have applied DL for the task of financial market forecasting are discussed. Next, the methodology section provides the theoretical and mathematical details of the models used. Finally, the analysis and results section shows the results obtained by both models followed by the conclusion of the study.

9.2 LITERATURE REVIEW

The literature on stock price forecasting is large. Most literature can be sorted into three main directions based on the choice of techniques and variables used for analysis and forecasting. The first and the oldest direction of studies uses mostly cross-sectional data analysis through regression-based techniques. Some of the notable works in this area can be epitomized through the works of Ma & Liu (2008), who use multivariate analysis for prediction of stock prices in the Shanghai Financial Market; Ivanovski (2016), who uses regression analysis for modeling stock returns for forecasting; and Khan et al. (2018), who use a robust framework for stock exchange forecasting based on regression analysis [19–21]. The second direction of research in the literature makes use of time-series models for forecasting stock returns using statistical techniques such as ARIMA, ARDL (autoregressive distributed lag model), and Granger causality test. Some representative works in this direction include Ariyo et al. (2014) and Mondal et al. (2014), who use the ARIMA model for stock price prediction [22,23]. Similarly, Jarrett and Kyper (2011) use the ARIMA model to forecast and analyse stock prices in the Chinese market [24]. The third and latest direction of research in stock price forecasting includes work using ML and DL models.

Some early examples in the third direction of research include Phua et al. (2001), who use a neural networks framework optimized with genetic algorithms for forecasting movements of stock price in the Singapore market achieving an accuracy of 81% [25]. Chen et al. (2003) proposed robust forecasting models for predicting the direction of returns by building a probabilistic neural network (PNN) based on historical stock market data from the Taiwan Stock Exchange and compared it with the output of two models: a random walk model and a parametric generalized method of moments (GMM) model. Their results showed that the highest returns were generated by investment strategies based on the output of the PNN model [26]. Zhang et al. (2007) used a multilayer backpropagation (BP) network for forecasting the data of data of the Shanghai composite index and generated buying and selling signals achieving about three times returns than a simple buy-and-hold approach [27]. Wu et al. (2008) proposed an ensemble model for predicting stock prices combining support vector machines (SVM) and Artificial Neutral Network (ANN). The ensemble approach followed by the authors produced more accurate results than the other two models applied individually [28]. Dutta et al. (2006) was one of the first studies to apply ANN models for forecasting Bombay Stock Exchange's SENSEX weekly closing values in the Indian stock market [29]. They illustrated how two neural networks with three hidden layers each could be applied to the forecasting problem and computed the performance of the two neural networks using root mean square error (RMSE) and mean square error (MSE) from January 2002 to December 2003. Hanias et al. (2012) conducted a study on the Athens Exchange (ASE) to predict the daily index price using a backpropagation neural network and reported an extremely low MSE value (0.0024) [30]. Some other examples in this area include Xiao et al. (2014) who use ARIMA and ANNs for forecasting market volatility [31]; Porshnev et al. (2013) who use machine learning for stock prediction using historical indicators and data from Twitter for sentiment analysis [32]; similarly, Tang and Chen (2018) use historical prices and news data for sentiment analysis to predict future stock prices [33]. Wang et al. (2018) in their work use both news data as well as social media sentiment data along with past prices for forecasting [34]. An extensive, comprehensive survey of machine learning techniques used in stock price forecasting can be found Obthong et al. (2020) [35].

Recently, the application of DL has gained prominence in the field of time-series data forecasting which is of particular application in many areas such as weather forecasting [36] and electricity load and price forecasting [37,38] among others. Most recent references in the literature report strong support for DL algorithms as they are a more powerful time-series forecasting tool compared to simple ANNs from earlier studies. DL models can accommodate both fundamental and technical frameworks and have the ability to adapt to non-linearity of datasets and do not requiring any static a priori assumptions [39]. Some of the work employing DL in financial data forecasting is discussed next. For example, Hossain et al. (2018) created a hybrid LSTM-GRU (Gated Recurrent Unit) model for forecasting the S&P 500 stock prices and found their hybrid model was able to outperform all other algorithms compared in the study [40]. Siami-Namini et al. (2018) compared the performance accuracy of ARIMA and LSTM for financial time series and showed that LSTM has much better performance to ARIMA for all metrics [15]. Fisher and Krauss (2008) found that LSTM model performed better than other algorithms used except during the 2008 financial crisis where the random forest model was performing better than LSTM. Overall, they showed how LSTMs can model useful signals from chaotic financial time series and are highly applicable for financial forecasting [16]. Chen et al. (2015) applied the LSTM network model on Chinese Stock Market data for stock return classification and found that compared to random predictions, the LSTM model showed much-improved performance [17]. In the Indian financial market, Mehtab et al. (2020) demonstrate how LSTM networks can be used for accurately forecasting the closing value of NIFTY 50 index stock price movements on a time horizon of one week and reported very promising results [18].

More recently, additive models have also been gaining popularity for time-series forecasting. These models may be termed as auto ML models where the parameters are auto-adjusted by the algorithms based on the data. The most popular representative example of additive model is the open-source FbProphet algorithm designed by Meta [41]. Since its introduction, it has been used in many tasks of forecasting and has also been applied in the field of finance. Indulkar (2021) uses deep learning and FbProphet for analysis and forecasting of cryptocurrencies [42]. Raheem and Nihla (2021) use fbProphet for foreign exchange rate forecasting [43]. Saiktishna et al. (2022) use it for stock market forecasting [44].

It is clear from the literature that time series forecasting literature has evolved from the use of traditional statistical techniques such as the ARMA and ARIMA models to the use of simple ANN (Artificial Neural Network) and ML models and finally, towards the direction of deep learning where the LSTM network models seem to be the most powerful technique. Therefore, in order to demonstrate the power and effectiveness of deep learning, this study compares the performance of the three representative techniques from the literature: the ARIMA model, the LSTM model, and the FbProphet model. The technical details of the models are discussed in the next section, followed by the results of the empirical analysis.

9.3 METHODOLOGY

9.3.1 Statistical Time-Series Models

Over the years, many classical time-series methods such as the ARMA, ARIMA, and exponential smoothing models have been proposed which readily achieve impressive results for time-series forecasting. These methods are easy to understand and their ease of implementation has contributed to their popularity over the years. ARIMA is arguably one of the most popular models in time series analysis [45]. Like many classic models, the ARIMA model is based on assumptions of linearity of time-series and assumes a known statistical distribution. It models a time series as a combination of three base processes: the autoregressive AR (p) process, the Integrated I (d) process (using the differencing of raw observations to induce stationary into the time series) and lastly the moving average MA (q) process. Mathematically, the ARIMA (p, d, q) model using lag polynomials is defined as follows:

$$\varphi(L)1 - l^d y_t = \theta(l)\varepsilon_t \qquad (9.1)$$

$$\text{i.e.} \quad (1 - \sum_{i-1}^{p} \varphi_i l^i)(1 - l)^d y_t = (1 + \sum_{j=1}^{q} \theta_j l^j) \tag{9.2}$$

Box and Jenkins generalized the ARIMA model to handle seasonality by proposing the Season-ARIMA or SARIMA model [46]. The SARIMA model uses seasonal differencing to remove non-stationarity from the time series. This model is mathematically formulated as:

$$\phi_p(l^s)\varphi_p(l)(1 - l)^d(1 - l)^D y_t = \Theta_Q(l^s)\theta_q(l)\varepsilon_t \quad \text{i.e.} \quad \phi_p(l^s)\varphi_p(l)_{Zt} = \Theta_Q(l^s)\theta_q(l)\varepsilon_t \tag{9.3}$$

where, Z_t is the time series differenced seasonally.

9.3.2 Long-Short Term Memory Networks

An ANN is a computational structure which is inspired from the same principle as the workings of the human brain [47]. It is designed to extract patterns and identify underlying trends in arbitrary data. ANNs are particularly suitable for handling incomplete and messy datasets. They do not need prior knowledge or assumptions about the distribution of the data and are capable of mapping approximate functions onto any data. Statistically, ANNs are considered as non-linear models. Usually, a standard ANN consists of three layers of connected processors called neurons: one input layer, a couple of hidden layers in the middle, and one output layer. Each neuron produces a sequence of real-valued activation functions. Input layer neurons get activated when data are passed into them, and other neurons activate as they are connected through weighted links passing data from previous layers. The output of the network is controlled by the weight assignments for each connection and the tuning procedure to achieve the desired output through weights adjustment is called 'learning' [48,49].

Figure 9.1 shows an artificial neuron. The neuron has 'm' inputs (x_i) and each input is connected to the neuron by a weighted link (w_i). The weights and inputs are all real numbered values. In this case, the neuron adds the inputs using the following equation:

$$A = \sum x_i w_i + b \tag{9.4}$$

where A is the net sum and b is the threshold value.

The output is produced using the net sum A using an activation function $F(A)$:

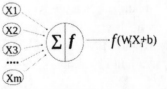

FIGURE 9.1 An artificial neuron.

Source: [48].

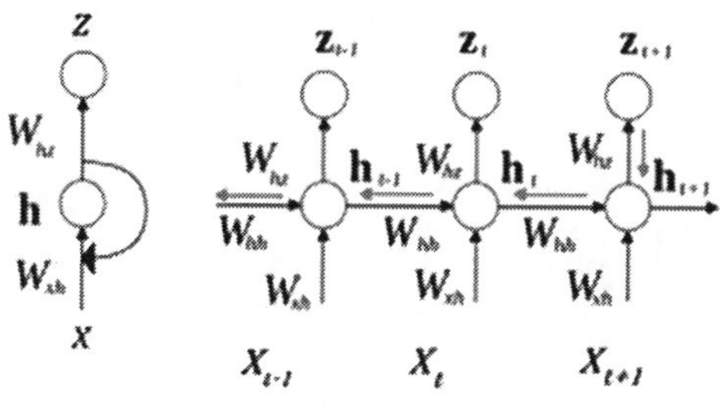

FIGURE 9.2   Recurrent neural network (RNN).

Source: [50].

$$output = F(A) \tag{9.5}$$

A special class of deep neural networks known as RNNs are highly useful for all types of sequential data making them perfect for modeling time series [50]. RNNs can also capture temporary dependencies over variable time periods. Unlike feed-forward networks, RNN structures have unique internal states whose output is looped back into the input using a feedback mechanism. Generally speaking, when feedback loops are present in a network, it is called an RNN. The famous back-propagation algorithm can be used to train any RNN by training the network in a way that it is able to encode prior information into hidden layers effectively capturing patterns in time series. Figure 9.2 depicts the conceptual structure of a standard RNN model.

A RNN can be said to have a memory. The information from each input sequence is kept in the hidden state of network, and this hidden information is inputted back recursively into the network as it moves forward to read new inputs. The input to hidden layer can be described by the following equation:

$$h_t = g_n(W_{xh}X_t + W_{hh}h_{t-1} + b_h) \tag{9.6}$$

where, h_t is the hidden layer at time t, g_n is the function, W_{xh} is the weight matrix for input to hidden layer, X_t is the input at time t, h_{t-1} is the hidden layer at time $(t-1)$, and b_h is the threshold value.

The equation for the output layer is given as:

$$Z_t = g_n(W_{hz}h_t + b_z) \tag{9.7}$$

where, Z_t is the output vector, W_{hz} is the weight matrix for hidden to output layer, and b_h is the threshold value.

LSTMs, a special category of RNNs, were introduced by Hochreiter and Schmidhuber in 1997 to deal with the long-term dependency problem associated with conventional RNNs. Conventional RNN structure contains a simple feedback loop, while LSTMs contain memory blocks or cells instead. Each memory cell comprises three gates and one cell state which regulates the information flowing through the cells.

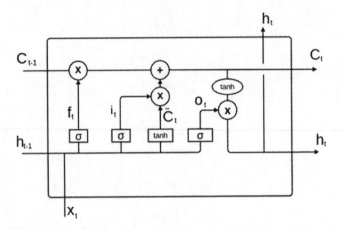

FIGURE 9.3   A typical LSTM cell.

Source: [17].

In figure 9.3, the line passing through the top is known as cell state (C_{t-1}, C_t) which runs through the entire network and transfers information between cells. The sigmoid or forget gate layer (f_t) decides how much information will be stored in a cell state. A point-wise multiplication operation is used to assemble the output from forget gate to cell state. Next is input gate which combines the sigmoid layer (i_t) and tanh layer outputs into the cell state. In the diagram $C̃_t$ is the new value created by tanh layer. The memory cell gets two inputs: the output h_{t-1} of the previous moment and the external information x_t of the current moment and combines them in a vector $[h_{t-1}, x_t]$ through sigmoid (σ) transformation. Mathematically it is expressed as

$$f_t = \sigma(W_f . [h_{t-1}, x_t] + b_f) \tag{9.8}$$

where W_f is the weight matrix, b_f is the bias of the forgotten gate, and σ is the sigmoid function. The main function of the forgotten gate is to record the amount of state C_{t-1} from the previous time to be reserved for the current time cell state C_t. The gate gives an output value between 0 and 1, with 1 indicating complete information reservation and 0 indicating no reservation. The input gate determines the amount of the input x_t information from the current network is reserved into the cell state C_t, thus, preventing non-significant information from getting into the memory cells. It has two main functions first, to find the cell state which must be updated using the sigmoid layer.

$$i_t = \sigma(W_i . [h_{t-1}, x_t] + b_i) \tag{9.9}$$

The second function of the input gate is to update the information to be loaded into the cell state. The tanh layer in the middle controls how much new information is added. Mathematically,

$$\widetilde{C_t} = tanh(W_c \cdot [h_{t-1}, x_t] + b_c) \tag{9.10}$$

Finally, the state of the memory cells is updated using the following equation:

$$C_t = f_t * C_{t-1} + i_t * \widetilde{C_t} \tag{9.11}$$

Next, using the point-wise multiplication of sigmoid gate and tanh gate, the output (O_t) information is formed by:

$$O_t = \sigma(W_o \cdot [h_{t-1}, x_t] + b_o) \tag{9.12}$$

The final output (h_t) of the cell is defined as:

$$h_t = O_t * tanh(C_t) \tag{9.13}$$

Overall, the unique structure of LSTM model makes it an excellent tool for time-series forecasting. LSTMs have comparatively lower cost to train and have emerged as the representative deep learning architecture for sequential data processing.

9.3.3 The FbProphet Algorithm

Facebook/Meta open-sourced its Prophet forecasting tool for the public in early 2017. FbProphet can be considered an 'auto' machine learning tool which helps to predict time-series data using the seasonality information present within a time series. It is an additive regression-based model where non-linear trends are fit using piecewise linear or logistic growth curve trends. It can detect changes in trends by automatically selecting change points from the data. The Additive equation for the FbProphet forecasting model is given by equation (9.14) which shows different components of the equation:

$$y(t) = g(t) + s(t) + h(t) + \varepsilon t \tag{9.14}$$

where, *y(t)* is the Additive Regressive Model, *g(t)* is the Trend Factor, *h(t)* is the Holiday Component, *s(t)* is the Seasonality Component and *et* is the Error Term.

9.3.4 Evaluation Measures

For evaluation of the results, two standard metrics are used: the MSE and the RMSE. MSE is the average of squared difference between the target and the actual output value while RMSE is the square root of the MSE. RMSE is usually employed to find error in the model on the same scale as the original data. The use of these evaluation metrics is common in literature and they make excellent general purpose error metrics for numerical prediction problems.

$$MSE = \frac{1}{N} \sum_{i=1}^{N} (\widehat{y}_i - y_i)^2 \tag{9.15}$$

$$RMSE = \sqrt{\frac{1}{N} \sum_{i=1}^{N} (\widehat{y}_i - y_i)^2} \tag{9.16}$$

where, N is the number of samples, $\hat{y}_i$ is the model prediction value, and y_i is the actual value.

9.4 EMPIRICAL ANALYSIS AND RESULTS

9.4.1 Data

To demonstrate the effectiveness of AI-based DL models over traditional statistical techniques for price forecasting, this study uses the SBI ETF NIFTY 50 fund, an ETF based on the NIFTY 50 Index as the test bed for empirical testing. The data contains a uni-variate series of daily closing price of observations spanning from 11 February 2019 to 2 May 2022.

For forecasting the time series, representative models from each class are chosen, the ARIMA model from traditional statistical models; the LSTM (long short-term memory) network model from deep learning; and the FbProphet model from additive models. The implementation of these models is discussed in the following part (figure 9.4).

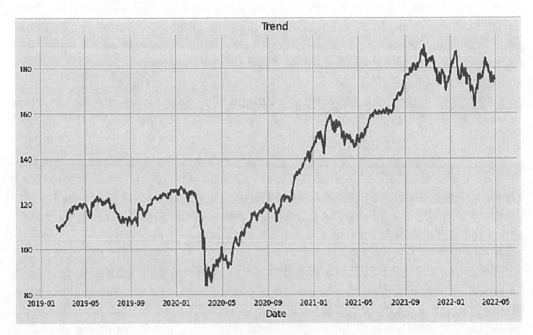

FIGURE 9.4   SBI NIFTY 50 ETF price chart in INR from 11 February 2019 to 2 May 2022.

Source: Author's construction.

9.4.2 Augmented Dickey Fuller Test and Stationarity

Before using any statistical model for time-series forecasting, it is important to determine the stationary of the time series and how many steps of differencing will be required for making the series stationary. Though, it is clear from looking at the price series that there is a presence of trend and the series is clearly not stationary, visual analysis is not the most robust method of finding out the stationarity of a time series. One of the best methods to test for stationarity is the Augmented Dickey Fuller Test. It is a type of Unit Root test with the null hypothesis (H0) that there is presence of unit roots in the series. The presence of unit roots determines stationary of a time series and the number of unit roots determines the number of differencing steps required for making it stationary. Looking at the ADF Test results in table 9.1, it is clear that for the analysis, the First-Differenced Closing Price should be used (figure 9.5).

TABLE 9.1   Results of ADF Test

	Closing Price Series	First-Differenced Closing Price
ADF Test Statistic	−0.7287	−11.04498
p-value	0.83917	5.250469309479673e-20
Null hypothesis(H0)	Accept	Reject
Stationarity	Non-stationary	Stationary

Source: Author's construction

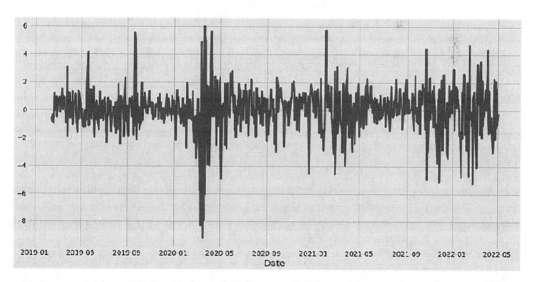

FIGURE 9.5   First difference closing price series from SBI NIFTY 50 ETF from 11 February 2019 to 2 May 2022.

Source: Author's construction.

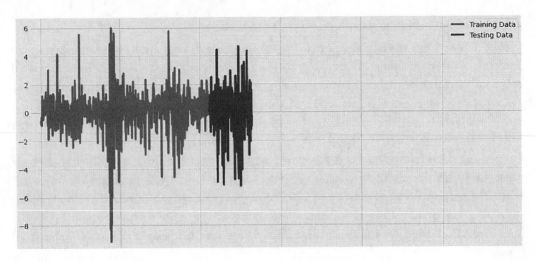

FIGURE 9.6   Training and testing splits.

Source: Author's construction.

9.4.3 Training and Testing Splits

In any statistical or ML model, the data is generally divided into two parts, the training period and the testing period. The models are trained using the training period where they learn to identify intrinsic patterns in the data and the validity of the trained model is evaluated on the testing period. This confirms the out-of-sample powers of the models. This study follows the same principle and divides the dataset into two parts using an 80/20 split where 80% of the data is used for training and the remaining 20% is used for testing purposes. Figure 9.6 shows the training and testing splits for the data used for both forecasting models. In order to keep the analysis consistent all three models are applied on the first-differenced closing price series.

9.4.4 Model Specifications

Any ARIMA (p, d, q) model requires the three parameters to be specified by the users where p is the number of lags chosen, d shows the number of steps required for differencing to make the series stationary, and q is the number of times the differencing is done. Since in this case only one differencing step was required, the value of d has been chosen as 1. The previous day's value is used for autoregression and, thus, a value of 1 has been assigned for p parameter and since only one differencing step was required and was performed on the series before putting it into the model, the value of q has been taken as 0.

LSTM requires two main parameters to be chosen by the users: the number of nodes and the number of layers. There are no particular rules that determine these values and they are chosen based on the particular intricacies of problems involved such as the number of time steps being taken and the number of future values being forecasted. Too big a value would lead to overfitting of the model on training data and too small a value would fail to learn the patterns adequately. Thus, keeping this in mind the model

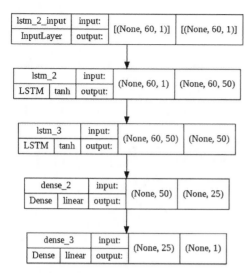

FIGURE 9.7   The architecture of LSTM Model.

Source: Author's construction.

TABLE 9.2   Forecasting Results of Both ARIMA and LSTM Models

	MSE	RMSE
ARIMA	5.428	2.330
LSTM	0.122	0.350
FbProphet	2.245	1.478

Source: Author's construction

parameters have been chosen for this study. Figure 9.3 shows the architecture of the LSTM model used in this study.

The model contains one input layer which provides data to the two LSTM layers each with 60 nodes as inputs 50 nodes as the Output. The LSTM layers' output is further passed into two dense layers with linear activation functions. MSE is used as the loss function and ADAM algorithm is used for optimization. Finally, the information from the dense layer is passed to a fully connected output layer (figure 9.7).

9.4.5 Results

The three models—ARIMA (1, 1, 0) model, the LSTM model, and the FbProphet model—are trained on the same training set data. The results of models are summarized in table 9.2 where the MSE and the RMSE values are compared for the three above-discussed approaches.

As evident from the results, both FbProphet and LSTM models are performing very well for the task of univariate time series forecasting much better than ARIMA. However, the performance of LSTM model with a 0.350 RMSE is clearly much superior to the 2.330 RMSE value given by the ARIMA model and 1.478 value given by Prophet. For ease of replication of analysis the study uses open source data taken from Yahoo Finance and for analysis uses the Python 3 programming language. ARIMA model has been implemented using the statsmodels package; the LSTM model has been implemented using the Keras

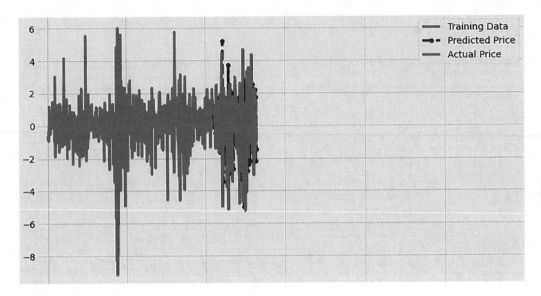

FIGURE 9.8   ARIMA model forecasting results.

Source: Author's construction.

DL library, the FbProphet algorithm has been implemented using the open source package by the same name, figures 9.8, 9.9, and 9.10 denote the graphical representation of results from both models. From the graphs it can be seen that the predictions made by the ARIMA model are more volatile than the other two models although the other models are able to predict the direction of movements quite well.

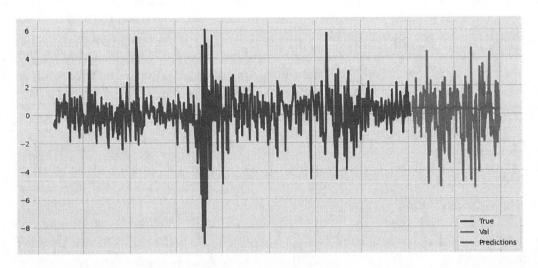

FIGURE 9.9   LSTM model forecasting results.

Source: Author's construction.

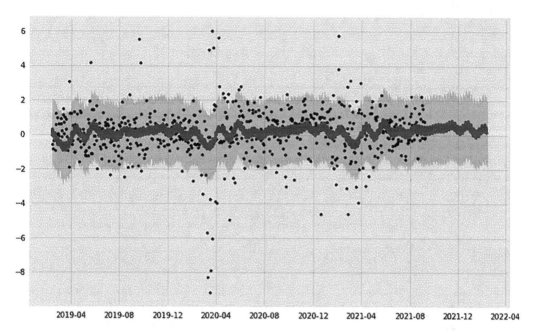

FIGURE 9.10   FbProphet results.

Source: Author's construction.

9.5 CONCLUSION

The development of AI and increased usefulness of DL models have inspired researchers to successfully apply these models for stock market prediction. This study reviews some of the most recent progress made in literature in the past few years for stock market prediction. Next, the theoretical underpinnings of the two representative models from statistical and DL are discussed in detail. The models are applied to a dataset containing closing prices of an ETF with NIFTY 50 as the underlying benchmark showing a practical example of how these techniques fare against each other when applied to real-world data. The forecasting results: MSE and RMSE clearly indicate the superiority of LSTM model over the ARIMA model and also over the FbProphet additive model.

Though this study provides a fairly detailed general overview and empirical example which can be understood and followed by beginners, there are certain limitations of the study. For example, this study only looks at univariate forecasting where the only input given to the model is the historical price information. Since stocks are generally affected by movements of other stocks as well as the whole market, future research in this area should consider adding more inputs (for example, market volatility, fundamental or technical indicators) to the models and make them more comprehensive. There is also another strand of research not covered in this study which uses alternate data sources such as the news and social media sentiment data [33]. Readers are advised to look into these directions of research for further exploration into how these state-of-the-art techniques could be further used to make better predictions. Overall, AI techniques have proven to be highly useful in the field of finance and will most definitely play a pivotal role in the future of finance research.

REFERENCES

[1] Fama, E.F. (1965). "The behavior of stock-market prices." *The Journal of Business* 38(1):34–105.

[2] Malkiel, B.G. (2003). "The efficient market hypothesis and its critics." *Journal of Economic Perspectives* 17(1):59–82.

[3] Hyndman, R.J., Athanasopoulos, G. (2018). "Forecasting: principles and practice." *OTexts.*

[4] Bollerslev, T. (1986). "Generalized autoregressive conditional heteroskedasticity." *Journal of Econometrics* 31(3):307–327.

[5] Rawat, W., Wang, Z. (2017). "Deep convolutional neural networks for image classification: A comprehensive review." *Neural Computation* 29(9):2352–2449.

[6] Monk, A., Prins, M., Rook, D. (2019). "Rethinking alternative data in institutional investment." *The Journal of Financial Data Science* 1(1): 14–31.

[7] Gu, S., Kelly, B., Xiu, D. (2020). "Empirical asset pricing via machine learning." *The Review of Financial Studies* 33(5):2223–2273.

[8] Chen, L., Pelger, M., Zhu, J. (2019). "Deep learning in asset pricing." *arXiv preprint arXiv:1904.00745.*

[9] Kyriakou, I., Mousavi, P., Nielsen, J.P., Scholz, M. (2019). "Machine Learning for Forecasting Excess Stock Returns–The Five-Year-View." *University of Graz, Department of Economics.*

[10] Wu, Q., Zhang, Z., Pizzoferroto, A., Cucuringu, M., Liu, Z. (2019). "A deep learning framework for pricing financial instruments." *ArXivorg.*

[11] Heaton, J.B., Polson, N.G., Witte, J.H. (2016) "Deep learning in finance." *arXiv preprint arXiv:1602.06561.*

[12] Dorffner, G. (1996). "Neural networks for time series processing." *In Neural Network World.*

[13] Sutskever, I., Vinyals, O., Le Q.V. (2014). "Sequence to sequence learning with neural networks." *Advances in Neural Information Processing Systems:* 27.

[14] Vargas, M.R., De Lima, B.S., Evsukoff, A.G. (2017). "Deep learning for stock market prediction from financial news articles." *In 2017 IEEE international conference on computational intelligence and virtual environments for measurement systems and applications* (CIVEMSA): 60–65).

[15] Siami-Namini, S., Namin, A.S. (2018). "Forecasting economics and financial time series: Arima vs. LSTM." arXiv preprint arXiv:1803.06386.

[16] Fischer, T., Krauss, C. (2018). "Deep learning with long short-term memory networks for financial market predictions." *European Journal of Operational Research* 270(2): 654–669.

[17] Chen, K., Zhou, Y., Dai, F. (2015). "A LSTM-based method for stock returns prediction: a case study of China stock market." *In 2015 IEEE International Conference on Big Data (Big Data):* 2823–2824.

[18] Mehtab, S., Sen, J., Dutta, A. (2020). "Stock price prediction using machine learning and LSTM-based deep learning models." In *Symposium on Machine Learning and Metaheuristics Algorithms, and Applications:* 88–106.

[19] Ma, J., Liu, L. (2008). "Multivariate nonlinear analysis and prediction of Shanghai stock market." *Discrete Dynamics in Nature and Society* Article ID 526734.

[20] Ivanovski, Z., Ivanovska, N., Narasanov, Z. (2016). "The regression analysis of stock returns at MSE." *Journal of Modern Accounting and Auditing.* 2016 Apr;12(4):217–224.

[21] Khan, U., Aadil, F., Ghazanfar, M.A., Khan, S., Metawa, N., Muhammad, K., Mehmood, I., Nam, Y. (2018). "A robust regression-based stock exchange forecasting and determination of correlation between stock markets." *Sustainability* 10(10):3702.

[22] Ariyo, A.A., Adewumi, A.O., Ayo, C.K. (2014). "Stock price prediction using the ARIMA model." *In 2014 UKSim-AMSS 16th International Conference on Computer Modelling and Simulation*, Cambridge, UK: 106–112).

[23] Mondal, P., Shit, L., Goswami, S. (2014). "Study of effectiveness of time series modeling (ARIMA) in forecasting stock prices." *International Journal of Computer Science, Engineering and Applications* 4(2):13.

[24] Jarrett, J.E., Kyper, E. (2011). "ARIMA modeling with intervention to forecast and analyze Chinese stock prices." *International Journal of Engineering Business Management* 3(3):53–58.

[25] Phua, P.K., Ming, D., Lin, W. (2001). "Neural network with genetically evolved algorithms for stocks prediction." *Asia-Pacific Journal of Operational Research* 18(1):103–107.

[26] Chen, A.S., Leung, M.T., Daouk, H. (2003). "Application of neural networks to an emerging financial market: forecasting and trading the Taiwan Stock Index." *Computers & Operations Research* 30(6): 901–923.

[27] Zhang, D., Jiang, Q., Li, X. (2007). "Application of neural networks in financial data mining." *International Journal of Computer and Information Engineering* 1(1): 225–228.

[28] Wu, Q., Chen, Y., Liu, Z. (2008, January). "Ensemble model of intelligent paradigms for stock market forecasting." In *First International Workshop on Knowledge Discovery and Data Mining (WKDD 2008)* Washington, DC, USA (pp. 205–208). IEEE.

[29] Dutta, G., Jha, P., Laha, A.K., Mohan, N. (2006). "Artificial neural network models for forecasting stock price index in the Bombay stock exchange." *Journal of Emerging Market Finance* 5(3): 283–295.

[30] Hanias, M., Curtis, P., Thalassinos, E. (2012). "Time series prediction with neural networks for the Athens Stock Exchange indicator." *European Research Studies Journal* 15(2): 23–32.

[31] Xiao, Y., Xiao, J., Liu, J., Wang, S. (2014). "A multiscale modeling approach incorporating ARIMA and ANNs for financial market volatility forecasting." *Journal of Systems Science and Complexity* 27(1): 225–236.

[32] Porshnev, A., Redkin, I., Shevchenko, A. (2013). "Machine learning in prediction of stock market indicators based on historical data and data from Twitter sentiment analysis." In *IEEE International Conference on Data Mining Workshops*, Dallas, TX, USA: 440–444.

[33] Tang, J., Chen, X. (2018). "Stock market prediction based on historic prices and news titles." In *Proceedings of the International Conference on Machine Learning Technologies (ICMLT'18)*: 29–34.

[34] Wang, Z., Ho, S-B., Lin, Z. (2018). "Stock market prediction analysis by incorporating social and news opinion and sentiment." In *Proceedings of the IEEE International Conference on Data Mining Workshops*: 1375–1380.

[35] Obthoong, M., Tantisantiwong, N., Jeamwatthanachai, W., Will, G. (2020). "A survey on machine learning for stock price prediction: Algorithms and techniques." In *Proceedings of the 2nd International Conference on Finance, Economics, Management and Business (IT FEMIB'20)*: 63–71.

[36] Grover, A., Kapoor, A., Horvitz, E. (2015). "A deep hybrid model for weather forecasting." In *Proceedings of the 21st ACM SIGKDD International Conference on Knowledge Discovery and Data Mining*:379–386.

[37] Ryu, S., Noh, J., Kim, H. (2016). "Deep neural network based demand side short term load forecasting." *Energies* 10(1): 3

[38] Lago, J., De Ridder, F., De Schutter, B. (2018). "Forecasting spot electricity prices: deep learning approaches and empirical comparison of traditional algorithms." *Applied Energy* 221: 386–405.

[39] Cavalcante, R.C., Brasileiro, R.C., Souza, V.L., Nobrega, J.P., Oliveira, A.L. (2016). "Computational intelligence and financial markets: A survey and future directions." *Expert Systems with Application* 55: 194–211.

[40] Hossain, M.A., Karim, R., Thulasiram, R., Bruce, N.D., Wang, Y. (2018). "Hybrid deep learning model for stock price prediction." In *2018 IEEE Symposium Series on Computational Intelligence (SSCI)*: 1837–1844.

[41] Taylor, S.J., Letham, B. (2018). Forecasting at scale. *The American Statistician*, 72(1), 37–45.

[42] Indulkar, Yash. (2021). "Time Series Analysis of Cryptocurrencies Using Deep Learning & Fbprophet." *International Conference on Emerging Smart Computing and Informatics (ESCI)*, pp. 306–311. IEEE, 2021.

[43] Raheem, F., qbal, N. (2021). "Forecasting foreign exchange rate: Use of FbProphet." *International Research Conference on Smart Computing and Systems Engineering (SCSE)*, vol. 4, pp. 44–48. IEEE, 2021.

[44] Saiktishna, C., Sumanth, N.S.V., Rao, M.M.S., Thangakumar, J. (2022). "Historical Analysis and Time Series Forecasting of Stock Market using FB Prophet." *6th International Conference on Intelligent Computing and Control Systems (ICICCS)*, pp. 1846–1851. IEEE, 2022.

[45] Cochrane, J.H. (2015). "Time Series for Macroeconomics and Finance." *University of Chicago* 15: 16.

[46] Box, G.E., Jenkins, G.M., Reinsel, G.C., Ljung, G.M. (2015). "Time series analysis: forecasting and control." *John Wiley & Sons*.

[47] Haykin, S.S. (2009). "Neural Networks and Learning Machines." *Pearson Education, Upper Saddle River*.

[48] Schmidhuber, J. (2015). "Deep learning in neural networks: an overview." *Neural Networks* 61: 85–117.

[49] Sibi, P., Jones, S.A., Siddarth, P. (2013). "Analysis of different activation functions using back propagation neural networks." *Journal of Theoretical and Applied Information Technology* 47(3): 1264–1268.

[50] Che, Z., Purushotham, S., Cho, K., Sontag, D., Liu, Y. (2018). "Recurrent neural networks for multivariate time series with missing values." *Scientific Reports* 8(1):1–12.

CHAPTER 10

Applications and Impact of Artificial Intelligence in the Finance Sector

Pokala Pranay Kumar, Dheeraj Anchuri, Syed Hasan Jafar,
Deepika Dhingra, and Hani El-Chaarani

CONTENTS

10.1 INTRODUCTION

The finance industry turned into a centre to incorporate the developments of artificial intelligence (AI) and using this cutting-edge innovation technology, companies ensure to protect their data by building hack-proof protection shields [1]. AI execution all through the financial industry is dictated by market factors such as monetary strategy, competitiveness with other companies, and profitability prerequisites, just as supply factors, for example, finance industry innovations and information accessibility and specialized progressions [2]. AI is an innovative emerging technology which makes machines think and act like a human. Several branches, such as machine learning (ML), robotics, deep learning, are a part of expert systems such as ML, genetic algorithms, natural language

DOI: 10.1201/9781003327745-10

processing, and so forth. [3]. This chapter discusses various applications in the finance industry using AI as well as its branches.

10.2 LITERATURE REVIEW

In this chapter, the authors explored how neural networks were used in various patterns between 1990 and 1996. The audit of the complete chapter focused on some particular fields in the finance field like the distribution year, utilizations of different areas, an ultimate conclusion measure, the board structure, IT/training improvement, techniques that are actualized in different areas, and so forth. The authors examined different procedures recommended by numerous analysts and researchers for the future extent of the work. The authors directed this by taking many example spaces of how the neural networks are utilized and how much precision these networks gained utilizing these neural organizations. For instance, in a similar investigation segment, they led a study on 37 articles that depicts the uses of neural networks. They utilized measurable strategies to break down the exhibition of neural networks in these 37 articles. The following model is a relative investigation in the joining of advancements where they coordinated various calculations such as genetic algorithms, expert systems, and a lot more with neural networks to examine the presentation of calculations and increase the exhibition which could be used to address issues in the financial sector. By probing these integrations they found that on the off chance that one innovation fizzled in execution, we can coordinate with another innovation to expand the presentation just as defeated the blunders. In their review of the examination, they noticed the reconciliation by taking 8 applications in which 7 are incorporated with the expert systems and one with the fuzzy logic. In this, they expounded by clarifying the tests led by different specialists, as Markham and Ragsdale advanced with their exploratory outcomes which examine the integration of neural networks with the Mahalanobis distance measurable method which is utilized for insolvency forecast of banks. The end depicts the progression of innovation and a combination of various advancements that could diminish and improve the proficiency of the calculations which helps in building various applications to tackle true issues in finance [4].

This chapter exposes the survey results conducted by the authors on what are the techniques used in financial market analysis and what are the best algorithms that are used in the prediction of market values. In this, the data studied is collected from the North American Market. The main objective of the introduction elaborates on the importance of stock market prediction. In this, he elaborated a review of ML techniques such as Support Vector Machine (SVM), Artificial Neural Networks (ANN), and Random Forest (RF). Exploratory research using AI generally falls into two main categories. The first determines the key factors and patterns of the environment, separates the informative part of the model's preparation and approval, and refreshes them. The next section uses the sophisticated model in the proposed information for testing, with a modest assessment of past performance. The SVM arrangement model can be adjusted as a regression to foresee values in monetary time arrangement for this situation, it is known as Support Vector Regression (SVR). Most monetary business sectors' expectation papers initially recognize the troublesome job needing to be done. Monetary business sectors' costs are impacted by a horde of elements and there has been an enormous number of propositions for their expectation. A few models convert into exchanging methodologies. For instance, heading expectation can be deciphered as a purchase/sell signals technique, contingent upon the bearing of the conjecture. Nonetheless, a few creators cease from educating a particularly viable utilization regarding their models, focusing on the report of results utilizing measures other than returns. In the event that monetary returns are utilized to assess models and systems, it is prudent to incorporate other down-to-earth measures, for example, drawdown and instability as danger boundaries [5].

Deep learning has been widely used in machine vision, natural language processing, and image recognition. The remarkable success of deep learning as just an information-handling procedure also boosted the value of an analysis domain. With the recent growth of Fintech, the use of deep learning in banking and finance departments has become much more popular. Nonetheless, throughout the present writing, an itemized analysis of the uses of deep learning in business and economics is insufficient. The whole research assessed and deconstructs the writings on the use of deep learning models within core finance or business environments to attempt to provide a thoughtful evaluation of system classification, inputs, or model assessment. Finally, they discuss three perspectives that could have an impact on the outcomes of financial deep classification algorithms. This study provides academics and experts with information and training about how to use deep learning models of business and economics to achieve the main objective. This study provides a comprehensive analysis of the literature on the application of Deep Learning (DL) in the finance and banking industry. A rational selection of scholarly knowledge bases is needed for both the research and refining. This article evaluates 7 F&B sections and establishes relations between the spaces and their commonly used DL models. Under our structure, they examine the complexities of each post. They often split down methodologies into concrete spaces and render suggestions based on the validity of various models. As a result, they summarize three main points: data preprocessing, data sources, and evaluation laws. They go on to look at the troubling consequences of computational complexity and supportability by using DL templates, as well as some possible solutions. This examination adds to the writing by introducing a significant gathering of information on related investigations and giving valuable suggestions to monetary investigators and analysts [6].

There has been escalated research from scholastics and experts in regards to models for anticipating insolvency and default occasions, for credit hazard the executives. The fundamental scholastic examination has assessed insolvency utilizing customary insights strategies and early man-made brainpower models. In this chapter, creators tried AI models, such as help vector machines, sacking, boosting, and arbitrary woods, to foresee insolvency one year preceding the occasion, and contrast their exhibition and results from the discriminant examination, strategic relapse, and neural organizations. The vital knowledge of the investigation is a significant improvement in expectation exactness utilizing AI methods, particularly when, notwithstanding the first Altman's Z-score factors. Contrasting the best models, with every single prescient variable, the AI procedure identified with irregular woods prompted 87% exactness, though calculated relapse and straight discriminant examination prompted 69% and half-precision, separately, in the testing test. Liquidation forecast is related to credit hazard, which has been pushed into the spotlight because of the new monetary emergency. AI models have been extremely effective in account applications, and numerous investigations analyze their utilization in insolvency expectations. The Altman and Ohlson models are as yet applicable, due not exclusively to their prescient force yet in addition to their basic, down-to-earth, and reliable systems. Hardly any examinations can enhance their outcomes concerning determining the exactness or the straightforwardness of the models. This current examination's results are intriguing in that they uncover how utilizing computational learning strategies can improve the prescient force of credit hazard models. Banks and danger chiefs can explore these AI models, which could improve their credit hazard investigation and consequently assist them with accomplishing better productivity with lower credit hazard openness [7].

The key advantage of using ML in the financial sector is that it encourages the development of information examination. AI (ML) could be useful in a variety of databases, including organized, semi-structured, and unstructured information. AI could be used precisely across the business process to differentiate risk, events, and company operations using cutting-edge precognition techniques. By identifying limitations, AI estimates will exclude errors and different hidden fraud schemes. Insurance companies rely on predictive models which take into account past incidents of skewed conduct. The AI estimates with new information also resulted in much more extraordinary fraud findings. Simulated intelligence-controlled scholarly frameworks should be prepared in a space. The nature of the information used to prepare prescient models is similarly significant as the amount, on account of AI. The datasets should be delegated and adjusted with the goal that they can give a superior picture and stay away from predisposition. This is critical to prepare prescient models. Present-day advances are moving very quickly making their way into different fields of business. Throughout this context, the security industry should not require the assistance of anyone. The application of knowledge to security does have a strong history. As a result, the approach insurance companies use in computational mathematics analysis was not particularly impressive. The aim of using data science analysis insecurity is the same as it is in other industry sectors: to simplify marketing procedures, improve revenue, raise pay, and reduce costs. They presented a few AI techniques throughout this article to accurately evaluate security assurances and evaluate their exhibits using various measures [8].

The private protection area is perceived as one of the quickest-developing businesses. This quick development has powered unfathomable changes over the previous decade. These days, there exist protection items for most high-esteem resources such as vehicles, adornments, wellbeing/life, and homes. Insurance agencies are at the front line in receiving forefront activities, measures, and numerical models to augment benefits while overhauling their client's cases. Customary strategies that are only founded on human-on top of it displays are tedious and off base. In this chapter, we build up a protected and computerized protection framework system that diminishes human collaboration, gets protection exercises, cautions and advises about hazardous clients, identifies fake cases, and diminishes money-related misfortune for the protection area. After introducing the blockchain-based structure to empower secure exchanges and information sharing among various cooperating specialists inside the protection organization, we propose to utilize the limit slope boosting (XGBoost) AI calculation for the previously mentioned protection administrations and think about its exhibitions with those of other best-in-class calculations. The acquired outcomes uncover that, when applied to an accident protection dataset, the XGboost accomplishes superior additions contrasted with other existing learning calculations. For example, it arrives at a 7% higher exactness contrasted with choice tree models when identifying fake cases. They got results to uncover that, when applied to an accident coverage dataset, the XGboost accomplishes elite increases contrasted with other existing learning calculations. For example, it comes to 7% higher exactness contrasted with choice tree models when identifying deceitful cases. Besides, we propose a web-based answer for naturally managing ongoing updates of the protection organization also, we show that it beats another online best in the class calculation. At last, we join the created AI modules with the hyper record texture writer to carry out and imitate the counterfeit knowledge and blockchain-based structure [9].

Financial supporters place a high value on precise stock trade expectations; however, finance exchange becomes influenced through volatile variables such as weblogs or reports, making it impossible can forecast stock trade lists based solely on factual information. The extremely unpredictable nature of financial markets emphasises the importance of thoroughly examining the role of external variables in stock forecasting. Equities markets could be predicted using AI estimates based on data from online media and financial news since this knowledge can influence the behaviour of financial supporters. They use statistics from online media and financial media data in this chapter to determine the impact of such data upon the accuracy of stock market forecasts for the next 10 days. Include options and reduce negative messages on the datasets to improve implementation and quality of predictions. They also conduct tests to identify stock markets that are difficult to predict and those that are more influenced through Internet advertising and financial media. With the aim of finding a stable classifier, they compare the aftereffects of different measures. Finally, deep learning is used to achieve the highest level of expectation accuracy, and several classification algorithms are ensembled. Our trial results show that the most noteworthy forecast correctness of 80.53% and 75.16% are carried out using internet media and financial news, respectively. They also reveal that the New York and Red Hat stock markets are difficult to predict, that internet media has a greater impact on New York and IBM stocks, and also that financial reporting has a greater impact on London and Microsoft stocks. The subjective classifier has been found to be accurate, with its troupe achieving the highest precision of 83.22% [10].

10.3 APPLICATIONS OF AI IN FINANCE

10.3.1 Personal Finance

Personal finance is managing your money as well as investing and savings. The user wants this facility to be user-friendly which they want to manage their activities in single applications. This thought created a revolution of creating AI-powered mobile application of personal finance. PRM is an application software which makes user manage their transactions. This software builds using AI, ML, intelligent automation, smart analytics, and so forth. The market size of this PRM will reach 343 million dollars [11]. There are many personal finance AI-powered applications. The following are the top five applications according to *Analytics India Magazine* [12].

1. Cleo: This is certainly not a customized versatile application. This is likewise an AI-powered informing application that gives all-day, everyday client care support. It functions as a partner to oversee exchanges with monetary exercises. This application furnishes the network of managing an account with a versatile application and gives the office to send cash through web-based media. This likewise furnishes the month-to-month banking proclamations with the use of cash utilizing graphical portrayal which assists with comprehension.

2. Eva money: It was made by Fintel labs which is a customized AI portable application intended to help IOS and android. The most recent component work in this application was the voice and chat collaborator which assists with lowing class individuals, they can undoubtedly control the application utilizing the voice aid. This application gives responses to inquiries identified with an individual budget and gives tips on the best way to utilize this application. This insight assists with improving financial administrations with security. This application gives the office to associate ledger with this versatile application and gives the most recent patterns, monetary news, current monetary market investigation, and so on.

3. MintZip: This application began in 2001 which gives a start to finish money-related arrangements. This application assembles an AI aide named 'misa' which assists clients with tackling their monetary issues. This is furnished with conversational AI and AI-based monetary help to clients. It is coordinated with social science and monetary insight chatbots which give all day, every day back to clients. This is an ML application that prepares the information consistently that is utilized to give forecasts monetary help to clients.

4. Olivia.ai: This was made by two business people from Silicon Valley in 2015. The additional benefit of this application is utilizing social financial aspects with AI. This application discovers examples of monetary patterns and gives guidelines on the best way to go through cash. These examples likewise assist clients with spending less sum. Be that as it may, the impediment of this application is this is rigorously upheld to IOS and confined to areas such as Brazil and the United States.

5. Wizely: This is a cash investment funds application that assists clients with setting aside their cash and permits them to go through less measure of cash. This gives an adaptable cash investment funds plan which is India's first computerized bank application. This gives limitless references and pre-appointments for wished buys. This application utilized ML and AI tech to embrace the most recent patterns and make them more intuitive to clients and customers.

10.3.2 Consumer Finance

Customer account helps individuals in their business. In this, clients seek a bank for credit for their business or their utilization. Be that as it may, the information is secure or not, how might we know? For this financial area, adjusted AI was their essential innovation to construct hack-verification machines and stop extortion exercises in the bank. In this field, JP Morgan Chase is the biggest bank that uses AI in various areas of financial exercises. For instance, they are utilizing natural language processing for the contributing values and utilized for remote helpers, and so forth. They utilize predictive analytics for keen documentation estimating. At long last, they are utilizing these innovations for fraud detection [13].

10.3.3 Corporate Finance

In this, AI has been used to anticipate the danger factor while giving credits. ML submodule to AI is utilized for hazard forecast of credits and used to spot bizarre exercises. Many US banks utilize this innovation in customer check to give loans. They utilize deep learning strategies to discover the danger factors and assist with distinguishing the extortion examination. After these innovation frameworks, reconciliation banks got high benefits and the fraud rate likewise decreased [14].

10.4 RISK ASSESSMENT

In this utilization of AI and ML, individuals are distinguishing Visa extortion subtleties. In this day and age, a credit score is vital to get a qualification for a credit card. To examine the individual's advance information and advance exercises, instalment records examination, the number of idle charge cards, and so forth. This data we need to examine to give a credit card just as a financial assessment to an individual. In any case, generally, an individual needs to check the information. A solitary individual or a group couldn't check lakhs of client information for examination, here AI is incorporated where shrewd frameworks break down the information utilizing ML and train the models with a lot of information which gives us the aftereffect of forecasts. The probability of mistakes is less while utilizing this ML and gives the best accuracies. This AI mechanization likewise assisted with building chatbots which are utilized to gauge consumer loyalty. There is another application in hazard evaluation is fraud detection. In this Citibank attached with an information science organization named Feedzai to investigate the information and anticipate the misrepresentation assessments. They planned the OpenML motor which assists engineers with making new ML models that help in improving accuracies. This ML programming investigates all exchanges and instalment history to foresee the extortion assessments which helps in making trustable exchanges to clients just as bank customers [15].

10.5 INSURANCE CLAIM

Claim automation is a cycle that utilizes AI innovation protection is asserted without human support. In this Lemonade, the organization began a portable application that utilizes AI as their significant programming. This application is a chatbot that is utilized for enrolling on insurance and guaranteeing the insurance is straightforward and simple advances. The advance sum will be credited in practically no time. This application utilizes facial acknowledgement, natural language processing and AI to examine the records. Lemonade utilizes the chatbot for the check of the reports and harmed property with video processing innovation. This framework works in a manner it begins with a fraud identification algorithm utilizing AI and afterwards it gauges the misfortune is right or not. In light of the information guarantee, cash will be attributed straightforwardly to the client's record. Another application in claim retainment is the decrease of excessive charges, for instance, Tractable is a software organization that gives software that will examine the given pictures of damaged items and anticipate the cost of the damaged parts. This product additionally gives the level of damage and recommends supplanting that damaged part with another one or supplant with cash to clients. This product utilizes predictive analytics and computer vision innovation to the assessment of cost dependent on the pictures. The cycle goes in a manner like specialists will upload the pictures into the software, at that point the product dissects the photos. For instance, if we have inserted a damaged car vehicle, then the AI framework will foresee it as a car and show us each part where the damage occurs and how much rate it damaged. This software relates the data points of prepared information and chooses to give an instalment or not [16].

10.6 TRADING AND SHARE MARKET

ML is the technology where statisticians are looking to utilize this technology in the prediction of share values based on previous stock data. The predictions-based approach is known as predictive analytics. Some companies are using this technology in trading and foreign exchange, investing in shares, and so forth. Many analysts predicting the market with better accuracies as well as trading companies are trying to find the risk factors in the market using this technology. Trading technologies which use ML and big data to find the patterns in the current market for forecasting and integrate AI systems in their platform which helps to make quicker decisions by clients based on the predictions. Green key technologies use NLP and voice recognition systems for trade search and are used to note the data analysis of trading. Kavout is a predictive analytics company that offers an intelligence platform that processes the previous history and gives predictions in the stock market. Auquan is an AI-developed trading company that uses the latest technology and gives suggestions to the investors as well as it provides trading investing companies. AI trading company uses this AI to analyse the patterns in the market and predict the changes in the trading market [17].

There are a few applications where numerous organizations are utilizing this AI as their key innovation which makes their business more productive and aiding them in expanding their worth on the lookout.

10.7 DISCUSSION AND FUTURE SCOPE

This finance area raises distinctive imaginative methodologies utilizing this AI. In future, there is a chance of foreseeing deals and offer worth, however, it could likewise anticipate the misrepresentation of organizations dependent on the information. The digitalization of archives made less responsibility for the representatives which helps in making the asset reports and other monetary records of the associations. The GPT-3 algorithm works with lakhs of layers which got well known in the late time where researchers and scientists utilize this algorithm to make machine-based accounting reports, similar examination articulations, make records, and so forth without labour and with precise computations. Numerous most recent calculations are building various examples in the offer market to foresee the exact offer worth. These calculations will be utilized in tracking down the budget summaries' extortion identification with digitalized documental verifications. The future of the finance industry going to change where fraud instalments and excessive charges will be decreased while protection asserting.

10.8 CONCLUSION

This article examined numerous applications that manage AI and its sub-innovations in different areas in the account business. The innovation gave numerous benefits to the account business which helps in overseeing cash-related issues to customers just as organizations. The most recent advancements improved portable banking and computerized banking instalments which makes human work simple. This creative and agreeable errand was fabricated utilizing AI just as it had given the trust to customers and clients by getting their information.

REFERENCES

[1] Burrell PR, Folarin BO. The impact of neural networks in finance. *Neural Comput Appl* 1997;6:193–200. 10.1007/BF01501506.

[2] Tadapaneni NR. Artificial intelligence in finance and investments *Int J Innov Res Sci Eng Technol* 2020;9(5).

[3] Tyagi N. 6 Major Branches of Artificial Intelligence (AI) | Analytics Steps. *Analytics steps* 2020. https://www.analyticssteps.com/blogs/6-major-branches-artificial-intelligence-ai (accessed April 14, 2021).

[4] Wong BK, Selvi Y. Neural network applications in finance: A review and analysis of literature (1990–1996). *Inf Manag* 1998;34:129–139. 10.1016/S0378-7206(98)00050-0.

[5] Henrique BM, Sobreiro VA, Kimura H. Literature review: Machine learning techniques applied to financial market prediction. *Expert Syst Appl* 2019;124:226–251. 10.1016/j.eswa.2019.01.012.

[6] Huang J, Chai J, Cho S. Deep learning in finance and banking: A literature review and classification. *Front Bus Res China* 2020;14:13. 10.1186/s11782-020-00082-6.

[7] Barboza F, Kimura H, Altman E. Machine learning models and bankruptcy prediction. *Expert Syst Appl* 2017;83:405–417. 10.1016/j.eswa.2017.04.006.

[8] Burri RD, Burri R, Bojja RR, Buruga SR. Insurance claim analysis using machine learning algorithms. *Int J Innov Technol Explor Eng* 2019;8:577–582. 10.35940/ijitee.F1118.04 86S419.

[9] Dhieb N, Ghazzai H, Besbes H, Massoud Y. A secure AI-driven architecture for automated insurance systems: Fraud detection and risk measurement. *IEEE Access* 2020;8:58546–58558. 10.1109/ACCESS.2020.2983300.

[10] Usmani M, Adil SH, Raza K, Ali SSA. Stock market prediction using machine learning techniques. 2016 3rd International Conference on Computer Information Science, ICCOINS 2016 – Proceedings of Institute of Electrical and Electronics Engineers Inc.; 2016, pp. 322–327. 10.1109/ICCOINS.2016.7783235.

[11] Phaneuf A. Personal finance management (PFM) app industry explained. *Insider* 2020. https://www.businessinsider.com/personal-finance-management-market?IR=T (accessed April 17, 2021).

[12] Sarmah Harshajit. 5 Most popular AI-powered personal finance apps. *Analytics India Magazine*. 2019. https://analyticsindiamag.com/5-most-popular-ai-powered-personal-finance-apps/

[13] Mejia Niccolo. Artificial Intelligence at JPMorgan – Current Initiatives | Emerj. *Emerj* 2019. https://emerj.com/ai-sector-overviews/ai-at-jp-morgan/ (accessed April 17, 2021).

[14] Phaneuf Alicia. AI in Finance 2021: Applications & Benefits in Financial Services. *Insider* 2020. https://www.businessinsider.com/ai-in-finance?IR=T (accessed April 17, 2021).

[15] Mejia N. Artificial intelligence at Citibank – Current initiatives | Emerj. *Emerj* 2019. https://emerj.com/ai-sector-overviews/ai-at-citi/ (accessed April 17, 2021).

[16] Azulay Dylan. Artificial intelligence in Finance – A comprehensive overview | Emerj. *Emerj* 2019. https://emerj.com/ai-sector-overviews/artificial-intelligence-in-finance-a-comprehensive-overview/ (accessed April 17, 2021).

[17] Thomas Mike. How AI trading technology is making stock market investors smarter. *Builtin* 2019. https://builtin.com/artificial-intelligence/ai-trading-stock-market-tech (accessed April 19, 2021).

Index